ALL ABOUT VEGETABLES

edited by Walter L. Doty

CONTENTS

Published by Chevron Chemical Company,
Ortho Division—Garden & Home
200 Bush Street
San Francisco, Ca. 94104

Acknowledgements

First we must acknowledge how this book was put together. In its beginnings we found ways through interviews, tapes and questionnaires to gather the first-hand experience of 237 vegetable gardeners scattered through every climate in the United States. Some were first-time gardeners, some long-time gardeners, a few were pros, and 3 were drop-outs.

We held to the idea that such first-hand experience, added to our own, would keep our feet on the ground while we absorbed the latest scientific information.

To bring more first-hand information into the book, we established test gardens — one in St. Helena, California, another in the Los Angeles State and County Arboretum, and dozens in home gardens, wherever we could find a cooperating gardener. We searched the catalogs for every variety of peppers, eggplants, corn etc. that looked interesting, bought seed and planted it.

We decided that three editions of the book were necessary to properly serve gardeners West, North and South. The principles relating to plant growth are universal but the application of the principles differs by the climate.

So, we worked with vegetable specialists and Agricultural Extension people in every climate. With their help we mapped the climates, charted planting dates, and recommended vegetable varieties for each region.

So many have contributed so much in the process of putting this book together that a page of brief acknowledgements is woefully inadequate.

Our debt to the vegetable specialists and researchers in State Universities is a big one. In preparing localized copy, climate maps and when-to-plant charts localized by climate zones, we leaned heavily on these good men:

Earl J. Allen—
   University of Arkansas.

James R. Baggett—Oregon State.

Kermit Hildahl—Iowa State.

John MacGillivray—
   University of California.

Bernard L. Pollack—
   Rutgers State University,
   New Jersey

Wayne Sitterly—
   Agricultural Experiment Station,
   Clemson University,
   South Carolina.

For special checking and answers to questions we and our amateur and not-so-amateur gardeners asked, we are grateful to:

E. Blair Adams—
   University of Wyoming.

Albert A. Banadyga—
   North Carolina State University.

Richard L. Bernard—
   U.S. Regional Soybean
   Laboratory, Illinois

Louis Berninger—
   University of Wisconsin.

James T. Garrett—
   Mississippi State University.

A. E. Griffiths—
   University of Rhode Island.

Herbert Hopen—
   University of Illinois.

Anton S. Horn—University of Idaho.

N. S. Mansour—Oregon State.

Dean Martin—South Dakota State.

Charles W. Marr—Kansas State.

Charles A. McClurg—
   University of Maryland.

R. R. Rothenberger—
   University of Missouri.

Donald Schuder—
   Purdue University, Indiana.

Raymond Sheldrake—
   Cornell University, New York

W. L. Sims—University of California.

Perry M. Smith—
   Auburn University, Alabama.

Cecil L. Thomson—
   University of Massachusetts.

James Utzinger—Ohio State.

Ben Vance—Iowa State.

George R. Williams—
   Virginia Polytechnic Institute.

For their stimulating ideas and encouragement when we needed them, we give a special thank you to:

Maggie Baylis, San Francisco, Calif.

Russell Beatty—
   University of California.

J. D. Carlisle, Columbia, So. Carolina.

J. R. Cheatham, Richmond, Virginia.

George Creed, Cleveland, Ohio.

George Dewey, Santa Clara County,
   California

Andrew A. Duncan—
   University of Minnesota.

Derek Fell—Gardenville, Penna.

W. A. Frazier—Oregon State.

Fred Peterson, Santa Clara, Calif.

Victor Pinckney, Jr., Fallbrook, Calif.

William Titus, Nassau County, N. Y.

Doris Tuinstra, Grand Rapids, Mich.

Walter Vodden—Blake Garden,
   Kensington, California.

Frits Went—Desert Research
   Institute, University of Nevada.

In acknowledging the contributions mail-order seed companies have made to this book we make note of the important service they perform in making available new introductions of disease resistant varieties.

To all companies listed on page 111, we thank you for your help. To the following who became more involved in the development of this book, a special thank you:

Gerald F. Burke—
   W. Atlee Burpee Co.,
   Riverside, California

Kenneth Relyea—Farmer Seed &
   Nursery, Faribault, Minnesota.

Donald Jacobson—Gurney Seed &
   Nursery Co., Yankton, So. Dakota.

Charles B. Wilson—
   Harris Seeds, Rochester, N.Y.

William Overbey—Earl May Seed &
   Nursery Co., Sheneandoah, Iowa.

Glenn G. Vincent—George W. Park
   Seed Co., Greenwood, So. Carolina.

Eldridge Freeborn—H. G. Hastings
   Co., Atlanta, Georgia.

Acknowledgement is hereby given to contributors who can't be classified: Francis Ching of the Los Angeles State and County Arboretum who found ways to make our test garden a part of the many practical educational functions of the arboretum.

Jack Chandler, landscape architect, who designed the St. Helena test garden and with total family involvement, brought it through a successful season.

Richard Westcott who checked copy and kept us and our photographers in touch with gardeners in South Florida.

John Matthias, architectural designer of San Rafael, California, who stirred a good chunk of imagination into the mix of this book.

Special Food Features: Lou Seibert Pappas

Art Direction: James Lienhart, Ron Hildebrand

Photography: Clyde Childress, William Aplin

Illustrations: Ron Hildebrand, E. D. Bills

Production: Richard Ray, William Montgomery, and the staff of Regensteiner Publishing Enterprises

John M. Bridgman of San Francisco and Yorkville, California, who brought 15 years of gardening experience, detailed and documented, into this book.

Aaron Keiss for his research and words about herbs, vegetable history, and climate.

How to use this book

If you have room for a small vegetable garden, one way to use this book is to put it aside, and think what you would do without it. You might go down to the garden center, buy a bunch of seeds, some fertilizer, some manure and a bale or two of peat moss. Then spade up the soil in the sunniest spot you can find. Spread the peat moss and manure over the soil and add the fertilizer over it according to the directions on the package. Work the manure, peat and fertilizer into the soil with cultivator, rake or rented tiller. Read directions on the seed package—for planting seeds, thinning and distance between rows, then go ahead and plant the seeds. Millions of gardeners have raised billions of pounds of beautiful vegetables with the aid of common sense and by trial and error.

You can believe that we know that vegetable growing doesn't have to be a complicated affair and we have no intention of making it so.

We just hope that the suggestions and ideas in this book help you avoid some of the errors you might make and at the same time add a little excitement to your gardening experience.

"Just give me the facts"

If you want to get right down to the basic how-to-plant information—"Just the lean facts—the nitty-gritty" —turn to the planting chart on pages 18 and 19.

You may need to turn to it not only when you plant but when you plan your garden.

Note that there is more information here than how to plant. The 3 columns headed "Needs cool soil," "Tolerates cool soil," "Requires warm soil" are good clues on when to plant. At least, if you have an assortment of seeds in your pocket, you won't plant peas and beans on the same day.

Then turn to the "when to plant" charts for each major vegetable and add the "when" to the "how to" plant.

Watch for the bold face line "Mistakes beginners make" throughout the book. They are simple warnings of hazards to avoid.

About the plants you can't grow.

Don't let this book upset you because it talks about plants you can't grow — or think you can't grow in your climate. We have met too many gardeners who find their gardening pleasure in growing what can't be grown. If the attachment to the plant is strong enough, they'll grow it even if they have to build a special climate around it.

Putting first things first.

Remember how you read about the ways to improve your soil, or how to plant seed, or how to fertilize or do anything about a plant growing in garden soil, and that all may be lost if one step in the operation is neglected? That important step is *weeding*.

It doesn't take many days of neglect after the vegetable seedlings emerge for weed growth to almost nullify the work and cost of preparing the soil, adding organic matter and fertilizer. All the time spent in choosing and finding the right varieties, all of the hours of planning the garden, can be wasted or made less fruitful by the competition of weeds.

The good gardener learns to enjoy hand weeding. Kneeling, squatting or sitting, he looks at the plants at eye level. Pulling a grassy weed that is about to strangle a carrot seedling is an act of kindness that is sure to be rewarded. If the tops of the weeds break off, the soil is too dry. Right before his eyes is proof of how quickly weeds can rob the seedlings of water and nutrient.

How to avoid disappointments.

Get acquainted with some of the gardeners we worked with. Read about their successes and disappointments in "The Spoilers" on page 20, and their discoveries in the "Good Ideas From Good Gardeners" in pages 98-101. Then elsewhere in the book as you come upon warnings such as "Mistakes Beginners Make" repeated with almost every vegetable, accept them as positive pointers to success rather than warnings of disaster.

In the experience of the majority of our gardening friends and workers, the successes outweighed the disappointments. As one gardener wrote in answer to the question, "Did anything surprise you?": "How well things grow under the right conditions and how poorly under the wrong conditions."

Planning the garden.

There is a world of difference between growing *vegetables* and *vegetable gardening*.

When you think *vegetable gardening*, a sequence of operations comes to mind. Planning what to grow in the space you have. What varieties? When should we start? When the first harvest? How can we stretch the harvest with a succession of plantings? It's a mind-bending exercise in juggling space and time. (You'll find help in planning gardens from box sizes to 25 x 30 footers on pages 30-33).

Growing *vegetables* without a conventional vegetable garden and without trying to supply vegetables in quantity offers many options; vegetables in the flower border, page 106; growing vegetables and growing kids, page 102; vegetables in boxes and tubs, page 5, 13 and all through the book.

Looking for the hard-to-find.

Each year more unusual "vegetables" are made available to seed companies. If a newly introduced vegetable is in the hard-to-find class, the catalog number or numbers is given following the item. This number is keyed to the number of the seed company on page 111.

The items carried by a number of the seed companies are not keyed. You'll find them in 4 or more of the catalogs from the seed companies on the list.

With a grain of salt

In this book we follow the ways of all conventional vegetable books and bulletins and give what appear to be precise measurements in pounds, square feet, and length of row for applying fertilizers, precise-looking dates or charts for the time to plant. The directions for planting seed are expressed in inches between plants and between rows, and sometimes in degrees of temperature.

At first glance a reader may assume that there is an exact formula, a scientifically tested recipe for the care and feeding of each vegetable.

Actually, giving exact recipes for growing plants is like writing a cookbook using an oven of unknown temperature controls, flour that varies from fine to coarse, milk that may be sweet or sour, and water of unknown quality.

That a gardener can follow the directions given and grow perfect vegetables proves that the measurements are not critical. There's plenty of room for error.

The good gardener uses the dates and pounds and inches as reference points and makes the adjustments needed in managing his particular piece of soil and climate. And only out of experience in growing plants can he make those adjustments.

Many are the gardeners who measure fertilizer by the handful or the look of it scattered on the soil, and let the plants give them the signal when to apply it, by color and size of leaf and rate of growth. The trouble with measurements by instinct is that when exceptional results are obtained, the gardener has no way of duplicating the treatment. And the trouble with fertilizing when the plant shows signs of needing it, is that it may be too late to do any good.

Challenge the authorities.

Don't accept the recipes and direction in this book or any other with blind faith. Only the plants in your garden can tell you the truth and the plant is always right, no matter what an authority has said. Dr. Frits Went says it this way:

"Once the amateur has realized that he himself is master of the situation in his garden, and that he is not the slave of a set of recipes, a great deal is gained. Gardening comes out of the realm of mystic beliefs, and becomes an adventure in adaptation. Each plant grown becomes an experiment, instead of a routine performance. That plant becomes the test whether the applied principle was right. If the plant does not grow well or dies, the application of the principles was not right, or the conditions were such that the principle did not work. If, on the other hand, the plant behaves well, it shows the applicability of the principle.

By looking at the plants in this way, a garden becomes immensely interesting, it becomes the testing ground of ideas, and it frees the mind from dogmatism. The gardener becomes aware of the fact that experiments can be carried out everywhere, and are not restricted to highly specialized laboratories.

Science is not a cult, it flourishes where these observations are faithfully recorded.

"Why always in rows?"

In the planting chart and in the planting directions for the individual vegetables, the space between plants in a row and the distance between rows is spelled out.

To the first time gardener anxious to make a small plot of ground produce a bumper crop, the distances between rows seem unnecessarily wide.

You can cheat on these distances but remember that weeding and harvesting will be difficult. You must compensate for lack of space for the roots to run by more frequent fertilizing and watering. Crowding also cuts down on air circulation and invites foliage diseases.

Using a small piece of ground for a mass planting of vegetables makes good sense.

For example, carrots can be grown in the same way you would start a lawn. Sow as you would grass seed, rake in lightly. Cover with a thin mulch of ground bark, peat moss or vermiculite and water as you would a new lawn. Seeds will sprout in about the same time as it would take a quality bluegrass.

The lawn of lettuce will need an initial overall thinning and then selective thinning as you eat them.

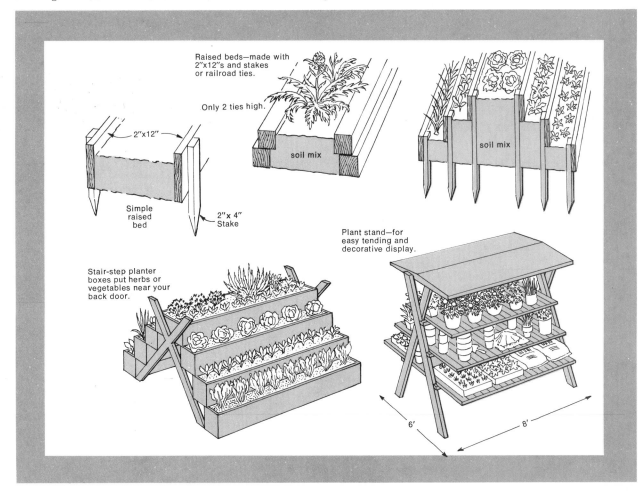

4

Fair is fair.

The superiority of home-grown over store-bought corn, snap beans, peas and all vegetables that lose their fresh sunshine quality quickly after picking is well advertised. Vegetables that must be picked green to allow for time in shipment, lack the taste quality the home gardener expects of his tomatoes and melons.

But, as we learned in working with home gardeners and in our test gardens, home-grown quality is not automatic.

At least the first-time gardener should know that he can grow a tough stringy beet or a bitter bunch of lettuce, and that home-grown turnips and kohlrabi can be almost inedible if not harvested at the young, half-grown stage.

There is no need to downgrade the commercially grown vegetables to elevate the home-grown varieties. Only when the best varieties are grown with the water and fertilizers the plants need *and harvested* at the right time, will the taste be something to brag about: "So much better than that store-bought stuff."

Getting along with nature.

On pages 26-29 you'll find a miscellany of suggestions on how to avoid battles with Nature you can't win, how to alter unfavorable environments Nature provides, and how to live with Nature's whims and tricks. And how the natural gardener swings with Nature's rhythm.

Growing without a vegetable garden

Gardeners, denied a luxury of rich, loamy soil, are not only finding ways to seed vegetables into very limited spaces but in doing so are finding ways to grow vegetables more effectively.

Many a gardener finds himself working with soil that won't support a vegetable garden. The soil may have a shallow layer of rocks or hardpan, or heavy clay that drains slowly or some other combination that is unfriendly to plants and hard to manage.

In such problem situations, growing plants above the soil is the best answer. The soil raised above ground level is held in place by 1" or 2" boards or with railroad ties as illustrated, or with brick or concrete.

If the raised bed is accessible from both sides, a width of 6 to 8' is practical. Planting, weeding and harvesting can be handled without walking in the bed. If the raised bed is alongside a fence or for any reason accessible from only one side, make the width 3 to 4'. The height of the bed should be at least 12" above the soil. If built 16" high and capped with 2 x 6" boards, you can weed while you sit.

When the bed is filled with a lightweight mix rich in organic matter, you have a very efficient vegetable growing factory. Drainage through the soil is good and with soil raised above ground level, drainage away from the bed is possible. Unless the soil around the bed is flooded, the soil and the raised bed will never be water logged.

In a wet, cool spring the soil in the raised bed will warm up and be ready for planting weeks before regular garden soils can be seeded.

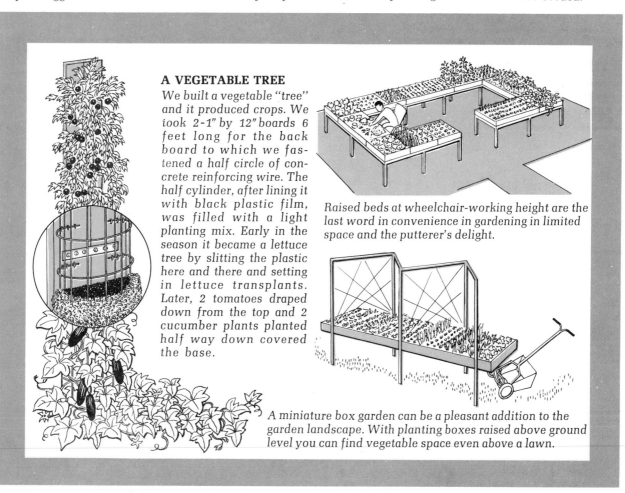

A VEGETABLE TREE

We built a vegetable "tree" and it produced crops. We took 2-1" by 12" boards 6 feet long for the back board to which we fastened a half circle of concrete reinforcing wire. The half cylinder, after lining it with black plastic film, was filled with a light planting mix. Early in the season it became a lettuce tree by slitting the plastic here and there and setting in lettuce transplants. Later, 2 tomatoes draped down from the top and 2 cucumber plants planted half way down covered the base.

Raised beds at wheelchair-working height are the last word in convenience in gardening in limited space and the putterer's delight.

A miniature box garden can be a pleasant addition to the garden landscape. With planting boxes raised above ground level you can find vegetable space even above a lawn.

A well built raised bed can support a lot of extras. Side boards can be used to hold wire frames to keep out birds and cats, or plastic covers to increase warmth or protect from frost. Plastic covers can be used to prolong the growth of lettuce and other salad makings well into the winter.

There is another advantage to the raised bed that is seldom appreciated. As a clean and neat structure the gardener is more likely to keep it cleaner than an equal amount of planting space in a corner of the garden. Weeds are more distracting in a raised bed.

If our prejudice for growing vegetables in raised beds shows in the pages of this book, know that we are not alone. See the raised bed endorsement in "Carrots," page 42 and in "Good Ideas," page 98.

Vegetable factory. A gardener with limited space can afford to take measures that increase production and remove some of the hazards of conventional vegetable gardening. Inventive gardeners are rediscovering the advantages of the old frame gardens, the raised bed, the cold frame and the hot bed.

As an example of what might be done with a space of just 3 x 9' we have diagrammed a combined raised bed, cold frame and greenhouse.

Call it what you want to, it illustrates one way to concentrate the growing of vegetables in an environment free from any of the hazards in open-space gardening. The use of such a structure will add weeks to the growing season, early and late. The hazards of heavy rains and blistering sun during a heat wave can be averted by a choice of frames and covers. Use plastic covers when it rains, lath or shade cloth when the summer sun is blazing hot. Wire coverings have their place when wind damage is critical.

Vegetables in containers
Growing vegetables when the garden is a balcony on the third floor of an apartment house or the patio of a mobile home, or a deck on a hillside or a roof top, is possible, practical and enjoyable.

By using one of the lightweight synthetic soils available at garden stores (see page 8) gardeners are finding that in boxes, baskets, plastic bags, clay pots, plastic pots, half-barrels, wire cages, they can create the ideal environment for root growth.

Tomatoes, free from infested soil problems, thrive so well in containers that gardeners with plenty of ground space are switching to pots, boxes and baskets. (see Tomatoes, page 62.)

Eggplants and peppers take the place of ornamentals on terraces and patios. A planter box 8" deep, 12" wide and 3' long will deliver enough beets or carrots or lettuce for many meals (see page 30.)

The dirt gardener with all the growing space he needs may laugh at the extreme measures some people will take to grow a few vegetables.

But as you can see in the illustrations below there is method in the madness.

When planting space is lifted waist high, weeding changes from chore to play. These planting beds invite frequent attention.

Grass and tree roots can't invade the above-ground garden. There are more ways to follow the sun when the garden is above ground and portable.

Planting beds that fit into the level area gracefully or playfully invite the putterer, amaze the visitor and prove that gardening doesn't have to be serious.

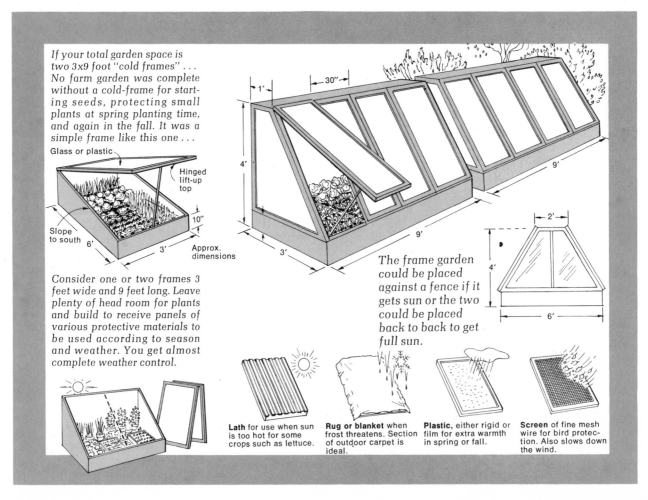

If your total garden space is two 3x9 foot "cold frames" ... No farm garden was complete without a cold-frame for starting seeds, protecting small plants at spring planting time, and again in the fall. It was a simple frame like this one ...

Glass or plastic
Hinged lift-up top
Slope to south
Approx. dimensions

Consider one or two frames 3 feet wide and 9 feet long. Leave plenty of head room for plants and build to receive panels of various protective materials to be used according to season and weather. You get almost complete weather control.

The frame garden could be placed against a fence if it gets sun or the two could be placed back to back to get full sun.

Lath for use when sun is too hot for some crops such as lettuce.

Rug or blanket when frost threatens. Section of outdoor carpet is ideal.

Plastic, either rigid or film for extra warmth in spring or fall.

Screen of fine mesh wire for bird protection. Also slows down the wind.

Vegetables grow up and hang down. The small-space gardener takes full advantage of vertical space. He looks at a fence 5' high and 20' long as 100 square feet of gardening space. He can cover it with vines of beans, cucumbers, tomatoes, squash or gourds without losing very much ground space. He can attach planter boxes to the fence for plants that drape, such as cherry and pear tomatoes or the miniature 'Tiny Tim' or 'Small Fry' or cucumbers. When growing vegetables in planter boxes on fences or at the base of the fence, he must compensate for the limited soil space. The more the roots are restricted, the more frequently water and nutrients are added.

The gardener without a vegetable garden by necessity avoids the over planting and wasted harvest so common in the conventional garden. He doesn't guess what a 20' row of beets will produce, he can sow seeds, a box or two of each, with the thinnings for greens and harvest just what the cook calls for.

A container gardener is more likely to plant a succession of a few green onions and a few head of lettuce than a dirt gardener will.

Planting for a succession of harvests with boxes is the very best way to approach planting a 3 x 9' garden or a 10 x 20' garden. See Planting the garden, pages 30-33.

Inquisitive gardeners find container gardening gives them new freedom. The dirt gardener might well hesitate to plant one sweet potato as a trial or 3 or 4 peanut seeds or $\frac{1}{2}$ dozen shallots or multiplier onions, or 2 or 3 miniature varieties of cabbage or one plant of the small lemon cucumber. The container gardener can always find room for one more pot or box. We have kept this inquisitive gardener in mind every time we tackled the presentation of a vegetable.

The container gardener can find ways to change the climate easier than the dirt gardener. In a climate too cool for eggplant, for example, the reflected heat of a house wall may give the eggplant all of the extra heat it needs to produce fruits.

From the standpoint of early harvest of vegetables, growing in containers offers many advantages.

Using a commercial planter mix as the soil, you can plant when it's time to plant. There is no wait for rain-soaked soil to dry out.

It's easy to give a planter box protection from wind and frost.

Plants in a sterilized planter mix are free from damage by nematodes and soil-borne diseases.

Remember if you plant a balcony garden and there is a balcony below you, don't forget that water is a part of gardening and it drips. Saucers under pots, a floor under planters of black plastic film will avoid neighbor trouble.

When using solid plastic pails and trash containers, don't forget to provide drainage. Drill holes, spaced evenly along the sides, near the bottom. Don't drill holes in the bottom itself.

You can use bags of Jiffy Mix, Pro-Mix, Peat-Lite and other lightweight mixes that are packaged in plastic bags as leak-proof planters on decks and balconies. Simply cut slits for planting "holes." Add water until all of the mix is wet. Don't overwater to the point of sogginess. Set in transplants of lettuce, tomatoes or whatever. Plants require far less frequent watering than when grown in pots or boxes. These lightweight mixes maintain good aeration even in the plastic bags.

If you think we are exaggerating the possibilities and enjoyments of growing vegetables without a garden, send for USDA Bulletin No. 163, *"Mini-gardens for Vegetables."* See page 111 for address and cost.

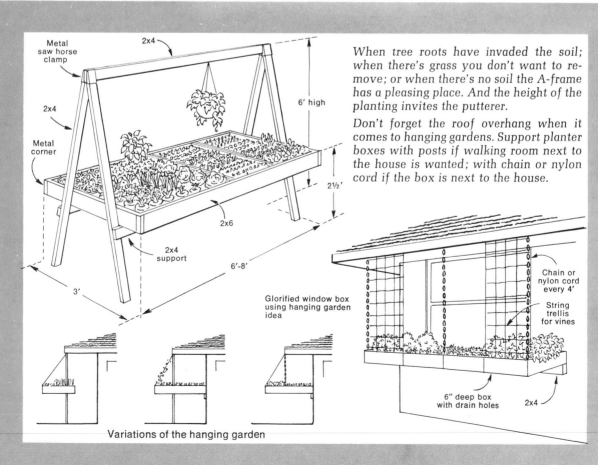

Metal saw horse clamp

2x4

2x4

Metal corner

6' high

2½'

2x6

2x4 support

3'

6'-8'

When tree roots have invaded the soil; when there's grass you don't want to remove; or when there's no soil the A-frame has a pleasing place. And the height of the planting invites the putterer.

Don't forget the roof overhang when it comes to hanging gardens. Support planter boxes with posts if walking room next to the house is wanted; with chain or nylon cord if the box is next to the house.

Glorified window box using hanging garden idea

Chain or nylon cord every 4'

String trellis for vines

6" deep box with drain holes

2x4

Variations of the hanging garden

The fundamentals

Soil

In this short chapter we look at soils from two viewpoints. One of the gardener planning to grow vegetables in containers of some kind, and one of the dirt gardener about to prepare a plot of ground for vegetables.

Soils and the dirt gardener. Anyone who has read the planting directions on a seed packet or a catalog is familiar with such instructions as "Sow seed in early spring as soon as the soil can be worked" and "Plant in a well-drained sandy loam."

How *early* is "as soon as the ground can be worked" in your garden? A rain-soaked heavy clay soil may not be ready for spading or tilling until spring gives way to summer. The best growing season for such crops as peas and lettuce may be lost.

Why the repeated emphasis on "good drainage"? When water replaces the air in the soil, roots suffocate. Roots will not develop without a constant supply of oxygen and a constant removal of carbon dioxide.

A well-drained soil is one in which the water moves through quickly, never completely shutting off the movement of air through the soil.

A sandy soil is well-drained but dries out quickly. Frequent watering washes nutrients through the soil.

The best advice a gardener ever had was "Don't try to live with an unfavorable soil." Nothing can dampen the enthusiasm of the beginner more quickly than a hard-to-manage soil.

The only quick way to change either a heavy clay soil or a light sandy soil to a substitute for a rich loam is through the addition of organic matter. Not just a little organic matter but lots of it.

The addition of organic matter—compost, peat moss, manure, sawdust, ground bark—makes clay soils more mellow and easier to work.

Organic matter opens up tight clay soils, improves drainage and allows air to move more readily through the soil, warming it up earlier in the spring.

In light sandy soils, organic matter holds moisture and nutrients in the root zone.

Don't confuse this massive addition of organic matter to the soil with the long-term improvement program that comes with the breakdown of organic matter into true humus (that final black sticky stuff that holds soil particles together in crumbs).

The quantity of organic matter must be large enough to physically change the structure of the soil. And *enough* means that at least 1/3 of the final mix is organic matter.

To add this amount, spread a layer of organic matter over the soil at least 2 inches thick and work it in to a depth of 4 inches.

Make the addition of organic matter when preparing the soil for planting. Spread the normal amount of fertilizer over the organic material (that would be 4 to 5 pounds of 5-10-10 per 100 square feet) and till it into the soil very thoroughly.

If you use peat moss, add ground limestone at the rate of 5 pounds per 100 square feet.

If you add raw sawdust that has not been composted or fortified with nitrogen, the amount of fertilizer will have to be increased to take care of the bacteria that go to work on the sawdust. Without additional nitrogen with the sawdust the bacteria will rob the soil of nitrogen while breaking down the sawdust.

For every 10 cubic feet of sawdust, add $1/2$ pound of actual nitrogen. That means 10 pounds of 5-10-10 or 4 pounds of blood meal. And that means 18 pounds of 5-10-10 per 100 square feet of sawdust 2 inches thick.

The following table shows how much sawdust or like organic material is needed to cover 100 square feet at various depths.

Depth (inches)	To cover 100 Sq. Ft.
6	2 cu. yds.
4	35 cu. ft.
3	1 cu. yd.
2	18 cu. ft.
1	9 cu. ft.
$1/4$	2 cu. ft.
$1/8$	1 cu. ft.
1 cubic yard = 27 cubic feet	

If measurements in cubic feet make you wince, see *teaching children garden math* page 108.

When setting out a few plants of tomatoes, eggplants, peppers, melons, cucumbers, zucchini, the preparation of soil in individual planting

What "mix thoroughly" means.
When you make your own planting mix (see text) remember that thorough mixing is essential. Each portion of the mix, down to a 2" potful, must have the same proportions of all the ingredients—and you can't get that by stirring.

Start with a pile of peat moss (dampened) and vermiculite. Mix a little and then scatter the other ingredients over the pile. Shoveling from this pile start a cone-shaped pile by pouring each shovelful directly on top so that each shovelful dribbles down the sides. Repeat the cone building three times.

The only way we know to get a more even mix is with a mechanical mixer.

holes is a good way to make the most of the addition of organic matter. Dig a hole for each. Make a 50-50 mix of the top soil and peat moss and back fill the mix. For good measure, put a shovelful of manure at the bottom of the hole.

If your soil is heavy clay and water doesn't drain through it, the hole may become a bathtub in which the plant will drown. In problem soils, plant above ground in raised beds.

The no soil gardener. For the mini-gardener, the roof-top gardener, the pot-box-tub gardener, the garden stores have soil substitutes or synthetic soils that have many advantages over soil. They are clean, free of weed seeds and plant disease organisms. They are very lightweight. Containers filled with these synthetic soils are easy to move.

As a growing medium for vegetables the mixes are almost foolproof. They can scarcely be waterlogged. Excess water drains through rapidly. Plant roots will spread throughout the well-aerated "soil," rather than develop at the edge of the containers.

Cornell and the University of California pioneered in formulating standard "soil" mixes for commercial plant growers. Mixes, following their formulas, are available under several labels. Some of the nationally distributed brands are 'Jiffy Mix,' 'Redi Earth,' 'Pro-Mix.' In the West several companies package the U.C. type mix under such brands as 'First Step' and 'Super Soil.'

The basic difference between the original U.C. mix and the Cornell version was in the use of vermiculite in

the Cornell mix and fine sand in the U.C. mix.

Use the mixes straight in small containers. Extend them with garden soil in large containers and raised beds.

You can make your own 'soil' mix. If you are going to fill a few planter boxes, a half dozen large pots or plan on using it in raised beds, mix the largest amount that can easily be handled in one mixing operation. That will be about a yard or 27 cubic feet. The mix is made up of equal amounts of peat moss and vermiculite. Peat moss comes in 6-cubic-foot bales and vermiculite in 4-cubic-foot bags. So you buy 2 bales of peat moss and 3 bags of vermiculite and call it a yard. The peat moss will expand to more than make up the difference between 24 and 27 cubic feet.

Dampen peat moss and roughly mix it with the vermiculite. Spread these fertilizers over the pile: 6 pounds of 5-10-10 commercial fertilizer; 2 pounds of superphosphate; 5 pounds of agricultural lime. Then mix and mix and mix again.

Best way to mix is to shovel first rough mix into a cone-shaped pile, allowing each shovelful to run down the cone as it builds up. See illustration.

If a smaller quantity will take care of your needs, cut down on all elements in proportion.

Composting

The objective of composting is to convert waste material into a sort of synthetic manure—dark brown crumbly stuff with the good-earth fragrance.

You take leaves, grass clippings, small prunings, straw, spoiled hay, sawdust, green weeds, dry weeds, vegetable harvest refuse, vegetable matter from the kitchen, coffee grounds, eggshells, shredded paper, wood ashes, and pile them in such a way that soil bacteria can thrive and multiply and break down these waste materials into a form you can use.

The bacteria are the converters of the raw material and they must have a workable environment. They need moisture, air, and food.

Grass clippings, green weeds, lettuce leaves, pea vines and other succulent materials contain sugar and proteins which are excellent nutrients for the bacteria. They decompose rapidly—sometimes too rapidly. However, dry leaves, small twigs, sawdust, and like woody dry materials decompose very slowly unless the bacteria are supplied with extra nitrogen.

The size of the woody material will affect the rate of decomposition. If leaves, large and small, go into the pile as they are raked up, decomposition will be much slower than when shredded by a rotary mower.

Prunings, clippings, wood chips will take months to break down even with extra nitrogen. However, when

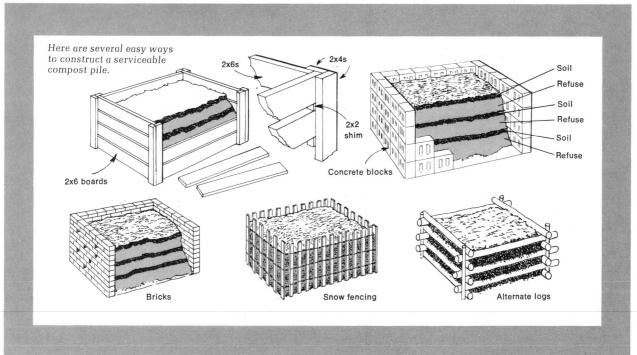

Here are several easy ways to construct a serviceable compost pile.

2x6s · 2x4s · 2x2 shim · 2x6 boards · Concrete blocks · Soil · Refuse · Soil · Refuse · Soil · Refuse · Bricks · Snow fencing · Alternate logs

put through a shredder, and mixed with green material, they will decompose rapidly.

If you have grass clippings in large quantities you must mix them thoroughly into the composting material to avoid odor and fly problems. A good load of fine grass clippings will make a soggy mass and putrify instead of decaying normally. Flies seem to regard the mass of clippings as an egg incubator. After mixing into the compost spread a layer of soil or old compost over the top.

The classic layer cake. Gardeners have found that some form of a series of layers of waste material with fertilizers, manures and garden soil between layers is the best way to build a compost pile.

The size of the pile will depend on the size of your garden. But two piles 4 by 6 are easier to manage than one 4 by 12.

You start the pile by spreading a layer of refuse about 6 to 8 inches thick over the 4 by 6-foot area. Spread over this layer a mixture of manure, garden soil and commercial fertilizers. This is the filling on the layer cake. And it's on the composition of this filling that composters have different opinions.

Both manure and a commercial fertilizer should be used to give the bacteria the food they need. The amount will be more if the waste material is dry rather than green. The greater the amount of fertilizer the richer will be the compost. A good average amount for each layer is 2 cupfuls of ammonium sulfate or blood meal.

Wet down the fertilizer layer just enough to carry the chemicals through the layer; don't wash them out with heavy watering.

In areas where the soil is on the acid side, the addition of a cupful of ground limestone, crushed oyster shell or dolomite lime to each layer will give you a less acid product and improve decomposition as well.

Add another layer of vegetable matter, spread the soil-manure-chemical layer over it and wet it down. Repeat the layering process until you run out of material or the pile is 4 to 5 feet high.

Form a basin at the top for watering and to catch rain.

Keep the pile as wet as a squeezed-out sponge. In a dry climate it may need water as often as every 4 to 5 days in warm weather.

Under normal conditions the pile should be turned in 2 or 3 weeks and again in 5 weeks. It should be ready to use in 3 months.

You can shorten that time to a few weeks if the material is put through a shredder before building the pile. The smaller pieces decompose faster since more surface is exposed to decay bacteria. Shredding also makes a fluffier mixture, allowing more efficient air and water penetration.

If the pile is built when the weather is warm you'll see heat waves rising above the pile in 24 to 30 hours. Turn the pile to mix the material and follow up with a thorough watering. It will heat again, and in a few days be hot enough to require turning again. Each time you turn it, move outer materials towards the center where heat and moisture encourage decomposition.

One advantage to the fast high-heat method of composting is the destruction of most of the weed seeds.

To get the most benefit out of composting it pays to have 3 piles going. One in which the compost is ready to use as a synthetic manure. Another that furnishes partially decomposed material for mulching. And one that's working in the first stages of the recycling process.

Use rotary mower to shred and bag fallen leaves and then add to compost pile.

Motorized shredder-baggers make everything from leaves to branches the right size for a mulch or fast breakdown in a compost pile.

Squash and pumpkins grow luxuriously in composting soil after the high heat stage is over.

The smaller the prunings and clippings, the faster the bacteria and molds can break them down.

Water

Of all the lines, chapters and volumes of *advice to gardeners* the most difficult to understand, the most frustrating and the most confusing, are on the subject of watering.

Ask why the tomato blossoms dropped and among other reasons you are told "either too much or too little water." Ask why the carrots are stumpy and you are warned against overwatering. Ask about bitterness in lettuce and you are warned against an uneven supply of water.

What's "too much" and "too little"? One answer: The phrase "too much water" is used in two ways. Too much water for the roots to grow in; and a supply of water (moisture) that gives the plant maximum leaf growth, rather than fruit.

Water has been called the "hazardous necessity." That means that you can kill a plant right fast with water. Plant roots require moisture and air for growth. They require a growing medium in which air can move through bringing oxygen for their growth and removing the carbon dioxide they respire.

Stop the supply of air by filling all of the air spaces in the soil with water and root growth stops. The longer time that air is cut off, the greater the damage.

Damaged roots have little defense against the entrance of rot-causing soil organisms. And so the plant dies of root rot.

Another series of warnings of the hazards of water comes at the reader of garden advice in the planting directions for the various vegetables. "Plant in a *well-drained*, rich loamy soil," or "Does best in a light, well drained soil."

Such warnings mean that the plant is easily damaged by too much water.

The gardener with good watering habits learns to apply water according to the nature of his soil. There is no way to half wet the soil. You prevent over-watering by making the intervals between watering fit the water holding capacity of the soil.

Soils on the clay side have a high water holding capacity, the air spaces are minute, and water moves through them slowly.

Such soils need infrequent watering. The gardener who manages them learns to use the spade test, to look at and feel the soil beneath the surface inches.

The very best way to solve the problem of water management is to prepare a garden soil that can't be overwatered. See "Soil" page 8.

The irrigation specialists have a useful word about water. A plant that is not getting its full quota of water is under *water stress*. As the moisture supply in the soil decreases, the plant must work harder. *Stress* is progressive, slight to severe.

Observant gardeners who have watched the quick flowering of annual flowers in a dry spell know what water stress will do. In growing herbs for a seed crop, putting the plant under water stress is normal procedure.

In the vegetable garden water stress is something you don't want—except on rare occasions such as the tomato that insists on vine production only.

Water stress affects various vegetables in special ways. A cucumber under stress just stops growing and when water is supplied, resumes growth.

Tomatoes, as they get near the size to harvest, will ripen all their fruits when put under stress.

Lettuce needs a steady supply of moisture and as its root system is shallow the frequency of watering will be high.

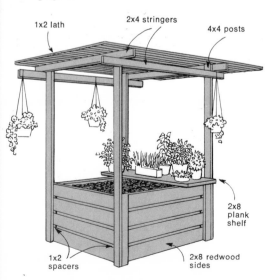
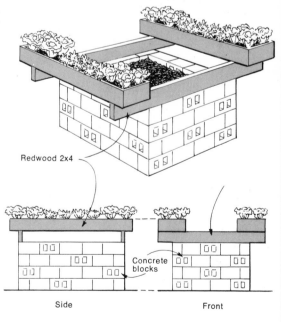

A properly managed compost pile is a small manufacturing plant turning out odorless synthetic manure. If there's no room to hide it, feature it with an overhead and call it a gazebo. Construction is basic "hammer-and-saw" taking off from the ordinary compost frame shown on page 9.

The compost pile made with concrete blocks (open at one end) can be relieved of the heavy masonry look with the addition of flower-vegetable boxes.

Muskmelons lose their sweetness if stressed for water in their ripening period.

It's difficult to say when in the life of any vegetable, watering is most critical. A report from Rutgers says that these are the periods when watering is most necessary for successful harvesting of the crop:

Vegetable	Critical Period
Asparagus	Brush—Fern
Broccoli	Head development
Cabbage	Head development
Carrot	Root enlargement
Cauliflower	Head development
Corn	Silking and tasseling, ear development
Cucumber	Flowering and fruit development
Eggplant	Flowering and fruit development
Lettuce	Head development
Lima bean	Pollination and pod development
Melon	Flowering and fruit development
Onion, dry	Bulb enlargement

The important fact about vegetables and water supply is that unlike flowers, vegetables never fully recover from a severe check in growth by the lack of moisture.

Wind protection in the vegetable garden pays off in several ways. Water loss is less with wind breaks; physical damage to plants is avoided; they take one negative factor out of the destructive combination of high temperatures, high light intensity, low humidities and strong winds.

Remember, too, that vegetable seedlings are poor competitors against weeds for their water supply.

The summer mulch of organic matter is important in maintaining a steady supply of moisture. See page 20 about mulches.

Fertilizers

The gardeners we worked with through the year handled their fertilizing program in many and, sometimes, strange ways. Every type of product from fish, blood meal, and manure, to commercial liquid and dry fertilizers was used. They talked about overfertilizing tomatoes and peppers and underfeeding cabbage. In three different locations where manure was free and easily available, they had trouble from a build-up of salts in the soil.

The first step in using fertilizer is to understand the label on bags and packages.

All commercial fertilizers are labeled by the percentages of nitrogen, phosphorus and potassium they contain.

There are many formulas, 4-12-4, 5-10-10, 6-20-10, 10-10-10 and so on, but the listings are always in the same order, with nitrogen first. In applying fertilizers, the percentage of nitrogen in the formula dictates the amount to be applied. The phosphorus and potassium just tag along. If the fertilizer you are using has a higher percentage of nitrogen, use less fertilizer. Gardeners who do not read directions on the package may double or treble the amount that should be applied if they don't watch the nitrogen percentage.

In the following chart you can see how the amount to be applied decreases as the percentage of nitrogen increases. (Assume that fertilizer recommendations call for 3 to 4 pounds per 100 square feet.)

Formula	Pounds per 100 sq. ft.
5-10-10	3.5
6-20-10	2.8
8-24-8	2.0
10-10-8	1.7
16-16-15	1.0

In applying fertilizer the amount to apply per square foot or length of row is easy to figure when you use liquid measurements. A pint is a pound, 1 cup is half a pound, etc. Read how one family solved the problem of gardening measurements on page 108.

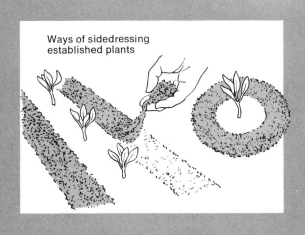

Ways of sidedressing established plants

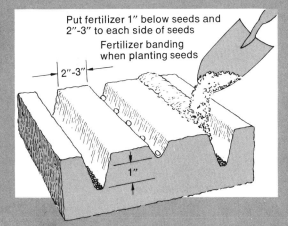

Put fertilizer 1″ below seeds and 2″-3″ to each side of seeds

Fertilizer banding when planting seeds

2″-3″

1″

When you look at the percent of water in various raw vegetables you can believe that water is important in the production of a crop. The percentages are not, of course, guides to the relative watering needs of the vegetables.

VEGETABLE	WATER %
Asparagus	91.7
Green bean pods	90.1
Beets—roots	87.3
Beets—greens	90.9
Broccoli	89.1
Cabbage	92.4
Chinese cabbage	95.0
Cauliflower	96.0
Celery	94.1
Swiss Chard	91.1
Chives	91.3
Cucumbers	95.1
Eggplant	92.4
Lettuce	95.0
Peas—shelled	78.0
Peas—edible pod	83.3
Peppers, hot (immature)	88.8
Peppers, sweet, green	93.4
ripe red	90.7
Potato	79.8
Radish	94.5
Squash, summer	94.0
winter	85.1
Tomato, ripe	93.5
Turnip	91.5
Watermelon	92.6

Ways to apply dry fertilizers.

(1) Mix with the soil before planting. Spread fertilizer evenly over soil at the rate called for on the fertilizer bag or box and work it into the soil with spade or power tiller.

(2) Apply in narrow bands of furrows 2 to 3 inches from the seed and 1 to 2 inches deeper than the seeds or plants are to be placed.

Careless placement of the band too close to the seeds will burn the roots of the seedlings. Best way is to stretch a string where the seed row is to be planted. With a corner of a hoe, dig a furrow 3 inches deep, 3 inches to one side of, and parallel to the string. Spread the fertilizer in the furrow and cover with soil. Repeat the banding operation on the other side of the string. Then sow seeds underneath the strings.

For plants widely spaced, such as tomatoes, fertilizers can be placed in bands six inches long for each plant or in a circle around the plant. Make the bands 4 inches from the plant base.

(3) Apply as a side-dressing after plants are up and growing. Scatter fertilizer on both sides of the row 6 to 8 inches from the plants. Rake it into the soil and water thoroughly. Banding is one way to satisfy the need many plants, especially tomatoes, have for a supply of phosphorus as the first roots develop. When fertilizers are broadcast and worked into soil, much of the phosphorus is locked up by the soil and is not immediately available to the plant. By concentrating the phosphorus in the band, the plant gets what it needs although much of the application is locked up.

Another way to satisfy the need for phosphorus is the use of a "starter solution" when setting out transplants of tomatoes, eggplant, peppers or cabbage. Any liquid fertilizer high in phosphorus can be used as a starter solution. Follow directions on the label.

Or you can make your own with the fertilizer you are using if it is high in phosphorus. When using 5-10-10, dissolve 1 pound in 5 gallons of water. It won't dissolve completely and must be stirred while using. Place the transplant in the planting hole, fill the hole half full of soil, pour in a cupful of the solution and finish filling the hole.

Take it easy with all types of fertilizers. Too much manure can cause as much trouble as any other kind of fertilizer. When using manure, cut down on the rate of fertilizers.

Follow label directions with liquid fertilizers.

Follow up dry fertilizer applications with a good watering to dissolve the fertilizer and carry it into the root zone.

When using large amounts of fertilizer for the heavy feeders such as cabbage and onions, apply half the amount before planting and side-dress with the remainder when growth is underway.

Check the timing for fertilizing application for each vegetable. With many crops the first application, aimed to protect early vigorous leaf growth, is all important. The yield of bush snap beans, for example, depends upon the size of the plant before flowering starts.

Plants grown in partial shade require less nitrogen than the same kind of plants grown in full sun.

Increase the amount of fertilizer when crowding plants by less spacing between rows and when grown in a random pattern in a small plot.

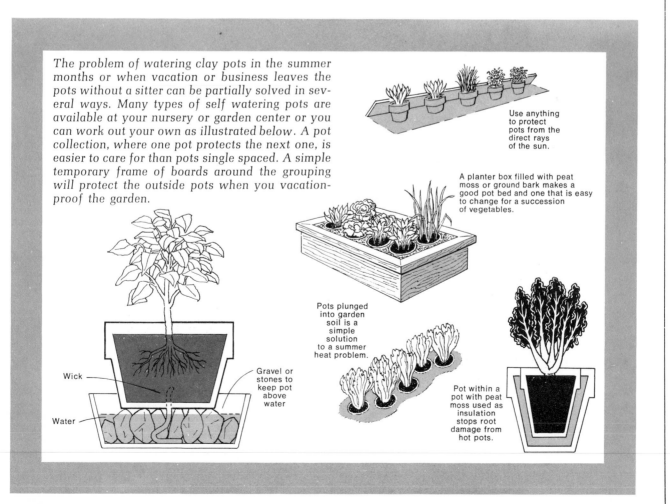

The problem of watering clay pots in the summer months or when vacation or business leaves the pots without a sitter can be partially solved in several ways. Many types of self watering pots are available at your nursery or garden center or you can work out your own as illustrated below. A pot collection, where one pot protects the next one, is easier to care for than pots single spaced. A simple temporary frame of boards around the grouping will protect the outside pots when you vacation-proof the garden.

Use anything to protect pots from the direct rays of the sun.

A planter box filled with peat moss or ground bark makes a good pot bed and one that is easy to change for a succession of vegetables.

Pots plunged into garden soil is a simple solution to a summer heat problem.

Pot within a pot with peat moss used as insulation stops root damage from hot pots.

Wick

Water

Gravel or stones to keep pot above water

Seeding and transplanting

Seeds

It's strange, but the simple business of sowing seed $1/4$ or $1/2$ or 1 inch deep, then covering the seeds with soil and finally keeping the soil around the seed damp, is not always successful.

One of our gardeners confessed, "For the first time in 13 years absolute failures were experienced. Diseases not before experienced were seen. Plants in excellent health from my greenhouse grew magnificently and then perished. Corn, cabbage, butter-nut squash, and onions did not even appear from seed."

Even the best of gardeners have experienced failure in germinating seeds now and then.

The first-time gardener sometimes kills by kindness. Don't overdo the preparation of a seed bed. Don't rake the soil until it is fine as dust. That's the way to make mud pies. When the soil dries out after watering the seeds will be imprisoned in a tight crust of soil.

Don't tenderly cover the seed with loose soil. Seed must have contact with soil.

Firm the soil over seed by tamping soil with side of rake or flat of hoe; tamp soil with a short piece of 2 by 4; or pat the soil.

If your soil is unfriendly because of heavy clay, and you don't want to improve the soil in the entire garden, add compost or other organic material to the row to be planted.

Don't rush the season. There's a race between rooting and rotting with many seeds. Corn, beans, especially limas in cold soil, for example. With such seeds the warmer the soil the better the chances for success.

If spring planting fever gets you while the soil is still cold, choose the seeds that tolerate cool soil. See planting chart page 18.

Depth of seed. The old rule of thumb is plant at a depth equal to 4 times the diameter of the seed. This rule and even the specific depth listed in the planting chart must be used with judgement. In wet weather or in heavy soils, plant shallow. If soils are light and sandy and dry weather is anticipated, plant deeper.

Several crops — parsnips, carrots, parsley, cress and, to a lesser degree, lettuce — benefit by very shallow planting $1/4$ inch or less.

Such shallow planting of seeds with a long germination period calls for close attention to sprinkling to prevent the soil surface from ever becoming dry.

Ways to prevent drying out and crusting of soil surface. Some gardeners cover soil rows with burlap sacks and sprinkle as necessary. With sacks there is always the danger of forgetting them for a few days at emergence time.

A $1/8$-inch mulch of vermiculite, bark or sawdust will prevent crusting and reduce the frequency of sprinkling. In windy weather, it's a good idea to contain the mulch in a slot to prevent it from blowing away.

Clear plastic is a good mulch but close watch for the emergence of seedlings is needed. Plastic must be removed as soon as seedlings show.

Bernard Pollack of Rutgers answered the question of mulch cover this way: "I think plastic is the answer. Make a shallow trough and plant seeds at bottom — cover trough with plastic (clear only) at an angle so water can run off. (See illus. below.)

"In New Jersey we call this 'trench

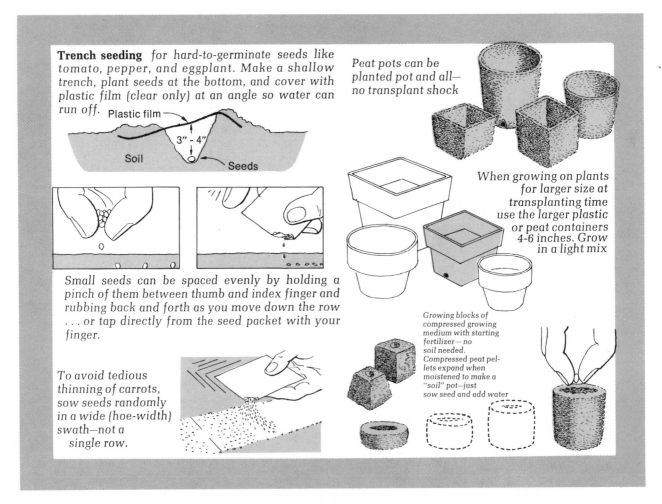

Trench seeding *for hard-to-germinate seeds like tomato, pepper, and eggplant. Make a shallow trench, plant seeds at the bottom, and cover with plastic film (clear only) at an angle so water can run off.*

Plastic film — Soil — 3" - 4" — Seeds

Small seeds can be spaced evenly by holding a pinch of them between thumb and index finger and rubbing back and forth as you move down the row . . . or tap directly from the seed packet with your finger.

To avoid tedious thinning of carrots, sow seeds randomly in a wide (hoe-width) swath—not a single row.

Peat pots can be planted pot and all— no transplant shock

When growing on plants for larger size at transplanting time use the larger plastic or peat containers 4-6 inches. Grow in a light mix

Growing blocks of compressed growing medium with starting fertilizer—no soil needed. Compressed peat pellets expand when moistened to make a "soil" pot—just sow seed and add water

culture' and we have had exceptionally good results with direct seeding of hard to germinate seeds like tomato, pepper, eggplant. The plastic cover prevents evaporation; heats the soil 20-30° higher than air temperature and makes the seed germinate fast and this prevents loss from disease. Plastic should be removed after germination to control weeds."

"Scatter" sowing. Consider the advantages of sowing seeds of carrots, beets and leaf lettuce in 3 or 4-inch wide bands rather than in a single line row. The problem of the first thinning is not as critical. With carrots, for example, there is less chance of tangled, malformed roots if the same number of seeds you normally sow in a foot of row are spaced out 3 to 4 inches wide. Some thinning will be necessary but much of it will be in pulling baby carrots. The disadvantage of the wide row is the necessity of hand weeding.

Commercial carrot growers spread carrot seeds in a 6-inch band by equipping the planter with a "scatter shoe."

All fine seeded vegetables that are used in the immature stage can be sowed in this fashion — beets and turnips for green tops, leaf lettuce and mustard for young leaves are examples.

Spacing seed in furrow. Some of the ways of dropping seed in the furrow are illustrated below. Here are a few more.

Sow small seeds in groups of 2 to 6 with a few inches between groups. It's said that the seeds help each other up when the soil is likely to crust over and it gives insurance against seed failures.

Mix small seeds and white sand in a saltshaker and shake down the furrow.

If you enjoy precision in spacing of small seeds, try this: Spread single sheets of facial tissue in the seed furrow. Seeds will show up clearly against the white paper and can be moved easily with pencil or toothpick. The tissue will rot away long before the seeds germinate.

A commercially available aid to precise sowing of fine seeds is the seed tape. Precisely spaced seeds are enclosed in water-soluble plastic.

Weeds. The competition with weed seedlings is always a problem. Every time the soil is worked, weed seeds are brought up to the surface where they find the best of conditions to germinate. And everything you do in the way of covering with clear plastic or a mulch will aid the weeds as well as the crop you are sowing.

First-time gardeners may wonder if their packet of seeds wasn't half weed seeds. In fact, Gerald Burke of the Burpee Company tells us that it is a frequent complaint. He writes: "One complaint we run into quite consistently is the story of the gardener who plants good seed out of the packet, but nothing but weeds come up. I guess this one bugs us as much as anything else. With today's highly developed techniques in cleaning vegetable and flower seed, the chance of weed seed appearing in any of these crops along with the good seed is negligible. There is a 1,000 times more weed seed in the soil than is ever going to be in a packet of seed."

Transplants

The root crops, beans, peas, corn, pumpkin and squashes are ordinarily seeded directly where they are to grow. Tomatoes, peppers, and eggplants are almost always set out in transplant size. Cabbage and its relatives, lettuce, onions, and melons are started both ways.

The most important reason for growing transplants is time saving. It permits the plant to grow before frost danger is over and before the soil is dry enough to work. It actually

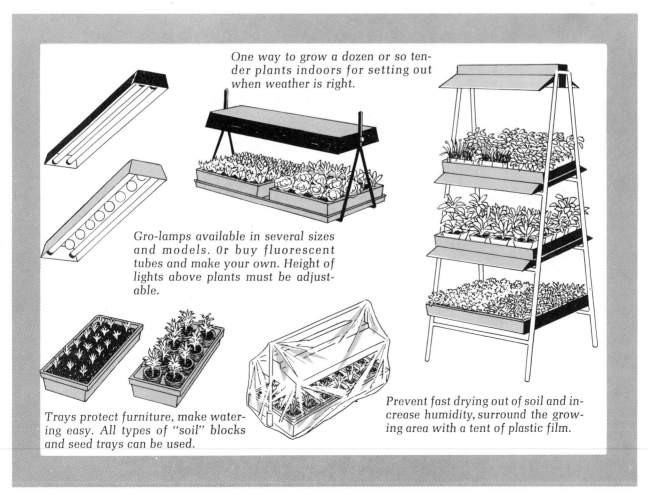

One way to grow a dozen or so tender plants indoors for setting out when weather is right.

Gro-lamps available in several sizes and models. Or buy fluorescent tubes and make your own. Height of lights above plants must be adjustable.

Trays protect furniture, make watering easy. All types of "soil" blocks and seed trays can be used.

Prevent fast drying out of soil and increase humidity, surround the growing area with a tent of plastic film.

lengthens the growing season by one to two months.

Starting from transplants avoids some of the hazards common to seedlings — birds, insects, heavy rain and weeds.

Whether you buy transplants or grow your own depends on whether you can buy the varieties you want and how you feel about starting from scratch. If it's fun, do it.

Methods of growing from seed to transplant size vary by the gardener. Some of the ways the gardeners on our panel handled the job are illustrated below.

Success in growing good transplants depends on how these basic requirements are met:

1. Disease-free growing medium.
2. Warmth and moisture for seed germination.
3. Adequate light for stocky growth.
4. An adjustment period to ready the indoor plant to open outdoor conditions.

These requirements can be met in several different ways:

Soil for seeds. Start seed in a medium that is free from disease-causing organisms.

Excellent germinating and growing materials, and plant containers are available at garden supply centers.

Vermiculite. A light weight expanded mica.

Synthetic soil mix. Jiffy Mix, Pro-Mix, Redi-Earth, etc. Seeds are sown in it, and seedlings grown in it.

Jiffy-7 Pellets. A compressed peat pellet containing fertilizer. When placed in water it expands to make a 1 3/4 by 2-inch container. Seed is placed directly in container after expanding.

BR8 Blocks. A plant growing fiber block containing fertilizer. Seed placed directly in block after block is thoroughly watered.

Kys-Kube. A ready-to-use fiber cube containing fertilizer. Seed placed directly in cube after cube is thoroughly watered.

Fiber Pots — Trays — Strips. Containers made of peat or other fibrous material. Fill with synthetic soil mix for growing on seedlings. No root disturbance, as container with plant is set out in garden soil.

Plastic. Pots or trays in various sizes and shapes. *Must* have drain holes in the bottom. Filled with synthetic soil

mix for growing seedlings. Root ball tipped out when transplanting.

Seeds in Vermiculite

Sow seeds about 1/4 to 1/2 inch deep in the moistened vermiculite. Pat lightly to firm vermiculite around seeds. Water lightly, cover with paper or slip the seed tray into a plastic bag.

When the first true leaves of the seedlings have formed, dig them out carefully and transplant into peat pots, plastic pot or whatever — filled with the synthetic soil. Make a small hole in the mix in the container and set the seedling in it so that the seed leaves are 1/2 inch from the surface. Press the mix firmly around the roots and stem. Water carefully. One advantage in starting seeds in vermiculite is the ease of lifting out the seedlings without damage to roots.

The use of vermiculite as the seeding "soil" and the mix of peatmoss and vermiculite as the "soil" for growing the seedlings avoids the death of seedlings from "damping off" caused by disease organisms in garden soil and composts.

If you wish to use compost or garden soil or to add either to the mix, it's a good idea to sterilize them.

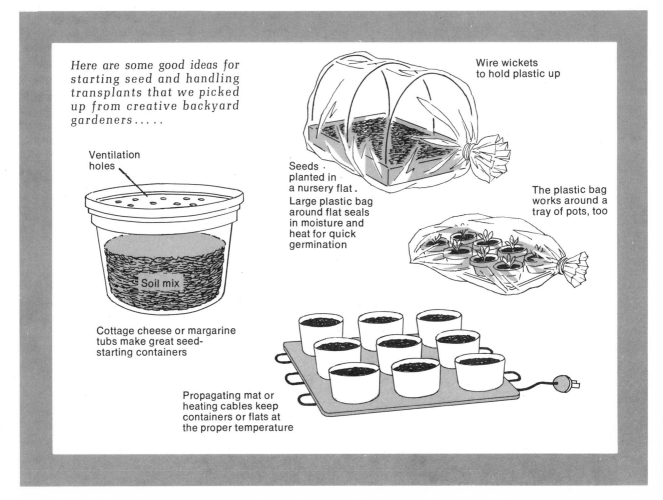

Here are some good ideas for starting seed and handling transplants that we picked up from creative backyard gardeners.....

Ventilation holes

Soil mix

Cottage cheese or margarine tubs make great seed-starting containers

Seeds planted in a nursery flat. Large plastic bag around flat seals in moisture and heat for quick germination

Wire wickets to hold plastic up

The plastic bag works around a tray of pots, too

Propagating mat or heating cables keep containers or flats at the proper temperature

Small quantities can be sterilized by baking the soil in the oven. Some experienced gardeners put the soil in coffee cans and bake at 350° for 1¹/₂ hours. Others place a potato in the soil and count it sterilized when the potato is done. The timing may be shortened if shallow containers are used. As soon as *all* the soil reaches 180° the job is done. In a shallow pan the soil may reach that temperature in 45 minutes with oven at 350°. Over cooking can release toxic substances in the soil.

Seeds in Blocks or Cubes

Seed is sown directly in the small blocks and in the expanding Jiffy Sevens. Of course the material should be thoroughly moist before seeds are sown. Give them the warmest spot you can find. For fast germination seeds of tomato, eggplant and pepper need a soil temperature of 75° to 85°.

Blocks should be covered with paper or slipped into a plastic bag to prevent drying out. There should be no need for watering until the seeds have sprouted.

Once the seedlings emerge, keep them in full sunlight — 12 hours a day if possible. The temperatures for seedling growth should be between 70° and 75° during the day and 60° to 65° during the night.

SETTING OUT

Transplants should go into the soil with as little root disturbance as possible. There will be very little with peat pots, cubes and blocks but be sure that all such containers are below soil level to prevent rapid drying out of the root ball.

It helps to pack soil down around the root ball. It also helps to "spot" water the root ball in addition to regular irrigation.

Plants in plastic or clay pots will tip out easier if the soil is wet.

Don't set a plant growing in a light soil mix in a small hole in heavy soil. Blend organic matter in a larger planting hole so that there is no abrupt change in soil texture.

See "Good Ideas from Good Gardening" page 99 for ways to protect transplants.

12 HOURS OF SUNLIGHT?

It's easy to give directions for the ideal way to grow transplants indoors, and the directions are easy to follow if "indoors" is a fully equipped greenhouse. But what do you do when you can't find a spot with 12 hours of sunlight and temperatures that fluctuate from 70° days and 65° nights throughout the growing period?

The answer is, you make do. We tallied some of the many ways our panel members carried out the transplant procedure. Some of them are sketched below.

"HARDENING" TRANSPLANTS

Young plants should not go directly from an indoor environment to the open garden. Take them outside in the daytime and bring them in again at night if frost is likely. In one way or another expose them to lower temperatures about 2 weeks before setting out. Also, gradually expose them to more sunlight.

Protecting the transplants with hot-caps or plastic covers in early plantings has more advantages than warming the soil and protection from frost.

Protecting the young plants from being ripped about by winds is equally important.

When using hot-caps or plastic covers, be sure there's some ventilation provided so that the young plants are not cooked by the heat build up.

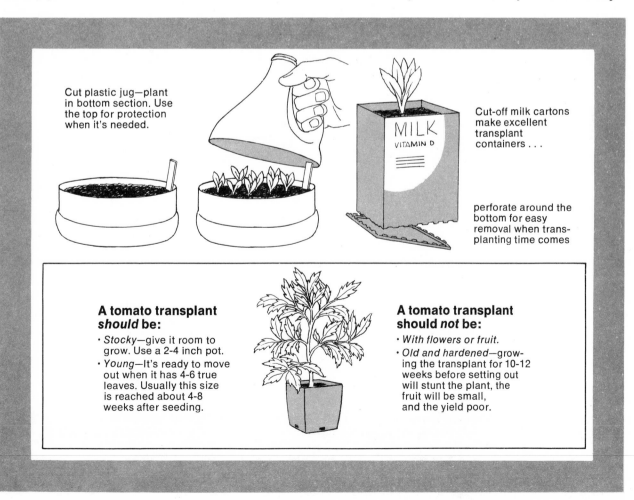

Cut plastic jug—plant in bottom section. Use the top for protection when it's needed.

Cut-off milk cartons make excellent transplant containers . . .

MILK VITAMIN D

perforate around the bottom for easy removal when transplanting time comes

A tomato transplant *should* be:
- *Stocky*—give it room to grow. Use a 2-4 inch pot.
- *Young*—It's ready to move out when it has 4-6 true leaves. Usually this size is reached about 4-8 weeks after seeding.

A tomato transplant should *not* be:
- *With flowers or fruit.*
- *Old and hardened*—growing the transplant for 10-12 weeks before setting out will stunt the plant, the fruit will be small, and the yield poor.

HOW TO USE THE PLANTING CHART

"Depth to plant seed." A quick look at the fractions and you know that many gardeners plant too deep.

"Number of seed to sow per foot." It's one answer to the question "How thick or thin should I sow seeds?" Our figures give the average of 6 expert seed-sowers — 3 pessimists and 3 optimists.

"Distance between plants." First figure is minimum. You get better growth at wider spacing. You cut down on the competition.

"Distance between rows." The minimum distance assumes that space is limited and weeding will be done by hand tools. Wider distance between rows is preferable and if power equipment is used, necessary.

"Number of days to germination." Number of days varies by soil temperature. Early spring sowings will take longer than later plantings. We give the range to answer questions like this one: "How long do I wait before I know I have to reseed?"

"Soil temperatures for seed." Seeds that "require cool soil" do best in a temperature range of 50°-65°; that "tolerate cool soil" in a 50°-85° range; those that "require warm soil" in a 65°-85° range.

"Weeks needed to grow to transplant size." The variation of 4-6, 5-7, 10-12 weeks allows for hot-bed, greenhouse, and window sill, and under grow-lamp conditions. Generally the warmer the growing conditions the shorter the time to grow transplants. However there must be allowance for a change from indoor to outdoor environment. See page 16.

"Days to maturity." Figures in this column show the *relative* length of time needed to grow a crop from seed or transplant to table use. The time will vary by variety and season.

Vegetable	Depth to plant seed (inches)	Number of seed to sow per foot	Distance between plants (inches)	Distance between rows (inches)	Number of days to germination	Needs cool soil	Tolerates cool soil	Needs warm soil	Weeks needed to grow to transplant size	Days to maturity	Remarks
Asparagus	1½		18	36	7-21		•		1 year	3 years	Sow in spring and transplant the following spring.
Beans: Snap Bush	1½-2	6-8	2-3	18-30	6-14			•		45-65	Make sequence plantings.
Snap Pole	1½-2	4-6	4-6	36-48	6-14			•		60-70	Long bearing season if kept picked.
Lima Bush	1½-2	5-8	3-6	24-30	7-12			•		60-80	Needs warmer soil than snap beans.
Lima Pole	1½-2	4-5	6-10	30-36	7-12			•		85-90	
Fava—Broadbean Winsor Bean	2½	5-8	3-4	18-24	7-14		•			80-90	Hardier than the common bean.
Garbanzo—Chick Pea	1½-2	5-8	3-4	24-30	6-12			•		105	
Scarlet Runner	1½-2	4-6	4-6	36-48	6-14			•		60-70	Will grow in cooler summers than common beans.
Soybean	1½-2	6-8	2-3	24-30	6-14			•		55-85 95-100	Choose varieties to fit your climate. See text.
Beets	½-1	10-15	2	12-18	7-10		•			55-65	Thin out extra plants and use for greens.
Black-eye Cowpea Southern Peas	½-1	5-8	3-4	24-30	7-10			•		65-80	
Yardlong Bean Asparagus Bean	½-1	2-4	12-24	24-36	6-13			•		65-80	Variety of Black eye peas. Grow as pole bean.
Broccoli Rabb—Italian Turnip—Sparachetti	½	6-10	8-12	24-30	3-10		•		4-6	45T	60 days from seed.
Broccoli, sprouting	½	10-15	14-18	24-30	3-10		•		5-7*	60-80T	80-100 days from seed.
Brussels Sprouts	½	10-15	12-18	24-30	3-10		•		4-6*	80-90T	100-110 days from seed.
Cabbage	½	8-10	12-20	24-30	4-10		•		5-7*	65-95T	Use thinnings for transplants. 90-150 days from seed.
Cabbage, Chinese	½	8-16	10-12	18-24	4-10		•		4-6	80-90	Best as seeded fall crop.
Cardoon	½	4-6	18	36	8-14		•		8	120-150	Transplanting to harvest about 90 days.
Carrot	¼	15-20	1-2	14-24	10-17		•			60-80	Start using when ½" in diameter to thin stand.
Cauliflower	½	8-10	18	30-36	4-10		•		5-7*	55-65T	70-120 days from seed.
Celeriac	⅛	8-12	8	24-30	9-21	•			10-12*	90-120T	Keep seeds moist.
Celery	⅛	8-12	8	24-30	9-21	•			10-12*	90-120T	Keep seeds moist.
Celtuce—Asparagus Lettuce	½	8-10	12	18	4-10		•		4-6	80	Same culture as lettuce.
Chard, Swiss	1	6-10	4-8	18-24	7-10		•			55-65	Use thinnings for early greens.
Chicory—Witloof (Belgian Endive)	¼	8-10	4-8	18-24	5-12		•			90-120	Force mature root for Belgian Endive.
Chives	½	8-10	8	10-16	8-12		•			80-90	Also propagate by division of clumps.
Chop Suey Green (Shungiku)	½	6	2-3	10-12	5-14		•			42	Best in cool weather.
Collards	¼	10-12	10-15	24-30	4-10		•		4-6*	65-85T	Direct seed for a fall crop.
Corn, Sweet	2	4-6	10-14	30-36	6-10			•		60-90	Make successive plantings.
Corn Salad	½	8-10	4-6	12-16	7-10		•			45-55	Tolerant of cold weather.
Cress, Garden	¼	10-12	2-3	12-16	4-10		•			25-45	Seeds sensitive to light.
Cucumber	1	3-5	12	48-72	6-10			•	4	55-65	See text about training.

* Transplants preferred over seed.

T Number of days from setting out transplants; all others are from seeding.

Vegetable	Depth to plant seed (inches)	Number of seed to sow per foot	Distance between plants (inches)	Distance between rows (inches)	Number of days to germination	Soil temperature for seed			Weeks needed to grow to transplant size	Days to maturity	Remarks
						Needs cool soil	Tolerates cool soil	Needs warm soil			
Dandelion	½	6-10	8-10	12-16	7-14		•			70-90	
Eggplant	¼-½	8-12	18	36	7-14			•	6-9*	75-95T	See page 16 about transplants.
Endive	½	4-6	9-12	12-24	5-9		•		4-6	60-90	Same culture as lettuce.
Wonder Berry Garden Huckleberry	½	8-12	24-36	24-36	5-15			•	5-10	60-80	
Fennel, Florence	½	8-12	6	18-24	6-17		•			120	Plant in fall in mild winter areas.
Garlic	1		2-4	12-18	6-10		•			90-sets	
Edible Gourds: Luffa; Vegetable Gourd; Lagenaria species; New Guinea Bean											See pages 68-69.
Ground Cherry Husk Tomato	½	6	24	36	6-13			•	6*	90-100T	Treat same as tomatoes.
Horseradish	Div.		10-18	24			•			6-8 mth.	Use root division 2-8" long.
Jerusalem Artichoke	Tubers 4		15-24	30-60			•			100-105	See page 71.
Kale	½	8-12	8-12	18-24	3-10		•		4-6	55-80	Direct seed for fall crop.
Kohlrabi	½	8-12	3-4	18-24	3-10		•		4-6	60-70	
Leeks	½-1	8-12	2-4	12-18	7-12		•		10-12	80-90T	130-150 days from seed.
Lettuce: Head	¼-½	4-8	12-14	18-24	4-10	•			3-5	55-80	Keep seed moist.
Leaf	¼-½	8-12	4-6	12-18	4-10	•			3-5	45-60	Keep seed moist.
Muskmelon	1	3-6	12	48-72	4-8			•	3-4	75-100	See page 16 about transplants.
Mustard	½	8-10	2-6	12-18	3-10		•			40-60	Use early to thin.
Nasturtium	½-1	4-8	4-10	18-36			•			50-60	
Onion: sets	1-2		2-3	12-24		•				95-120	Green onions 50-60 days.
plants	2-3		2-3	12-24		•			8	95-120T	
seed	½	10-15	2-3	12-24	7-12	•				100-165	
Parsley	¼-½	10-15	3-6	12-20	14-28		•		8	85-90	
Parsnips	½	8-12	3-4	16-24	15-25		•			100-120	
Peas	2	6-7	2-3	18-30	6-15	•				65-85	
Peanut	1½	2-3	6-10	30				•		110-120	Requires warm growing season.
Peppers	¼	6-8	18-24	24-36	10-20			•	6-8	60-80T	See page 16 about transplants.
Potato	4	1	12	24-36	8-16		•			90-105	Start hilling after emergence.
Pumpkin	1-1½	2	30	72-120	6-10			•		70-110	Give them room.
Radish	½	14-16	1-2	6-12	3-10	•				20-50	Early spring or late fall weather.
Rutabaga	½	4-6	8-12	18-24	3-10		•			80-90	
Salsify	½	8-12	2-3	16-18		•				110-150	
Salsify, Black	½	8-12	2-3	16-18		•				110-150	
Shallot	Bulb—1		2-4	12-18			•			60-75	
Spinach	½	10-12	2-4	12-14	6-14	•				40-65	See page 76.
Malabar	½	4-6	12	12	10		•			70	
New Zealand	1½	4-6	18	24	5-10		•			70-80	
Tampala	¼-½	6-10	4-6	24-30				•		21-42	Thin and use early while tender.
Squash (summer)	1	4-6	16-24	36-60	3-12			•		50-60	
Squash (winter)	1	1-2	24-48	72-120	6-10			•		85-120	
Sunflower	1	2-3	16-24	36-48	7-12			•		80-90	Space wide for large heads.
Sweet Potato	Plants		12-18	36-48				•		120	Propagate from cuttings.
Tomato	½		18-36	36-60	6-14			•	5-7	55-90T	Early var. 55-60. Mid 65-75, Late 80-100.
Turnip	½	14-16	1-3	15-18	3-10	•				45-60	Thin early for greens.
Mango Melon Vine Peach	1	2-4	12	48	3-12			•		90	
Watermelon	1		12-16	60	3-12			•		80-100	Ice-box size mature earlier.

* Transplants preferred over seed.

T Number of days from setting out transplants; all others are from seeding.

The Spoilers

In one of the questionnaires we used with gardeners throughout the United States we included these questions:

"What disappointments did you have in last year's garden? Crop failure? Mistakes? Why?—or where do you think you went wrong?"

"What success did you have?"

"Did anything surprise you? We are interested in both good and bad surprises—as well as what caused them if you know."

Replies came from gardeners of all faiths as to use of insecticides and fungicides. Several had tried getting by without any attention to any insects and diseases.

Here are a few answers, typical of many. Note that all of the spoilers were not insects or diseases.

From Massachusetts
Failure: "We had a great deal of rain and cold weather during May. Quite a few different kinds of seeds didn't come up and had to be replanted. The bugs ate the plants as fast as they came up." *Success:* "The cucumbers and pole beans and corn are going good now after the second planting."

New Jersey
Failure: "I watered and weeded and felt we would have good vegetables but we were disappointed. Worms in the radishes. Tomatoes not so good."

(In answer to the question: "What varieties did you buy?"— the answer was, "Don't remember, went mostly by the pictures.")

New York
Failure: "Trouble with fusarium wilt on tomatoes, and corn borer and corn earworm." *Success:* "Insect control other than corn. I tried to stick to a 10-14 day schedule through the growing season."

Did anything surprise you? "Results from succession of plantings; replanting of areas already planted.

"The amount of produce you can obtain from a 10 by 20-foot garden.

"How much better my garden looked than the organic garden next door."

Mistakes beginners make: Use grass clippings from a lawn that has been treated with 2-4,D weed killer.

Louisiana
Failures: None to speak of. *Success:* Produced 27 vegetables — over $900 (at retail) worth on a 45 by 60 foot garden.

Did anything surprise you? Marvel at nature's way of producing vegetables with a little help from the gardener.

Mistakes beginners make. Plant too thick. Wrong varieties. Poor insect and disease control. Poor drainage. Lack of irrigation.

Ohio
Failure: Didn't pick cabbage in time —heads split open. Didn't spray soon enough for cabbage worms. Though trained on stakes, many of the tomatoes touched the ground where they either rotted or were riddled with slugs. *Success:* Second planting of cucumbers a great success. Planted them alongside an arborvitae hedge upon which they climbed. Had a fine bean crop. A few bean plants had bacterial blight, but these I destroyed as soon as there was evidence of the disease.

Michigan
Failure: All of first sweet pepper blossoms set and a good later crop resulted. About half of my potato seed rotted in the ground. I think I planted too early when the ground was wet. *Success:* The garden was a great success. Picked 150 cantaloupes. Picked over 4 bushels of tomatoes from 12 plants.

Michigan
Failure: All of my cauliflower, most broccoli, all cabbage plants were infested with root maggots, and as a result bolted and formed very small heads. My lettuce, endive, and escarole was riddled by larvae. *Success:* In my 50' x 50' garden I raised 3000 lbs. of table-ready vegetables, most of which my wife canned or froze.

South Carolina
Failure: Had a great deal of trouble with okra — mainly due to cold, wet weather. Eggplant got eaten up by flea beetles — that was my own fault for neglecting them. *Success:* This is the first year I have successfully grown melons, due I think to mulching and picking disease resistant varieties.

Indiana
Failure: Baby Limas. Very little production late in the season probably due to small insects. Cucumbers — lost all plants either to wilt or insects. *Success:* Followed early plantings with late plantings. "Double-cropped" peas and beans, and peas and corn. Excellent beans, tomatoes, beets, broccoli, corn, cucumbers, peppers, spinach, carrots, and flowers. *Surprises:* How much we saved on groceries after September 1st.

Southern California
Failures: Summer crop was pretty much a failure. Tomatoes suffered from wilt and failure to set fruit. Green peppers and eggplant not good. Bush beans started out well then turned yellow and died. Failure attributed to too much horse manure, too much water, too many insects, too many gophers. *Success:* The results with zucchini and Swiss chard were excellent. The winter crop of beets, cabbage, broccoli, radishes, lettuce and turnips were excellent.

After reading a hundred or so reports on successes and failures in the garden it becomes obvious that this small book should not pretend to solve all of the problems created by insects and diseases. Check your County Agricultural Agent for special problems in your area.

The 50 page booklet, *Insects and Diseases of Vegetables in the Home Garden,* is available for 30¢ by writing to the Superintendent of Documents, Government Printing Office, Washington, D.C. 20402.

The chart on the following page gives you ways to control the most common insects. Missing on the chart are the root maggots. As many of our gardeners testified, they are disastrous on cabbage and all its relatives and radishes.

To stop the cabbage maggot from drilling holes in radishes, turnips and rutabagas, either dust or sprinkle *Diazinon* over the seeded row after seeding. This mild treatment will kill the maggots as they hatch.

The same maggots bore into the stems of cabbage, cauliflower and broccoli. Damage is more severe in spring than in fall plantings. To prevent their damage, pour a cupful of a solution of liquid formulation of *Diazinon* around the stem of the transplants when you set them out.

When using insecticides on vegetables check label for number of days before harvest to stop spraying. They differ by the kind of vegetable. In a small mixed-up garden a separ-

INSECTS	CROP	HOW TO CONTROL
Aphids	General feeder but especially **Cabbage, Cauliflower, Brussels Sprouts, Broccoli**	Spray with Malathion 50 Insect Spray.
Leafhoppers	Lettuce, Potatoes, Beans, Carrots, Celery, general feeders	Piercing and sucking insects that may need weekly applications for control. Most frequently recommended controls are Malathion Spray or SEVIN Garden Dust. Leafhoppers feed on blossoms of beans and cause a poor pod set.
White Flies	Tomatoes, Beans, and many more	Get at them at first sign. Nymphs do most damage. Use Malathion Spray and be sure to thoroughly cover underside of leaves. Spraying 4 times at weekly intervals may be necessary to clean them out.
Cabbage Looper / Cabbage Worm	Broccoli, Brussels Sprouts, Cabbage, Cauliflower	Spray or dust on appearance and apply weekly as needed. First choice is SEVIN. Bacillus thuringiensis (Dipel, Biotrol Thuricide)— start using when worms are small; worms must ingest the material; very safe to use; no restrictions.
Colorado Potato Beetle, Bean Leaf Beetle, Mexican Bean Beetle	Beans, Peppers, Eggplant	Same controls as Cucumber Beetles. Young plants of eggplant are vulnerable to Potato Beetle attack. Look for damage when first leaves unfold.
Cucumber Beetles, (Stripped and Spotted and Diabrotica)	Cucumbers, Squash, Melons, Pumpkins	Spray or dust when beetles appear and weekly as needed. Use SEVIN dust or spray, Methoxychlor, or Diazinon.
Flea Beetle, Blister Beetle	Peppers, Potatoes, Tomatoes	Spray or dust when damage first noticed. Same controls as Cucumber Beetles.
Cutworm	At night cuts off small plants at soil level. Tomatoes, cabbage, peppers, beans, corn may be destroyed.	Dust or spray in a band along the row with SEVIN. Or control before planting with a soil application of DIAZINON Soil & Foliage Dust. This will also stop wire worm damage. See label.
Squash Vine Borer, Squash Bug	Cucumber, Melons, Pumpkins, Squash	Look for appearance after June 15. Dust with SEVIN to get nymphs. Apply 3 times at 10-day intervals.
Corn Earworm, Corn Borer	Corn	First generation shows up in June and July; second generation August. Dust foliage with SEVIN for corn borer. For corn earworms dust silks when they emerge and repeat every 2 to 3 days until silks turn brown.

21

ate treatment for each vegetable is difficult, so the best way is to stop spraying or dusting 2 weeks before harvest.

CHOOSE RESISTANT VARIETIES

The very best way to avoid crop failure due to diseases is to plant disease resistant varieties. The number of varieties bred for resistance to diseases is increasing every year. In the text in each vegetable suspectible to diseases we have noted the varieties which have some disease resistance.

If you have had trouble with diseases or want to avoid trouble, check the variety list of these vegetables, here and in catalogs, and look for mention of resistance to the diseases damaging to the following vegetables:

Tomatoes—Fusarium, verticillium

Cucumbers—Scab, mosaic, downy mildew, powdery mildew, anathracnose.

Muskmelon—Fusarium, powdery mildew.

Snap beans—Mosaic, powdery mildew, root rot.

Cabbage—Virus Yellows.

Spinach—Blight, blue mold, downy mildew, mosaic.

Our consultant Raymond Sheldrake of Cornell emphasizes the importance of resistant varieties in his radio program and in a follow up note to us:

"So many people tell me that their cucumber vines just up and die, even though they sprayed them. Well, the big problem is that their plants be-

came infected with mosaic, virus disease known as cucumber mosaic virus. The only way to escape it is to use mosaic resistant varieties.

"In my radio programs I stress, for example, mosaic resistance in cucumbers and suggest mosaic resistant varieties, but when someone who heard the program would go to a garden store, all they might find is a pretty picture of a cucumber on the outside of a seed packet. The variety might be 'Straight 8' with no resistance to anything but the picture on the front of the package is what sells it. It's an open-pollenated cheap seed. Education is a slow process and I think we are closing the gap between what our breeders are doing and what our gardeners are using mainly because some of these diseases have become so severe that the gardener just can't get by with any old variety."

ROTATION-FUMIGATION

Controlling diseases by rotation of crops is good and often-repeated advice in all garden literature. Rotation is most effective when the garden site is changed every few years. Rotating crops within the garden so that the same crop does not occupy the same space year after year will help some. (See rotation plan in "Good Ideas From Good Gardeners" page 101). But in the 10 by 20-foot garden, rotation is out.

Several of our gardeners who have been forced to use the same plot of ground year after year asked about the feasibility of fumigating the soil.

We have fumigated all potting soil for many years with methyl bromide.

It's a simple operation but since a poison gas is used, we do not recommend this method of fumigation to gardeners who are careless in following printed directions.

U.S.D.A. Home and Garden Bulletin No. 180 on *Growing Tomatoes in the Home Garden* has this to say about soil fumigation:

"Fumigating the soil with methyl bromide before planting is an excellent way to control practically all weeds and nematodes and many diseases in the tomato garden.

"Plow or spade up the soil, then work it over with a harrow or rake. Place a plastic sheet over the area to be treated. Cover the edges of the sheet with soil to keep the methyl bromide from escaping; release the gas (in the quantity recommended by the manufacturer) under the plastic sheet. Keep cover in place 48 hours, then remove it. Cultivate the soil for aeration.

"Tomatoes may be planted 72 hours after aeration. Precautions for the use of methyl bromide are given on the manufacturer's label and should be carefully followed."

THE HABIT OF CLEANLINESS

The garden that is always clean and neat suffers less damage from diseases than a sloppy one. When a crop is harvested all the vines, leaves, and fruit are cleaned up and spread on the compost pile or spaded under. There's never a weed over two weeks old. In a really clean garden an infected plant stands out and is quickly removed and destroyed. For the gardener with the cleanliness habit only a healthy plant is a "clean plant" and he waters and fertilizes to make it so.

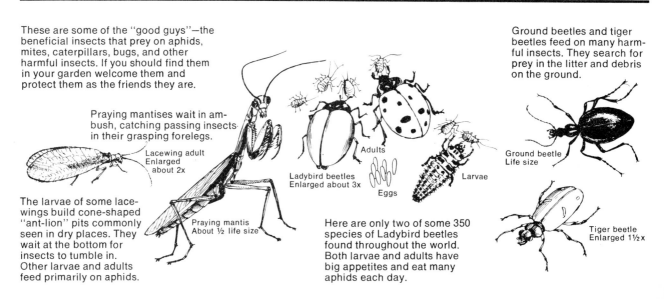

These are some of the "good guys"—the beneficial insects that prey on aphids, mites, caterpillars, bugs, and other harmful insects. If you should find them in your garden welcome them and protect them as the friends they are.

Praying mantises wait in ambush, catching passing insects in their grasping forelegs.

The larvae of some lacewings build cone-shaped "ant-lion" pits commonly seen in dry places. They wait at the bottom for insects to tumble in. Other larvae and adults feed primarily on aphids.

Lacewing adult Enlarged about 2x

Praying mantis About ½ life size

Ladybird beetles Enlarged about 3x

Adults

Eggs

Larvae

Here are only two of some 350 species of Ladybird beetles found throughout the world. Both larvae and adults have big appetites and eat many aphids each day.

Ground beetles and tiger beetles feed on many harmful insects. They search for prey in the litter and debris on the ground.

Ground beetle Life size

Tiger beetle Enlarged 1½x

The vegetable climates of the North

In the following 2 pages you'll find a map of the northern tier of states, showing the changing pattern in last and first-frost dates and length of season in 7 zones. These zones are used in the "When-to-plant" charts with the discussions of the individual vegetables.

Considering that the frost dates are the "normal" or "mean" dates, the chances of the frost hitting that date are exactly 50%. The gambling gardener bets that the last frost of spring will be earlier and the first frost of fall or winter will be later.

Within each zone the length of the growing season will vary as much as 20 days due to differences in elevation, air drainage, and many other factors.

With all their faults, it will pay any gardener to locate himself in his zone and use the "When-to-plant" charts as a reference point.

Look at the planting dates in your zone in relation to the planting pattern of the vegetable in all zones. You can see at a glance the nature of the vegetable's adaptability.

Garden climates vary, not by the mile but by a few feet.

For instance, the influence of a gentle slope in your garden is illustrated in the following quotation from Robert Moore Fisher's book, "How About the Weather," published by Harper & Brothers, New York.

"Suppose, for instance, your home is located in Ohio. If the back yard is *level*, on a clear day at noontime in late winter it will receive an amount of sunshine normal for that date. If, however, your back yard slopes moderately toward the *north* at an angle of 1 foot in 12, it will receive a less-than-normal amount of sunshine. In fact, it will face the sun in about the same way that a level plot does in Ontario, Canada. Consequently, the 'private climate' of your sloping back yard will be as wintry as the 'private climate' of a level back yard in Ontario.

"On the other hand, should your back yard slope *southward* at an angle 1 foot in 12, it will receive more sunshine than normal. In this case, your back yard 'private climate' will be similar to the 'private climate' of a level back yard in warm, springlike South Carolina.

"The slope of land, therefore, influences the 'private climate' of back yards as much as latitude influences the 'public climate' of entire states." Only by living in a garden for years, keeping some kind of records of the yearly swing of temperatures, can you learn to grow each vegetable in its most favorable time slot.

Beating the averages, planting earlier or later than a sensible person should, has its rewards. One freak early freeze may cut short the late planted beans and corn one year out of three, but out-of-season vegetables in the other years make up for the one failure.

The little climates. You can't do much about the big overall climate but you can do a lot with the microclimates in your garden. You can make a warm area warmer by a wind-break, or bring in more sunlight by thinning out overgrown trees. You can lengthen the growing season by planting in raised beds with a soil that drains quickly and warms up early in the spring.

The mini-gardener can enjoy a much longer growing season than the dirt gardener. There's no waiting period for the soil to dry. Pots and boxes can be moved to give protection from frost at night and into a warm spot during the day.

Zone 1

These are the warmest areas along the southern borders of Missouri, Kentucky, and Virginia. The growing season, about 200 days, is long enough to allow summer plantings of snap beans, carrots, sweet corn, and tomatoes; as well as fall plantings of the cool season crops.

Zone 2

April 20 usually signals the last frost of spring here. Inland areas have a fairly high amount of clear days while coastal portions see less sun. The amount of rainfall varies greatly throughout the zone. Parts of the western area receive only 20 inches of rain annually, while areas along the east coast receive twice that amount. As in zone 1, the climate is versatile enough to allow spring and summer plantings of cool season crops. The summer season is long enough and temperatures high enough to allow commercial growing of sweet potatoes.

Zone 3

Stretching through the mid-section of the Northern region, this zone is great corn and tomato country and offers a wide choice of vegetables for both early spring and fall gardens. Take full advantage of the 160 day growing season by planting lettuce, endive, turnips, broccoli, Chinese cabbage, and kale in Midsummer for fall and early winter harvest.

Zone 4

To make the most of this short, but fast growing season of about 140 days, give the warm-season crops a headstart by growing from seed indoors or by buying transplants to set out as soon as warm weather arrives. The early varieties of all long-season crops should be favored. Nights are cool enough to permit full season crops.

Zone 5

Gardeners in this zone find themselves pressed in a fairly short time period between spring and fall frost —about 120 days. Cool season crops grow well during the summer. Potatoes and rutabagas are among the vegetables that like it cool and thrive in this climate. Check the seed racks and catalogs for early, short-season varieties of the long-season crops, such as the midget muskmelons that ripen in 60 days, and early 'Sunglow' corn that matures in 62 days.

Zone 6

Many vegetable fit this climate although there are only about 100 frost-free days on the average. Again, as in zone 5, look for short-season varieties of long-season crops such as sweet corn, tomatoes, and melons. Look also to hot-caps, clear plastic row covers, and black plastic mulch as extenders of the growing season (see pages 26 through 29). Lettuce, cabbage, and other cool season crops do well through the summer here.

Zone 7

Although the growing season is short, 75 days or less, it is a merry one with long warm days and cool nights. Canadian Experiment Stations have bred many vegetable varieties especially for this climate.

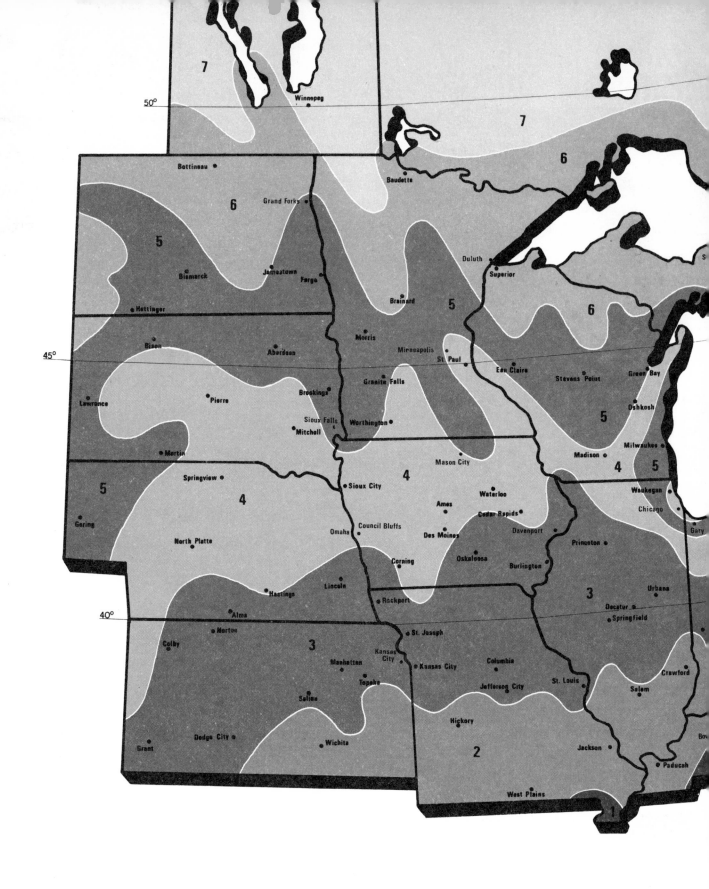

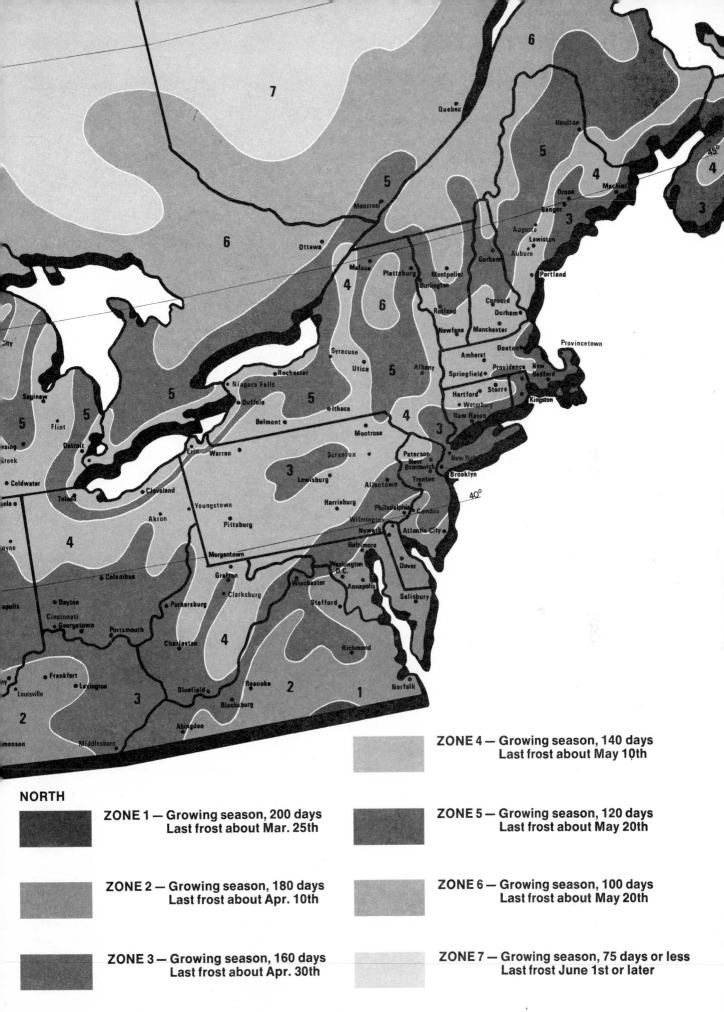

ZONE 4 — Growing season, 140 days
Last frost about May 10th

NORTH

ZONE 1 — Growing season, 200 days
Last frost about Mar. 25th

ZONE 5 — Growing season, 120 days
Last frost about May 20th

ZONE 2 — Growing season, 180 days
Last frost about Apr. 10th

ZONE 6 — Growing season, 100 days
Last frost about May 20th

ZONE 3 — Growing season, 160 days
Last frost about Apr. 30th

ZONE 7 — Growing season, 75 days or less
Last frost June 1st or later

Getting along with nature

It's easy to get along with Mother Nature when you learn to expect the unexpected and accept anything she does as a part of gardening.

For a pleasant relationship in the vegetable garden it's good to know something about how she influences the behavior of the vegetables in your garden.

Each vegetable has its own set of requirements for day length, day and night temperatures. light intensities, and heat units and the requirements change in the various stages of growth of the vegetables.

Changing the natural climate to protect or further the growth of vegetables is one of the most rewarding exercises in gardening. In this endeavor the resourcefulness of gardeners is astounding. The good gardeners who contribute their good ideas for vegetable protection (see page 98) prove the point.

How can the temperature level be raised? Some additional gain can be made by planting warm-season crops just south of a tall reflective surface such as a tall fence, or a row of corn or sunflowers. Planting on the south side of a ridge increases heat for young plants.

Plastic cottage cheese containers and the like from the market, and plastic jugs with the bottom removed, are used in many ways for early protection of seedlings.

Polyethylene plastic film, both clear and black, are efficient temperature changers. The use of black plastic film as a mulch has worked miracles with some vegetables.

MULCHING

Few actions in the vegetable garden are so rewarding as mulching. Even the sound of the word seems to soften up the soil.

The mulches may be organic material such as leaves, peat moss, straw, manure, sawdust, ground bark, compost and the like; or manufactured materials such as polyethylene film, aluminum foil, paper.

When you follow the best use of both, you join hands with the ancients and today's agricultural technologists.

Remember that in all discussion of the value of organic mulches in the vegetable garden we are talking about *summer* mulching.

An application of an organic mulch in early spring will slow up the natural warming of the soil as spring advances. As an insulating blanket it reduces solar radiation into the soil. As a result, frost hazards are greater with a mulched soil.

Summer mulching vs. cultivation. If you find yourself going over the soil after a rain or a sprinkler irrigation with a cultivator to break up the well-known surface crust, you need a mulch. Raindrops do a cementing job by packing the small particles between the larger ones so that the pores are plugged and neither water nor rain can enter. A mulch breaks the pressure of the water drops and pore spaces remain open.

Weed control. For weed control the organic mulch must be thick enough so that weed seedlings can't go through it on their own stored food. Perennial weeds will thrive in spite of organic mulches, or because of them. Black plastic will take care of all kinds of weeds and grasses.

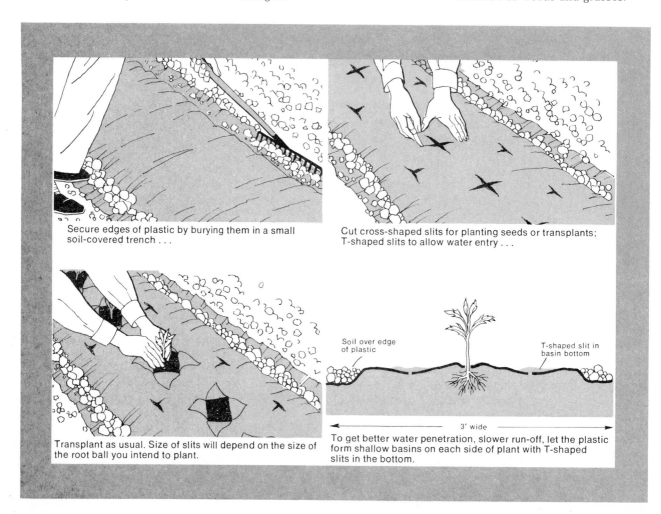

Secure edges of plastic by burying them in a small soil-covered trench . . .

Cut cross-shaped slits for planting seeds or transplants; T-shaped slits to allow water entry . . .

Transplant as usual. Size of slits will depend on the size of the root ball you intend to plant.

Soil over edge of plastic

T-shaped slit in basin bottom

3' wide

To get better water penetration, slower run-off, let the plastic form shallow basins on each side of plant with T-shaped slits in the bottom.

Conserves moisture. Mulches slow down the evaporation of water from the upper 6 to 8 inches of soil. Tests show that merely shading the bare soil will reduce evaporation as much as 30 percent, but a straw mulch will reduce evaporation as much as 70 percent.

A mulch not only saves on water but it helps maintain a more even moisture supply.

Adds to plant root system. By insulating the top few inches of the soil from the sun's heat and maintaining soil moisture to the surface of the soil, a mulch gives the roots a free run in the richest layers of the soil. Tests show that plant roots under the mulch develop as extensive a root system as they do under bare soil, and the surface roots are an added bonus.

Of course, if the lower layers of the soil are unfavorable to full root development such as tight clays that drain slowly, the plant will concentrate most of the roots near the surface.

Less danger of rot. A mulch beneath unstaked tomatoes, summer squash and cucumbers lessens the loss of fruit through rot. A tomato sitting on damp soil invites the soil bacteria to do their normal thing. Muddy splashes of rain may start rot in lettuce.

How thick the mulch? Apply organic mulches 1 to 2 inches thick for the fine materials such as sawdust, to around 4 inches thick for the coarse ones such as straw.

Untreated sawdust will cause some degree of nitrogen shortage. Soil bacteria go to work on the sawdust, take their necessary supply of nitrogen from the soil. The loss is not as great as when sawdust is mixed in the soil. A good rule of thumb measurement is to increase the amount of fertilizer regularly used for the crop by ¼ when using a sawdust mulch.

Black plastic film. Black polyethylene has built itself a solid reputation for increasing yields and speeding up ripening of melons, eggplant, peppers and summer squash. In areas where early season temperatures are less than ideal for these warm weather crops, yields of muskmelons in experimental plots have been increased up to 4 times over that of non-mulched plants.

The increase in soil temperature is given credit for the remarkable speed up of growth. However, temperature readings show that the increase is generally in the 3 to 6 degree range, sometimes only 2 degrees.

The temperature of the film soars high on a warm sunny day and kicks back a great deal of heat to the air above it, rather than transferring it to the soil.

Black polyethylene is generally available in 1-1½ mils thickness, in rolls 3 to 4 feet wide. Get the 1½ thickness. The usual method of spreading the film is illustrated below.

In one of our test gardens we spread the plastic, wall-to-wall over the entire 20 by 30-foot plot. We had fought a losing battle with Bermuda grass the previous season and figured the plastic worthwhile as weed and grass control alone. Seeds of melon and corn were sown in cut holes in the plastic according to our planting plan.

"EARLY" VARIETIES AND TEMPERATURES

Gardeners in short season climates get along with nature and grow vegetables that normally require a long warm growing season by planting "early" varieties.

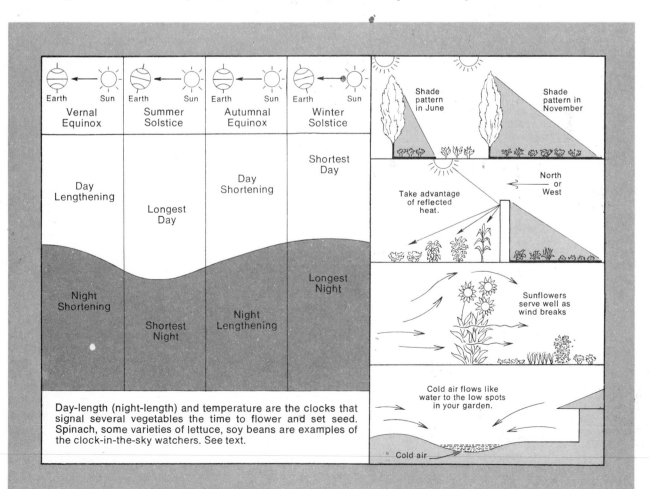

Day-length (night-length) and temperature are the clocks that signal several vegetables the time to flower and set seed. Spinach, some varieties of lettuce, soy beans are examples of the clock-in-the-sky watchers. See text.

When listing varieties of vegetables throughout this book the number of days from seeding or transplanting to maturity is indicated after the name of the variety.

The date is of value to gardeners who grow both "early" and "late" varieties, but it is all important to a gardener in a cool-summer or short-season area.

To these gardeners the word "early" means more than early. It means that the vegetable will grow and produce a crop with less total summer heat than the later maturing varieties. The "early" variety might not mature in the number of days indicated but it would produce in his climate.

The development of the "early" variety of the Crenshaw melon expanded the plantings of this famous melon into relatively short-season areas.

The "midget" vegetable varieties enthusiastically advertised as space savers for the mini-garden, are extra early varieties bred to grow with less total heat than others.
Frustration in growing vegetables can be avoided if you accept the

natural rhythm of plant growth rather than trying to make plants fit your rhythm. Spring fever in the first warm days of the season is not the best guide for when to plant. The full enjoyment of the vegetable garden comes when you are in step with beets, lettuce, beans and all the vegetables you grow.

Check the planting chart on pages 18-19. Are the vegetables you are thinking about in the cool-season or warm-season group? Some of the cool-weather crops may need to be planted before you *feel* like gardening.

"Cool-season" means more than that the vegetable can be planted early. The quality, the good taste of peas and beets, for example, depends on the temperatures in which they ripen. The first picking of garden peas and the first harvest of beets are the great ones.

Waiting for the soil to warm up for the planting of beans and corn or night temperatures to rise for setting out transplants of tomatoes may

seem like nonsense on the first warm day of spring, but if the soil temperature is below 55°, beans will rot and tomatoes and eggplant just sit and sulk. Lima bean seed is likely to rot if soil is below 62°; so will okra.

DAY LENGTH

The length of day influences the growth habit of several annual vegetables. Spinach and Chinese cabbage are notorious examples. As days lengthen beyond the 12 hour day and 12 hour night of the vernal equinox they get a signal that it's time to flower. Rising temperatures along with the longer days play a part in this flowering habit. Gardeners learn about the influence of day length by crops "bolting" to seed before they are ready to harvest.

Gardeners who have tried to grow Chinese cabbage in the spring rate it among the difficult-to-grow vegetables. When grown to mature in the short days of fall, it is as easy to grow as any vegetable.

In spinach, long days, especially if the plants were subjected to cool conditions when they were younger,

Make the most of the swing of the seasons. This chart of seasonal planting dates was prepared for the growing seasons of Long Island, New York. In principle it applies to all areas where the last frost date in spring is in April and first frost date of autumn in October. Planting for fall and winter crops extends the harvest.

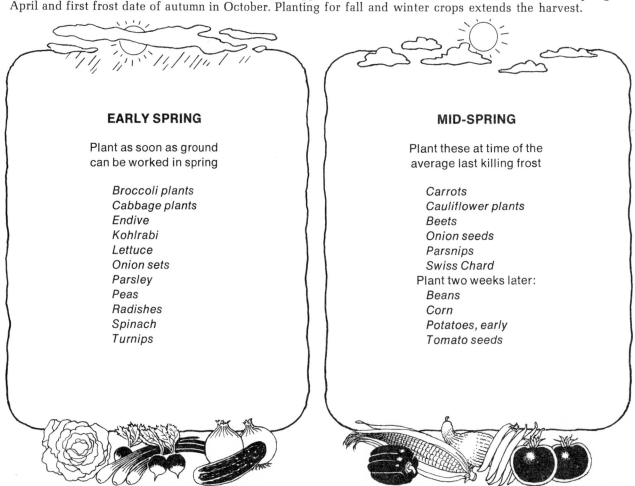

EARLY SPRING

Plant as soon as ground can be worked in spring

Broccoli plants
Cabbage plants
Endive
Kohlrabi
Lettuce
Onion sets
Parsley
Peas
Radishes
Spinach
Turnips

MID-SPRING

Plant these at time of the average last killing frost

Carrots
Cauliflower plants
Beets
Onion seeds
Parsnips
Swiss Chard
Plant two weeks later:
Beans
Corn
Potatoes, early
Tomato seeds

cause bolting. Plant in early spring and use a "long-standing" variety or, in mild winter climates, plant in fall.

Premature flowering also occurs in lettuce but the cause is more that of hot weather than day length. The choice of varieties to fit the season is all important. Check the variety list for bolting-resistant varieties.

HEAT UNITS

Each vegetable has its own range of temperatures for maximum growth. Each has its minimum temperature at which it will not grow. The minimum for peas is $40°$; for corn, $50°$; peppers and eggplant will live at $60°$, but the optimum for growth is much higher. With these warm-season plants, fruit size and quality are poor at low temperatures.

The temperature requirements of warm-season vegetables are sometimes expressed in "heat units." Heat units have been used as one of the guides to the selection of a corn variety. Many other factors are involved. However, comparison of the heat units required for varieties of corn and the heat units provided by various climates, illustrates the one reason why "early" varieties of corn are the best bets for the cool or short season areas.

SHADE

Locating a vegetable garden in a small area with a tree or two is impossible if you believe what gardeners have been told since the first garden book was written, namely: "Locate the vegetable garden where it will get full sun."

Of course, gardeners have grown many kinds of leafy vegetables in partial shade quite successfully. The official sanction for planting in partial shade comes from the U.S.D.A. in House and Garden Bulletin No. 163 —Minigardens for Vegetables. These vegetables tolerate partial shade: beets, cabbage, carrots, chives, kale, leeks, lettuce, mustard, green onions, parsley, radish, Swiss chard, and turnips.

You will note that all of these vegetables are in the cool season class. The warm season crops, such as peppers, eggplant, and melons, require full sunlight.

Our consultant, A. E. Griffith, of the University of Rhode Island, suggested that all "part shade" advice should be qualified everywhere. Partial shade is one thing in a climate with a full quota of clear sunny days and something else again when a cloud cover or fog reduces sunlight. He explained why: "My reference to 'part shade' relative to cloud cover reflects a somewhat parochial thinking on my part.

"Item: Most vegetables do best in full sun in the cool, stormy summer climate of New England.

"Item: Most vegetables will tolerate shade for 2-3 hours per day although they will not perform quite as well as they should.

"Item: Much of the coast of New England from eastern Connecticut eastward to New Brunswick is subjected to fog or cloud overcast in May and June, as well as September and October, resulting in only about 65% of available sunshine.

"Item: Low solar energy plus partial shading would often seriously delay the maturation of many warm weather crops.''

EARLY SUMMER

Plant when soil and weather are warm

Beans, Lima
Cantaloupe
Celery plants
Crenshaw melons
Cucumbers
Eggplant plants
Pumpkins
Pepper plants
Potatoes for winter
Squash
Tomato plants
Watermelons

MID-SUMMER—FALL

Plant in late June or early July

Beets
Broccoli
Cabbage
Cauliflower
Kohlrabi
Lettuce
Radishes
Spinach
Turnips

Released by Cooperative Extension Association of Nassau County, N.Y.

Planning The garden

Our panel of first-year vegetable gardeners answered the question about mistakes in planning their gardens with almost one voice — "We got too much of one thing at one time." "We grew more squash than we could give away."

Planning for a continuous supply of fresh vegetables — not too much and not too little — is no easy task. And the limited-space gardener has a far more difficult problem than the farm-space gardener.

In the farm garden you can block out space for the spring garden and hold back space for the summer garden. By the time the spring garden is harvested you can plan the fall garden. But consider the gardener on a city or suburban lot, caught in the enthusiasm of the first planting of spring: He has prepared a piece of ground about 20 by 30 feet. He pictures the future row upon row of beautiful plants. He clutches a dozen packets of seeds, each holding enough to plant 50 or 100 feet of row.

It's easy, when planting a row of head lettuce — sowing seed or setting out plants — to conclude that 20 or 30 heads might not be enough for the salads the family will eat. That 30 foot row looks short. But when 30 heads come into the kitchen in a 10-day period the short row is long.

A dozen cabbage plants look quite innocent in their little trays at the nursery. But when 36 to 40 pounds of cabbage come knocking at the kitchen door. . . . someone must learn how to put down sauerkraut.

Fortunately all vegetables do not have short harvest periods. And you'll find that by selection of 2 or 3 varieties of the short harvest kinds you can spread the harvest period. (See text on cabbage and corn for examples.)

Vegetables with long harvest period

The vegetables that provide a long harvest period by storage in the soil are carrots, beets, parsnips, salsify, and Florence fennel.

Of these, carrots and beets provide a succession of harvests from baby beets and baby carrots up to mature

When garden planning is concentrated on a 24 by 32 inch box you begin to appreciate what can be planted in small space.

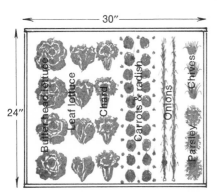

ing between bands was followed in planting the 3 by 9-foot gardens. Add the two variations of the 3 by 9 plan to see what can be done in a 3 by 18-foot space garden. A trellis for cucumbers adds a crop without adding

much ground space. Plants in tubs, boxes and 5 gallon cans are the planner's best friends when it comes to bringing the concentrated 3 by 9 garden up to meaningful production.

Bell pepper   Tomato   Eggplant

In the carrot-onion-radish box we sowed the carrots in 4 inch-wide bands spaced 5 inches apart. After thinning and eating baby carrots we had 2 rows of mature carrots in each band—a total of 66 carrots. The planting of onion sets yielded more than 50 green onions.

In the "salad box" we managed to get 4 heads of Bibb lettuce and 4 heads of leaf lettuce in addition to carrots and onions. Plantings of lettuce in 6 and 8 inch pots were made a week after planting the box. The ground rules for planting in bands and spacing

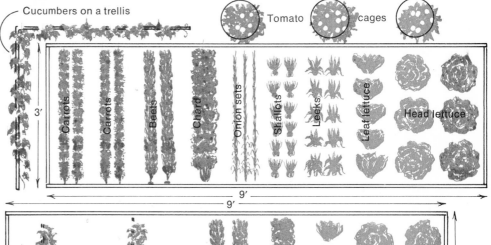

size and then a storage period of weeks or months depending upon time of year and storage conditions. Leaf lettuce and Swiss chard have a long harvest period since they can be picked a leaf at a time.

Make a succession of plantings. One answer to the feast and famine problem is successive plantings of small quantities.

For example, if the first planting of lettuce is in March, make another planting in April and again in May.

Successive plantings of snap beans, 4-6 weeks apart will give you fresh beans for 5 months or more.

But to get a continuous harvest of a vegetable the second planting must go in before the first is harvested. And there is the problem of the small-space gardener. How does he find room for the second or third planting?

The no-soil-space garden. The balcony, deck, or patio garden is planned in boxes, tubs, bushel baskets, cans, and planters of all shapes and sizes.

One way to plan for a reasonable supply of vegetables from a container garden is illustrated below. We take a 24 by 32-inch box 6 inches deep as one basic unit and a container 12 inches square as another. Larger sized units could be used to advantage but in this place we hold to a size that is readily portable.

The choice of vegetables for the box gardens would be those you like, conditioned by the highest return per square foot of space — or the vegetables with the closest spacing in the row.

If you turn to the planting chart on page 18 and check the "Distance in the row" column, you'll find these vegetables in the close-spacing group: carrots, beets, chives, leaf lettuce, mustard, green onions, radish, turnips. Let's assume that you'll favor one or more of these but insist on head lettuce, too. So you check that planting distance and you are all set on distance in the row.

To get a continuous harvest we plant a total of 6 boxes: 2 with the vegetables that can take early planting; 2 duplicates planted 3 weeks later; 2 more 2 weeks later. The behavior of the vegetables in your climate will dictate your choice in late spring and fall plantings. In such box plantings it's easy to think of harvests in terms of the number of meals rather than total quantity.

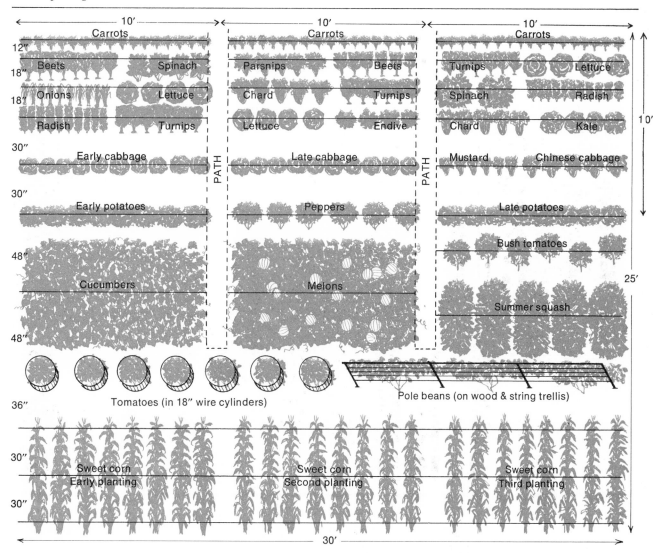

Here is a no-nonsense 25 by 30 foot garden planned to bring a succession of crops throughout the growing season. A block 10 feet wide and 30 feet long is set up for succession plantings starting with the early cool *weather crops in the first 10 by 10 foot block. Second 10 by 10 block is for succession planting a month later. The 3rd block takes care of the crops that will mature in the fall. As space opens in the first block by har-* *vesting early maturing crops, it also is planted for late fall maturing.*

The warm season vegetables occupy the rest of the space. The corn is planted in 3 blocks of 3 rows in 3 plantings 2 weeks apart.

But plants have tops, therefore the distance between rows must be considered. So you look down the column "Distance between rows" in the chart. The shortest distance is 12 inches and most call for 18 inches. How much can we cheat on those distances in the box garden?

Since there is no need to walk through plants, and cultivating and weeding are done by the fingers rather than a hoe, such distances as 12-18 inches shouldn't be necessary.

But if the vegetable is to reach normal size it must have normal head room. If you crowd head lettuce, for example, much closer than 10 inches you harvest 3 poor heads and no more lettuce than 2 good heads would give you. So we allow for head room and allow 5 inches between the wide rows.

SUCCESSION CHARTED

When you chart on paper a succession of plantings, the goal of a long harvest season appears easy to reach.

The starting dates in your garden will vary from the dates on the sample chart shown here but the idea of successive plantings is valid every-

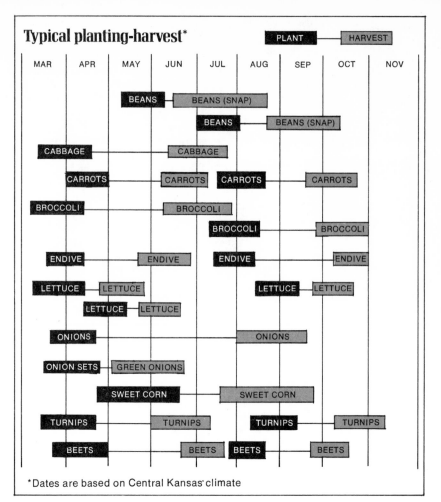

Typical planting-harvest*

PLANT ▬▬ HARVEST

MAR | APR | MAY | JUN | JUL | AUG | SEP | OCT | NOV

BEANS — BEANS (SNAP)
BEANS — BEANS (SNAP)
CABBAGE — CABBAGE
CARROTS — CARROTS — CARROTS — CARROTS
BROCCOLI — BROCCOLI
BROCCOLI — BROCCOLI
ENDIVE — ENDIVE — ENDIVE — ENDIVE
LETTUCE — LETTUCE — LETTUCE — LETTUCE
LETTUCE — LETTUCE
ONIONS — ONIONS
ONION SETS — GREEN ONIONS
SWEET CORN — SWEET CORN
TURNIPS — TURNIPS — TURNIPS — TURNIPS
BEETS — BEETS — BEETS — BEETS

*Dates are based on Central Kansas climate

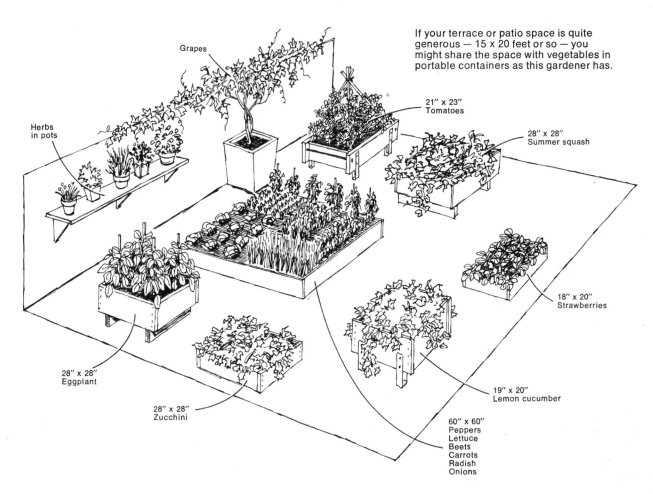

If your terrace or patio space is quite generous — 15 x 20 feet or so — you might share the space with vegetables in portable containers as this gardener has.

Grapes

Herbs in pots

21" x 23" Tomatoes

28" x 28" Summer squash

18" x 20" Strawberries

19" x 20" Lemon cucumber

28" x 28" Eggplant

28" x 28" Zucchini

60" x 60" Peppers Lettuce Beets Carrots Radish Onions

where. The problem of the small space gardener is to find a place for the second or third planting. He can't plant lettuce on top of lettuce.

Planting quick maturing crops between slow growers — it's called intercropping — is one solution. From the experiences of our panel gardeners we found these suggestions for successive plantings:

Lettuce transplants in the shade of bush snap beans.

Turnips broadcast between cabbages.

Green onion sets tucked in almost everywhere.

Thinning of lettuce transplanted for a later crop.

And of course radishes can grow alongside almost any vegetable.

The 3 by 9 foot garden. Whether the garden space is 3 by 9, 4 by 9 or 3 by 27, the planning problem is about the same.

You will do the best job of planning of a 3 or 4 foot wide garden if you visualize it as a series of planter boxes similar to those illustrated. As the length increases the variety of vegetables increases.

To get continuous harvests in such a small garden, stand-by plants growing in 4 inch pots should be ready to pop into the garden when any crop is harvested.

The large small garden. The plan shown on page 31 for no-nonsense 25 by 30 garden shows succession of planting from early season to late. The dates of planting each block will vary according to your climate. See "When to plant" for each vegetable.

If more space is available, the space-requiring vegetables such as vines of winter squash and melons, would find space. Corn would be given wider blocks.

If you analyze the progression from a garden in a box, to a 25 by 30, or 30 by 50 square foot garden you will find the areas with the high concentration per square foot do not increase in proportion to size. For example, the 25 by 30 garden is three 9 by 12 gardens planted in succession. The choice of vegetables and the number of each is a personal thing. Looking at the 25 by 30 plan you can see that the planner loves carrots.

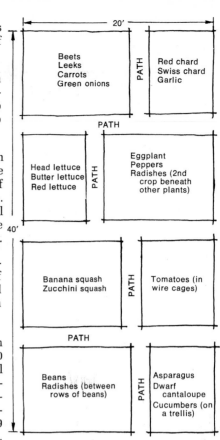

In an area 20' x 40' you have room for eight raised beds with ample paths between—similar to the garden shown below.

About the individual vegetables

It is the fashion in conventional vegetable books to present the individual vegetables in some sort of order: Alphabetical; or by major and minor crops; or by the warm-weather and cool-weather crops; or by families. We have a non-pattern arrangement. In the next 32 pages you'll find the vegetables no gardener should overlook. In the following 6 pages we pick up the unusual and those not so frequently found in the small garden. And then we let the gardening-cook choose the salad vegetables, greens, stalks, roots, and herbs that play an important part in international cookery. The quick way to find the vegetable you are looking for is to use the index. In these pages you'll meet vegetables that are next to impossible to grow in your climate. In deference to the gardeners we know who enjoy growing the impossible, we include every vegetable found in some 30 catalogs.

Note: *Where the availability of a variety is limited, the name is followed by a number. For exampel: 'White Beauty' (9) and 'White Italian' (19). See page 111 for seed catalog corresponding to these numbers.*

Asparagus

As early as 200 B.C. the Romans had how-to-grow directions for asparagus. They enjoyed it in season and preserved it for later use by drying.

Its characteristics were so well-known to the ancients that 1st century Emperor Augustus described haste to his underlings as being "quicker than you can cook asparagus."

A 16th century Englander said of 'sperage': "It is delicious eaten with oyl and vinegar." Records of plantings in American gardens attest to the long life of this vegetable. From the Middlebury, Vt., Register in 1917: "There is an asparagus bed on the Elios Lyman farm . . . which was started 101 years ago and continues to this day to yield a generous crop."

When you grow asparagus you are joining Mother Nature in a classic demonstration of her growth power. What a manufacturing plant!

In summer, its graceful, fern-like foliage stands tall to the sun. The leaves are manufacturing food in excess of their needs for growth and are storing the excess in the roots. The big transfer to storage will come when the tops die.

Asparagus ferns in summer

With the warming of the soil the following spring, stalks rise from the crown to renew the plant. All growth now is on stored food in the roots. (The manufacturing plant is on battery power.)

Many more shoots will form than are needed for the renewal of the plant. So you prune the shoots — a few or more the first year. More the second. The third year should give you 4 weeks of cutting.

Prepare soil. When planting asparagus you are building the foundation for 10 to 15 years of production. So take the time to work the soil a foot or more deep and mix in large amounts of manure, compost, peat moss or like organic material, plus 4 to 5 pounds of 5-10-10 fertilizer per 100 square feet.

Planting transplants (root crown). You save a year over starting from seed by buying one year old plants (crowns) from garden centers or seed companies.

Dig trenches 8 inches deep and 4 to 5 feet apart. (Asparagus roots spread wide). Spread some compost or manure in the bottom of the trench and cover with an inch of garden soil.

Set the crowns 18 inches apart in the row and cover with 2 inches of soil. As the new shoots come up, gradually fill in the trench.

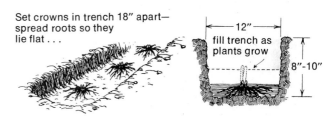

Set crowns in trench 18" apart— spread roots so they lie flat . . .

12"
fill trench as plants grow
8"-10"

Fertilizing · For high production and thick spears follow a twice-a-year feeding program. Make one application before growth starts in the spring and a second as soon as the harvest is finished to encourage heavy top growth.

Don't skimp on water when the top growth is developing.

Harvesting. Cut or snap off spears when 6 to 8 inches high. "Snapping"— bending the spear over sharply until it breaks — avoids injury to other shoots below ground. When cutting spears the asparagus knife is a handy tool.

Early in the season the shoots may require cutting only every third day, but as the growth becomes more active it may be necessary to cut twice a day, especially if the asparagus is growing on very light warm soil.

VARIETIES

Choose rust resistant varieties such as 'Mary Washington' and 'Waltham Washington.'

Serving ideas:

Fresh young asparagus is excellent raw, sliced thinly on the diagonal into green salads or included on a relish platter with a sour cream dip.

Or nestle asparagus spears in a basket of *crudites:* fresh raw vegetables arranged like a nosegay in a small wicker basket. Serve with mayonnaise or a French *tapenade* sauce composed of mayonnaise seasoned with chopped ripe olives and anchovies.

Serve hot cooked asparagus spears with browned butter, sieved egg yolk, and chopped watercress to lavish over each serving as the Dutch do.

Beans

Beans originated in Central America, but were well distributed in many parts of the western hemisphere before Columbus arrived. Several varieties used in the United States today were developed from beans grown by the American Indians.

If you turn to the planting chart on page 18 you will find directions on planting these beans: snap bush and pole; lima bush and pole; fava beans, garbanzos, scarlet runner, soybeans and the yardlong bean. All are discussed here except soybeans (page 67), scarlet runner (page 107), and yardlong (page 57).

Snap beans are said to be the foolproof vegetable for the beginning gardener. Members of our panel found them easy to grow but not foolproof.

TIME TO SOW SEEDS IN PLACE

(Usually direct seeded but can be started in pots 3 weeks earlier. See pg. 18 for planting directions.)

ZONE	JAN.	FEB.	MAR.	APR.	MAY	JUNE	JULY	AUG.	SEPT.	OCT.	NOV.	DEC.
1				———		———	———					
2				———		———						
3				———								
4				———								
5				———								
6				———								

MISTAKES BEGINNERS MAKE

Plant too early. Seeds will not germinate in cold soil. If you want to rush the season, sow indoors in peat pots and set out when soil warms up.

Plant too deep and too shallow. In spring plant no more than one inch deep. Increase the depth in follow-up plantings to 2 inches in summer plantings.

Allow soil to crust over. A sprouting bean must pull folded leaves through the soil and spread them above ground. In crusted or heavy soils you'll notice broken shoots where they have tried and failed.

Apply a light mulch over seed row to prevent crusting or if crust forms at emergence time, soften it by a light sprinkling.

Leave over-mature pods on the vines. To get a full crop of snap beans pick beans before large seeds develop. A few old pods left on a plant will *greatly* reduce the set of new ones. Keep snap beans picked in the young succulent stage.

Let soil dry out. Lack of moisture in the soil will cause the plant to produce "pollywogs" — only the first few seeds develop and the rest of the pod shrivels to a tail.

Fail to feed bush beans early enough in the season. Plant must make strong early growth to be of good size before flowering starts. Feed by mixing a 5-10-10 fertilizer at the rate of 3 pounds per 100 square feet into the soil before planting.

Placing fertilizer too close to bean roots.

Don't forget that feeding and watering is a continuous affair with pole beans. It's possible to get a second crop after the main crop is finished. Remove all pods, fertilize and water deeply.

VARIETIES

Bush Beans require only about 60 days of moderate temperatures to produce a crop of green pods. With such a short growth period they can be grown in nearly any place in the United States. In most areas you can keep them coming to the kitchen over many months by making small plantings every 2 weeks.

There are many varieties of green bush beans. These are near the top of all recommended variety lists: 'Tendercrop,' (53 days to maturity); 'Topcrop,' (49 days); 'Bush Blue Lake,' (58 days); 'Spartan Arrow' (52 days); 'Greensleeves' (56 days); 'Tenderette' (53 days).

'Romano 14' (52 days). A bush form of the popular pole 'Romano.' Large, broad flat pods are as thick, succulent and flavorful as the regular Romano.

Bush wax beans most frequently recommended are: 'Resistant Kinghorn Wax,' (54 days) 'Cherokee Wax,' (52 days) and 'Eastern Butterwax,' (53 days).

Purple podded 'Royalty' (55 days). This tender, stringless purple podded bush bean is gaining a reputation for flavor and ability to grow in colder soil than other snap beans. Furthermore, bean beetles seem to avoid it. When cooked in boiling water for 2 minutes, pods turn deep green, providing a built-in indicator for home freezing.

Pole snap beans. The small-space gardener may find that going vertical with a trellis, teepee, or fence of pole beans solves his garden planning better than a succession of bush beans. You'll get production over a longer period with pole beans.

'Kentucky Wonder' is still the favorite. 'Blue Lake' is praised for its thick flesh and small seeds that are slow to mature.

The variety 'Ramono,' a broad flat bean of distinctive flavor, is increasing in popularity.

Lima Beans need warmer soils to germinate properly and higher temperatures and a longer season to produce a crop. But they fail to set pods in extremely hot weather.

Of the bush lima varieties, 'Fordhook 242' (70 days) is widely adapted and sets pods under higher temperature than most varieties. 'Henderson Bush' (65 days) is a good producer of small baby limas. 'Thaxter' resembles 'Henderson Bush' but has better disease resistance.

The popular pole lima variety is still the old timer 'King of the Garden.' (88 days from seed to maturity.)

Horticultural Beans. These are large seeded beans grown to be used in the green-shell stage. The fiber is too tough to be cooked as snap beans. Pods are colorful, striped and mottled in red. There are always displays of them at county fairs.

Varieties are 'Dwarf Horticultural' and 'Bush Horticultural.' The pole variety is 'King Horticultural.'

Broadbeans, Fava, Horsebean, Windsor are not true beans. They are related to vetch and will grow in cool weather unsuited to snapbeans. In mild winter areas they are planted in the fall for a spring crop. Will not produce in summer heat.

Varieties 'Long Pod' and 'Broad Long Pod' have 5 to 7 large flat seeds. Can be used as a substitute for pole limas, green shell or dry, in short season areas.

Garbanzo, Chick Pea, Chestnut Bean. Botanically, garbanzos are neither beans or peas but *Cicer arietinum,* Chick Pea or Gram. The gram is as important to the food of India as the bean is to the United States.

Garbanzo, a bush type, produces 1 or 2 seeds in each puffy little pod. It is picked in the green-ripe stage or allowed to ripen for dry beans. When cooked they have a chestnut-like flavor and add a pleasant touch to a green salad or a mixed bean salad. The pureed cooked beans are notable blended with garlic, lemon juice, and sesame paste in an Arabian dip.

Seed source [4], (19). See page 111.

Serving ideas:

The many kinds of fresh and dried beans comprise a basic staple food in many cuisines throughout the world. These legumes vary greatly in size and style of cooking. Many are available both fresh and dried.

When cooking with dried beans, it is not necessary to soak them overnight. A short-cut method is to place them in a kettle, cover with water, and bring to a quick boil. Boil for 2 minutes, remove from heat and allow to stand 1 hour, still covered with water. Then cook until tender as the recipe directs.

For broadbeans, peel the shelled beans before cooking in boiling salted water. Serve hot with butter or pureed with heavy cream.

Purple Pod Pole

Romano Pole Beans

Blackeyed Peas

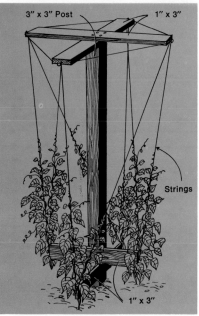
3" x 3" Post   1" x 3"
Strings
1" x 3"

The cabbage family

Cabbage

Cabbage as we know it developed gradually from leafy, non-heading forms growing wild in various parts of Europe. Hard heading types were not definitely recorded until 1536. They were brought to the United States in 1541.

How to grow. Plan for a succession of a few heads at a time. Buy transplants for the earliest planting then sow seed directly in the garden for follow-up crops.

To produce large heads, space plants 20 inches or more in rows 36 inches apart. Smaller, normally developed heads big enough for family use can be grown spaced 12 inches between plants.

Cabbage is a heavy user of nitrogen and potash. Before planting add 6 to 8 pounds of 5-10-10 for 100 square feet and work it into the soil. Follow up, in 3 to 4 weeks, with a side dressing of about 1 pound of ammonium nitrate per 100 feet of row.

Problems. The heads of early varieties split soon after they mature in warm weather. So plant at one time only the number you can use in a 2-3 week period.

To slow up splitting hold off on water or partially root prune the plant when the heads are formed. Some gardeners simply twist the plant to break some of the roots. Splitting is seldom a problem with late varieties maturing in cool weather.

A number of our gardeners reported trouble with young plants bolting and failure of overwintering plants to form heads.

Cabbage is a biennial, forming a leafy head the first year and flowering the second.

The change from leaf stage to flowering (bolting) will occur in young plants if they are exposed to temperatures below 50° for 2 or 3 weeks. Large transplants, subjected to low winter temperatures will flower in the spring.

There will be less trouble with bolting if you use transplants with stems the size of a lead pencil.

TIME TO SET OUT PLANTS
(Sow seed indoors 5-7 weeks earlier)

ZONE	JAN.	FEB.	MAR.	APR.	MAY	JUNE	JULY	AUG.	SEPT.	OCT.	NOV.	DEC.
1			────			──────						
2			──			────						
3			────			────						
4				──								
5					────							
6					──							

The Cabbage Family

Varieties that are yellows resistant are indicated (YR).

Early to medium

'Early Jersey Wakefield' (63 days). (YR). 2½-3 pounds.
'Golden Acre' (64 days). (YR). 4-5 pounds. Quick to split.
'Copenhagen Market' (72 days). (YR). 4-4½ pounds.
'Marion Market' (75 days). (YR). 5½-7 pounds.
'Market Prize' (76 days). (YR). 4-5 pounds.

Late

'Danish Ballhead' (105 days).

Red

'Red Acre' (76 days). 4 pounds. Slow to split.

'Red Danish Ballhead' (97 days). 5 pounds.

Savoy

'Chieftain Savoy' (88 days). Standard savoy, densely curled, crumpled leaves.

'Savoy King' (90 days). (YR). 4 pounds. All America Selection.

THE MIDGETS

'Dwarf Morden' (53 days). (YR). Firm, round, tender 4-inch heads. Seed sources: (9), (21). See page 111.
'Little Leaguer Cabbage' (60 days). Round, 4-inch softball-sized heads. Seed source: (5).

'Baby Head' (72 days). Very small. 2½-3 pound heads. Holds well without splitting. Hard as a rock. Thick leaves. Seed sources: (10), (27).

Serving ideas:

A combination of both white and red cabbage, shredded, makes a striking coleslaw. Include fresh pineapple chunks or diced apple, if you wish.

Include this leafy vegetable in a classic French *pot-au-feu* (see page 86) and Spanish and Italian boiled dinners. Stuff the head with ground pork and veal, in the Danish manner or turn it into a Hungarian strudel. Offer it sweet and sour in the German way or shred and cook it with applie slices to go with duck, as it's done in Normandy.

Pickle it for sauerkraut to savor in such diverse dishes as the French *choucroute garni* (sauerkraut with pork and sausages), Russian sauerkraut soup, and Hungarian layered pork and sauerkraut.

Kale

Kale and collards are close kin of wild cabbage. And as long as man has grown any vegetable they have been cultivated. Similar in many ways, collards and kale differ in one respect: collards produce through hot summers; kale can't take the heat. Both are extremely hardy.

How to grow. Kale grows best in the cool days of fall. And the flavor of the leaves is improved by frost. Since kale thinnings are good eating scatter seeds in a 4-inch band and thin finally to 8 to 12 inches in rows 18 to 24 inches apart.

For early planting in the spring transplants are often used but direct seeding is best for fall planting.

VARIETIES

These varieties of kale deserve a place in the flower border:

'Blue Curled Scotch' (55 days to maturity). Leaves, as curled as parsley, are a distinct blue-green.

'Dwarf Siberian Curled' (65 days). Grayish-green leaves held like plumes.

Both grow to 12-18 inches tall and as wide.

Collards

This perennial is one of the oldest members of the cabbage family. Vegetable historians claim that it has been used for food for more than 4,000 years and cultivated in its present form for 2,000 years. European writers described it in the 1*st*, 3*rd* and 4*th* century and it was noted in early American gardens in 1669.

Collards have been a favorite in the South for generations. Actually they are widely adapted and are finding their way into more and more northern gardens. Collards, unlike their close relative kale, withstand hot summer weather, and will take much more cold than cabbage.

Broccoli

Brussel Sprouts

How to grow. Same fertilizing and water requirements as cabbage. Several planting methods are followed. (1) In spring sow seed or set out plants to stand 10-15 inches apart. (2) Or set plants close, 5-7 inches apart, to dwarf them into small bunchy plants. Harvest leaves as needed. (3) In summer plantings sow seed thinly and let seedlings grow until large enough for greens, then harvest seedlings to give the normal distance between plants.

When to plant. Try a planting in the spring and then in late July for fall harvest. Collards can take short periods of cold as low as 10 degrees. A light freeze sweetens the flavor.

VARIETIES

'Georgia' (Southern, Creole). Matures in 70-80 days. Old standard variety. Plants 24-30 inches tall with very broad, slightly crumpled, medium to blue-green leaves.

'Louisiana Sweet'. 85 days. Larger leaf area than 'Georgia,' with thick tender leaves of an appealing color.

'Vates'. 75 days. Low growing, broad and spreading. Thick, very broad bladed, grassy green leaves.

'Morris Heading'. 83 days. Leaves broad and wavy forming a moderately tight head good for winter planting.

Serving ideas:

We pick the leaves when young and with small midribs. Chop them finely and boil in salted water until tender and serve them dressed with butter or hot bacon drippings. Collards have a pleasant relationship with ham and pork and are often cooked with a ham hock or salt pork. Use them in a hearty pea soup seasoned with green pepper, onion and ham bone.

Sprouting Broccoli

Sprouting broccoli is grown in the same way as cabbage. It is more tolerant of heat than cauliflower.

Broccoli can be harvested over a long period. After the center cluster of buds is cut, the side shoots develop small clusters for a month or more.

VARIETIES

Strains of 'Italian Green Sprouting'—'De Cicco' (65 days) and 'Calabrese' (65 days) — are widely available. Frequently recommended varieties are: 'Green Comet' (55 days); 'Spartan Early' (55 days); 'Waltham 29' (74 days).

Brussels Sprouts

Sprouts require cool weather and are best grown for fall and winter harvest. Set out transplants in June or July.

The sprouts mature in sequence as long as weather permits. Remove the leaves from beneath the lowest sprouts and twist them off. The sprouts above will continue to develop.

In cold winter areas you can make sure of a full harvest by pinching out the growing tip in early fall. All of the sprouts will be ready about the same time.

The principal varieties are 'Jade Cross Hybrid' (95 days) and 'Long Island Improved' (90 days).

Serving ideas:

Boil these diminutive mild cabbages and dress with butter or sour cream or turn into a nutmeg-scented cream sauce or cheese sauce. For an interesting Oriental stir-fry, combine sprouts and thinly sliced beef, seasoning with soy and fresh ginger root.

Cauliflower

More demanding than broccoli or cabbage. Cauliflower will not head up properly in hot weather or stand as much cold as cabbage. Culture and planting dates are generally the same as cabbage.

When the curds (heads) develop and begin to show through the leaves, it's time to blanch them. Gather the leaves together over the curd and tie them with soft twine or plastic strips.

VARIETIES

Strains of 'Snowball' are the most practical. 'Early Snowball' (60 days). 'Snowball Y' (68 days). 'Snow King' (50 days). All America Selection.

'Purple Head' (85 days). Large heads. Turns green when cooked. No need to blanch.

Serving ideas:

The raw cauliflowerets are ideal for dips and the Italian *Bagna Cauda*, an anchovy-garlic-butter sauce (page 81).

Steam the cauliflowerets and serve hot with a delicate nutmeg-spiced cheese sauce in the Scandinavian manner.

Cook cauliflower whole and coat with a mixture of three parts olive oil to one part lemon juice. Sprinkle lightly with oregano. Place on a platter and surround with hot baby artichoke hearts in the style of Greek cooks.

Chinese Cabbage—Celery Cabbage

The name Chinese Cabbage covers a number of "greens" quite different in character. All are cool weather crops and bolt to seed in long days of late spring and summer. Grow as a fall and early winter crop.

How to grow. Sow seeds thinly and thin to stand 18 inches apart in rows 24 to 30 inches apart. Takes about 75-85 days from seed to harvest.

When to plant. Start seed in July. Figure 75-85 days before first frost for the heading types; 45 days for the loose-leafed.

VARIETIES

'Wong Bok'. 85 days. This is the Chinese cabbage most frequently available at supermarkets. Heads are about 10 inches tall, 6 inches wide and completely blanched.

'Michihli'. An improved form of Chihli. 75 days. Forms a tall 18-inch tapering head 3-4 inches thick with dark green wrapper leaves and well blanched inner leaves.

'Burpee Hybrid'. (Wong Bok type). Heads are round, 13 inches tall and 8 inches thick.

'Pac-Choy'. Non-heading type. One of the most popular of the oriental vegetables. Widely grown in Hawaii as one of the "Spoon Cabbages." They resemble Swiss chard (without heavy stalks) in growth habit.

Serving ideas:

The pale whitish-green cabbage is favored for soups, sukiyakis, and stir-fry medleys. It is also well-suited to Western dishes. Shred it for a cabbage slaw with fresh pineapple and a sour cream dressing. Boil wedges to accompany corned beef or other pot-au-feu type of dishes. Or shred and toss it with macadamia nuts and avocado chunks, bound in a creamy tart dressing. Or shred and butter-steam it to accompany roast pork or duck.

Use the broad leaves for cabbage rolls, stuffed with a minced pork and water chestnut filling.

The root crops

Beets

The original home of the beet was around the Mediterranean, where it first occurred as a leafy form, without enlarged roots. Improved types of these early beets are now grown as Swiss Chard. Large-rooted beets were first noted in literature around 1550 in Germany, but there was only one variety listed in the U.S. in 1806.

How to grow. Plant beets directly in rows a foot or more apart. Thin them to 2 inches. Some thinning can be postponed until the extra plants are large enough for eating the greens, roots and all. Unless you use a monogerm (single seeded) variety, each beet seedball produces 3-5 plants in a tight clump, so thinning should be done early.

Though beets prefer cool weather, they are tolerant of a wide range of conditions. The planting date chart shows they can be planted early, but additional plantings can be made for a long period. In very hot weather special attention to watering and mulching may be needed to get a good stand for seedlings.

TIME TO SOW SEEDS IN PLACE

ZONE	JAN.	FEB.	MAR.	APR.	MAY	JUNE	JULY	AUG.	SEPT.	OCT.	NOV.	DEC.
1			———	———								
2			——	———								
3			———	—								
4				———	—							
5				———								
6				———								

Mistakes beginners make. The usual overplanting and under-thinning. Stringy tough beets are the result of lack of moisture or competition from weeds or other beets. Beets must be grown full-speed without a single let-up.

VARIETIES

The choice of varieties for garden use is not very critical. Downy mildew resistance is needed in certain areas, however. All varieties can serve both for roots and greens, but if greens are needed to any extent it would be better to plant chard or a variety of beets designed for that use. Sugar beets, if seed can be found, are excellent for greens.

'Detroit Dark Red' (63 days). Dark color, neat globe shape. Downy mildew resistant strains available.
'Early Wonder' (55 days). Semi globe.
'Ruby Queen.' (60 days). Globe, deep red.
'Mono-King Explorer' (50 days). Monogerm type, single seed to each seedball. Deep red.
'Ruby Queen' (60 days). Globe, deep red.
'Burpee Golden' (55 days). Unusual golden yellow root, good quality; may average higher in sugar. Pigments do not bleed out in cooking as in red beets.

Beets for greens listed by various seedsmen include: 'Sugar Beets,' 'Green Top Bunching,' 'Beets For Greens,' 'White Beet,' 'Lutz Green Leaf.'

Serving ideas:

Serve hot cooked, sliced beets in an orange sauce or with dollops of sour cream. Shred raw beets and cook quickly in butter. Cooked beets are good in herring salad or borsch.

Carrots

Our carrots originated from forms grown in the Mediterranean. By the 13th century carrots were well established as a food in Europe and came to America with the first settlers, where Indians soon took up their culture.

Carrots are adaptable, tolerant of mismanagement and are unequaled for supplying food for a long period of time, using nothing more complicated for storage than the soil in which they are grown.

How to grow. In the Nichols Nursery Catalog you'll find this paragraph headlined "How to raise carrots without using a spade or hoe. It is simple, and here is how it is done: Build a raised bed made of 2 x 8 lumber (length optional) but width should not exceed 4 feet. Fill bed with 1/5 garden loam, 2/5ths clean sand and 2/5 compost, rotted manure, or peat moss. For every 10 feet length of bed spread 5 pounds of bone meal. Mix thoroughly all ingredients, then rake down into a fine seed bed. Broadcast the carrot seed, cover with 1/4 inch fine sifted peat moss. Water, and keep bed well moistened, but not soggy wet. Pull carrots as they are ready. July sown seed will give you carrots in the fall."

This is another way of saying what we have been preaching throughout the early chapters of this book.

The only question we have about the above soil mix is the inclusion of manure. Manures, unless very well rotted, cause roughness and branching carrots.

The raised beds reduce cracking and decay problems from excess water in the fall. Digging is no trouble in the light soil mix. Soil warms up early in raised beds and carrots can be started earlier than the regular garden soil can be worked.

Kohlrabi

Burpee Golden

See chapters on sowing seed (page 14) and planning the garden (page 30) for specifics on handling carrots.

VARIETIES

Choose varieties by your preference for shape and size. The short-to-medium or very short types are better adapted to heavy or rough soils than the long types, and are easier to dig.

Short-to-medium — good for wet fall and winter and heavy soils. 'Red Cored Chantenay (70 days to maturity). Medium length, heavy, widely adapted. 'Royal Chantenay' (70 days). Longer than Red Cored Chantenay. An improved strain. 'Spartan Bonus' (75 days). Medium long and heavy; good producer.

Long, slender—better in light sandy soils, need deep loose soils. 'Nantes.' Good quality, cracks in wet fall weather. 'Imperator' (75 days). Standard market carrot, 8-9 inches long, good quality. 'Gold Pak' (76 days). Deep color, 8-9 inches long.

Very short — 'Oxheart' (75 days). Good for heavy soils. Plump and short.

Serving ideas:

This brilliant vegetable is widely popular in a range of dishes, from appetizers to desserts, in many cuisines. Include diagonally sliced carrots on the *Bagna Cauda* tray (see page 81). Or prepare in the manner of Vegetables a la Grecque (see page 88). They lend color to many international stews and boiled dinners. They are a surprise ingredient in Continental nut cakes.

Kohlrabi

Kohlrabi is a relatively recent development from wild cabbage in northern Europe. It was not known about 500

years ago, and was first recorded in the United States about 1800.

This unusual but little known vegetable deserves to be grown and appreciated more. It looks like a turnip growing on top of the ground and sprouting leaves all over.

Often described as a turnip growing on cabbage roots. The flavor reminds of both turnip and cabbage but is milder and sweeter than either.

How to grow. Grow in the same way as turnips, see page 79. Woody stem fibers develop through the edible portion when fully developed. This is usually when they are about 2-3 inches in diameter.

VARIETIES

Only two varieties are grown: 'Early White Vienna' (55 days). Light green color, most commonly grown. 'Early Purple Vienna' (60 days). Light purple. Both of these forms are attractive and unusual enough to include in the ornamental vegetable border.

Serving ideas:

Prepare it in the same manner as you might turnips. It is excellent on a *Bagna Cauda* tray (see page 81) or as a vegetable relish with sour cream dips. Cube and add it to stews or mash it with butter and cream.

Radish

Give a youngster a package of radish seeds and say "go plant" and you'll have radishes. But to get crisp, mild, non-pithy radishes the fundamentals of fertilizing and watering must be met. Fertilizers must be worked into the soil before planting to be quickly available to the young seedlings. Spring radishes mature in 3 to 4 weeks from seeding so there's little time to correct mistakes.

Thin seedlings 1 or 2 inches apart very soon after emergence to reduce competition because roots begin to expand when only 2 weeks old. Scatter seeds spaced out in a 3 or 4 inch wide row to reduce need for thinning. For a continuous supply of crisp roots start early with small plantings and repeat every 10 days.

Mistakes beginners make. Most frequent disaster among our panel gardeners was damage from the cabbage maggot. For how to control see page 20.

VARIETIES

For early and fall planting there are many shapes and sizes:
'Cherry Belle' (22 days to maturity). Round, cherry size, all red.
'Burpee White' (25 days). Round. Pick them when 1/4 to 1 inch.
'French Breakfast' (24 days). Red with white tip, oblong.
'Sparkler' (25 days). Red with lower third white. Round.
'White Icicle' (28 days). 5-inch long roots.

Winter varieties. Plant in late summer or fall to mature in fall or winter; become quite large but remain solid and non-bolting. May bolt if planted in spring and early summer.
'White Chinese' (50 days). Long. Usually mild.
'China Rose' (52 days). Long, hot.
'Round Black Spanish' (56 days). Black, globe, hot.
Oriental fall and winter varieties: 'Takinashi' (65 days). 1 foot long, white, brittle fleshed. 'Sakurajima Mammoth' (70 days). Giant sized to 70 pounds. Seed sources (19). See page 111.

Serving ideas:

Though traditionally considered a salad vegetable or relish, trimmed radishes are excellent butter-steamed until crisp-tender, about 5 minutes.

Clockwise from here: Country Gentlemen Yellow Hybrid, Indian corn, An inferior early variety, Purple Husk, Silver Queen, Indian corn, Popcorn, Indian corn.

Corn

"Corn" as a word has meant many things. Originally it meant any hard particle or grain, sand, salt. Our "corned" beef earned its name because it was cured with salt. Both wheat and barley were called corn in the Old World. Maize, the main cereal of the New World, was first known as "Indian corn" and later just "corn."

Corn supported the early civilizations of the Americas. Fossils show that corn was grown in North America more than 2,000 B.C. Following the discovery of America, corn spread rapidly throughout the Old World.

How to grow. Plant seed 2 inches deep, 4 to 6 seeds per foot in rows 30-36 inches apart. Thin to 10-14 inches between plants. Plant early, midseason and late varieties or successive plantings every 2 to 3 weeks for a continuous supply of sweet corn through summer and into the fall.

TIME TO SOW SEEDS IN PLACE

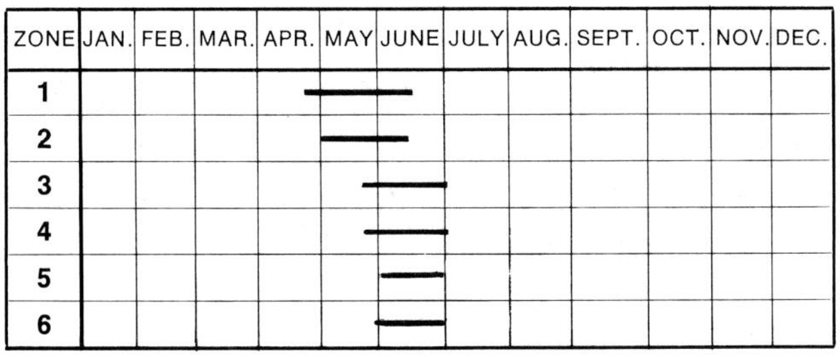

ZONE	JAN.	FEB.	MAR.	APR.	MAY	JUNE	JULY	AUG.	SEPT.	OCT.	NOV.	DEC.
1					—							
2				—								
3					—							
4					—							
5					—							
6					—							

More corn per foot of space? A number of gardeners on our panel argued about the need for spacing corn 10-14 inches in the row and 30-36 inches between rows.

Here's how the specialists reacted:

"More home garden corn plantings are *ruined* by overcrowding than any other factor.

"When seedlings are up, everyone hates to pull them out and throw them away. Actually too many seedlings in a row act just like weeds.

"The smaller-growing early varieties might be spaced 8 inches apart in rows 30 inches apart, but with the later varieties such as 'Golden Cross Bantam,' I like to get them spaced out to a good 12 to 15 inches for good ear production.

"If you overspace corn you generally are compensated by more useable ears and some sucker production."

How much fertilizer and when? The schedule that most specialists approved:

"At planting time, fertilize in bands on both sides of seed row, 2 inches from seed in the furrow and an inch deeper than seed level. Use 3 pounds of 5-10-10 (in each band) per 100 feet of row.

"When corn is 8 inches high, side dress with same amount. Repeat when knee-high (18 inches).

"Nitrogen deficiency is easy to spot because the lower leaves of the plants turn yellow very quickly."

Watering. It's water all the way for corn. Here's what the corn specialists said:

"The water need is greater from tasseling time to picking time.

"Sweet corn makes very rapid growth during the time of maturing the crop. No check in watering should occur.

"In very hot and dry weather, rolling of the leaves may occur in midday even when soil moisture is adequate. Plants will transpire water faster than the roots will absorb water. But if leaves roll (edges turn upward), check the soil for moisture."

Do's—Don'ts. Corn is wind pollinated. Plant in short blocks of 3 to 4 rows rather than a single row.

Don't worry about the suckers, the number vary by variety. They do not "take strength from the main stalks." Tests have shown that removing suckers may reduce yields.

In most areas, damage from the corn earworm takes the joy out of growing corn unless steps are taken to stop them. See page 21 for ways to control.

Ears with tight husks and a good tip cover are damaged less by the corn earworm. They do not prevent the entrance of the worms but the damage is less. In the list of varieties that follow we have noted those with tight husks.

Tight husks and good tip cover have another advantage. A corn specialist reports:

"We have a terrible time with birds eating the kernels on the tip of the ear. The damage is worse on ears with a loose husk. And such damage to the ornamental Indian corn make it worthless. We solved the problem by slipping a paper bag over each ear after it's pollinated."

VARIETIES

If you have found the corn that fits your garden and your taste, consider the following list an invitation to sample a new taste or a new color.

The "bi-colors" with their mixture of white and yellow kernels should be experienced at least once. The 'Xtra Sweet' varieties do contain more sugar than the standard varieties and their sugar changes slowly to starch.

In every trial of varieties the variety 'Silver Queen' is rated as "the highest quality corn ever developed."

In the following chart resistance to bacterial wilt is indicated by the letter "R." Varieties with tight husks receive letters (T.H.).

The number of days to maturity is a relative figure. It varies by the total amount of heat the corn receives. Varieties listed as 65 days may take 80 or 90 when planted early. Corn does not get up and grow until the weather warms. The same variety will come close to its cataloged 65 days if planted a month later.

When planting for a succession of harvests, the effect of cool spring weather should be considered. Rather than planting every 2 weeks, let the height of the first planting set the date for the second.

Variety	Color	Days	Ear Length	Rows	Height	—
Earliking	Y	60	7-8	12	5½	—
Spring Gold	Y	66	7	12-16	6	T.H.
Golden Beauty	Y	67	6-7½	14	5½-6	R.
Marcross Golden Belle	Y	69	6½-8	12-14	6	R.
Sugar & Gold	Bl	70	6-6½	8-10	4-6	—
Gold Cup	Y	77	7½	14-16	6½	—
Butter & Sugar	Bl	78	7½	12-14	4-6	T.H.
Seneca Chief	Y	80	8-8½	14	6-7	T.H.
Golden Cross Bantam	Y	80	7½-8	10-14	6-7	R.
Illinichief	Y	83	7-9	12-14	5-6	—
Iochief	Y	85	9-10	14-18	6½	R.
Silver Queen	W	96	8-9	14-16	7-8	R.

Cucumber

Probably has its origin in India. Vegetable historians say that it was introduced into China the second century before Christ. The French, in 1535, found the Indians growing them in what is now Montreal. De Soto found them being cultivated in Florida.

Because of its short growing season (55-65 days from seed to picking size) the cucumber can find the warm slice of climate it needs almost everywhere. It does well with less heat than melons.

TIME TO SOW SEEDS IN PLACE
(Can be started in pots indoors 4 weeks earlier.)

ZONE	JAN.	FEB.	MAR.	APR.	MAY	JUNE	JULY	AUG.	SEPT.	OCT.	NOV.	DEC.
1				—			——					
2				——								
3				——								
4				——								
5					——							
6												

How to grow. Sow seed 1 inch deep, 3 to 5 seeds to 1 foot of row. Thin to 12 inches between plants. Distance between rows 48 to 72 inches. If grown in hills, sow 9 to 12 seeds in each hill and when plants are up, thin to 4 or 6 and finally to 2 or 3 per hill. Hills are spaced 24 to 36 inches apart in rows 48 to 72 inches apart. There is no advantage in spacing in hills.

Where growing season is short, start seed indoors 4 to 6 weeks before time to set out transplants (See "Seeds and Transplants" page 14). When setting out transplants, cover plants with "hot caps" or plastic to increase temperatures and protect from frost.

Fertilizing and watering. Cucumbers respond to generous amounts of organic matter in the soil. For special treatment, dig the planting furrow 2 feet deep and fill the first foot or so with manure mixed with peat moss, compost, sawdust or other organic material. Fill rest of the furrow with soil, peat moss, and 5-10-10 fertilizer at the rate of 2 pounds to 50 feet of row.

Since roots will grow to a depth of 3 feet if soil is normal, watering should be slow and deep. If the plant is under stress from lack of moisture at any time it just stops growing. It will pick up again when moisture is supplied. It is normal for leaves of cucumbers to wilt in the middle of the day during hot spells, but check the soil for moisture at the below-surface levels.

When space is limited. Cucumbers trained on a trellis take very little ground space and you will harvest more attractive fruits and fewer culls. Cucumbers that are curved when grown on the ground, such as "Burpees Hybrid," grow almost straight when trained on a trellis.

Consider the midget varieties when space is limited. They can be grown on the ground, in tubs and boxes or as hanging baskets. Two such varieties are:

'Tiny Dill Cuke'. 55 days. Vines spread only 2 feet. Produces near finger-length cukes. University of New Hampshire development.

'Patio Pik'. 60 days. Vine is very dwarf, spreading only 18 to 24 inches. Pick small for dills, larger for slicing. Up to 7 inches long.

Don't worry about the failure of the first early flowers to set fruit. The male flowers open first, then about a week later you'll see flowers with baby cucumbers at their bases. The male flowers supply the pollen which is transferred by insects to the female flowers.

If this delayed setting worries you, try one of the new all-female (gynoecious) hybrids. They set fruit with the first blossoms and thus bear fruit closer to the base of the plant.

Most important. Keep all fruit picked from the vines as they reach usable size. The importance of this can't be overstressed, because even a few fruit left to mature on the plant will completely stop the set of new fruit. If you can't keep up, and want to have the fruit keep coming, invite the neighbors to share the harvest.

VARIETIES
Disease resistance is important in cucumbers, depending on locality. Disease resistance or tolerance is indicated as follows: Scab (S), Mosiac (M), Downy Mildew (DM), Powdery Mildew (PM), Anthracnose (A). Name of Experiment Station that developed the variety is included. Gynoecious hybrids (Gyn.) are all or nearly all female, produce fruits on the early flowers, usually have about 12% normal plants mixed in for pollination.

'Gemini Hybrid' by Clemson. (Gyn.), (DM), (M), (PM), (A), (S).
'Meridian.' Cornell. (Gyn.), (S), (M).
'Marketer Hybrid.' Cornell. (DM), (M).
'Marketmore.' Cornell. (S), (M).
'Triumph Hybrid.' All-American Selection. (DM), (M).
'Ashley.' Clemson. (DM).
'Burpee Hybrid.' (DM).
'Poinsett.' Clemson. (DM), (PM), (A).

Picklers: Many varieties available. These have the advantage of disease resistance:

'Pioneer.' (Gyn.), (S), (M), (DM), (PM).

'SMR 58.' (S), (M).

'SMR 18.' (S), (M).

Many kinds. Cucumbers come in a wide variety of shapes and colors. There's a white one available—'White Wonder' catalog (26). The 'Lemon Cucumber' is the size and shape of a lemon and at maturity turns a lemon yellow and then a golden yellow. This old timer is easy to grow, always sweet, and as burpless as any we have grown. Available: (5), (16), (19), (27), (31).

The very long, narrow cucumber you see in the produce markets is the English type, seedless when grown in greenhouses without pollination. Similar looking — long and slim are 'China Long' and 'China Hybrid' (4).

'Burpless Hybrid' (60 days) is an excellent producer of 8-10 inch long fruits, 30 to 40 per plant. Mild and nearly seedless.

Serving ideas:
This is a popular salad and pickle vegetable.

Slice and serve cucumbers in a white vinegar-sugar-dill bath for a Scandinavian "wilted" salad. Or serve sliced cucumbers in a yogurt and mint dressing for a Near Eastern meal. Or mix fresh slices with sour cream and chopped parsley.

Female cucumber bloom

Patio Pik

Armenian

Armenian

Japanese Yamato

Purpless

Japanese Eggplant

Dwarf Golden Eggplant

Eggplant

One of the oldest references to eggplant is in a 5th Century Chinese book. A black dye was made from the plant and was used by ladies of fashion to stain their teeth. When polished they gleamed like metal.

Wild eggplant occurs in India and was first taken into cultivation there. The Arabs took it to Spain; the Spaniards took it to the Americas, and the Persians to Africa.

The eggplants received in various European countries in the 16th and 17th Centuries varied greatly in shape and color. The first known appear to belong to the class now grown as an ornament, the fruit resembling an egg. Later, the varying shapes were described as long, pear-shaped, oblong, round or spherical. The colors reported were purple, yellow, white, ash-colored, and variegated. The purple and the white ornamental were growing in American gardens in 1806.

Today only the large-fruited varieties are grown on a commercial scale. Florida, Mexico and California supply the markets in the winter and spring months. In September and October New Jersey, Ohio, Colorado, Michigan, Illinois, Missouri, New York and Texas make their contributions.

TIME TO SET OUT PLANTS

(Sow seed indoors 7-10 weeks earlier)

ZONE	JAN.	FEB.	MAR.	APR.	MAY	JUNE	JULY	AUG.	SEPT.	OCT.	NOV.	DEC.
1				—								
2				——								
3					——							
4					——							
5					——							
6												

Eggplant has a very high heat requirement. Thrives best at 78° day, 68° night temperatures. The large-fruited kinds are more demanding than varieties with smaller fruits. Select early varieties where summers are short.

VARIETIES

More than 30 varieties are available. Some of the most popular are:

'Black Beauty' (75-80 days to maturity) is the most frequently recommended large-fruited variety. However the hybrids, such as 'Black Magic' and 'Burpee Hybrid' are favored for their earliness, vigor and disease resistance. They are taller growing than 'Black Beauty' and hold their fruit well off the ground. 'Jersey King Hybrid' produces elongated cylindrical fruits. 'Early Beauty Hybrid' is a compact grower with short oval fruits similar to 'New Hampshire Hybrid.'

Some of the old fashioned and unusual varieties you'll find listed in various catalogs (see page 111) are:

'Golden Yellow' (19) and 'Golden Egg' (12): Highly ornamental. Our plants produced more than 20 lemon-sized

(At left) 'Black Beauty' is the largest of the eggplants, 'Burpee Hybrid' next, then 'White Beauty,' 'Egg,' 'Early Beauty Hybrid.'

eggs per plant. 'Apple Green' (9): Fruits are non-acid, don't require peeling.

'White Beauty' (9) and 'White Italian' (19): Medium-sized fruits. Delicate flavor.

'Morden Midget' (9) (21). Medium-sized deep purple fruits on sturdy, small bushy plants. Developed at Morden, Canada, Experiment Station.

How to grow. Buy plants or start seed indoors 6 to 9 weeks before time to set out transplants. See transplanting procedure page 16. Set plants 18 inches apart in rows 36 inches apart.

Fruits will be ready to harvest in 75-95 days from setting out transplants.

Eggplant is more susceptible to low temperature injury — especially cold nights — than tomatoes. Don't set out plants until daily temperatures are in 70° range. Plants that fail to grow because of cool weather become hardened and stunted. Once stunted they seldom make the rapid growth necessary for quality fruit.

Plants heavy with fruit may need staking.

Apply a side dressing of fertilizer a month after planting and repeat in a month.

Mistakes beginners make. Setting out plants before weather is warm. Failure to give protection against cold with hot caps or plastic covers. Failure to protect young plants against damage by flea beetles and Colorado potato beetles. See "Insects and Diseases" page 20.

Special handling. The eggplant is well adapted to container growing. We have grown a half dozen varieties in 5-gallon size containers without a failure. The use of one of the synthetic soil mixes in containers is good insurance against the diseases that plague eggplant in some areas. See page 16. In containers the medium to small sized fruits carried high on the plant are more interesting than the lower growing heavy fruited varieties.

Where summers are cool, give containers the hot spots around the house — reflected heat from a south wall for example.

Harvest. For best eating quality, pick fruits when young at any stage from 1/3 to 2/3 their normal mature size. Good fruit has a high gloss. One test for maturity is to push on the side of the fruit with the ball of the thumb. If the indentation does not spring back the fruit is slightly mature. Fruits in which seeds have turned brown are past the eating stage. The stem is woody; so harvest with pruning shears.

Serving ideas:

Please don't make up your mind about liking or not liking eggplant until you have tried a few more recipes.

France, Italy, Greece, and the Near East have their ways with eggplant. Prepare it in a baked vegetable casserole called *ratatouille* from the south of France (see page 84). Simmer spears in a court bouillon a la Grecque style (see page 88).

Bake a whole eggplant for a Near Eastern salad. Place the whole eggplant in a shallow pan and bake in a 375° oven for 1 hour, or until tender. Place under cold water and peel off skin. Dice and mix with chopped green onions, tomatoes, garlic, and oil and vinegar. Serve cold on Romaine leaves.

Eggplant soaks up considerable oil or butter when fried. An easy way to cook the slices to avoid frying them in oil is to lay the 3/4 inch thick slices in a lightly oiled baking pan. Then bake in a 425° oven for 30 minutes, turning several times.

Lettuce

Leaf lettuce, native to the Mediterranean and Near East is a plant of great antiquity. More than 2500 years ago it was cultivated in the royal gardens of the Persian Kings. Forms of head lettuce appeared in the 15th Century. Lettuce seeds were carried by Columbus to the New World and were the first seeds sown in American colonial gardens.

As lettuce grows, so grows the gardener. Success with lettuce, in the full sense of the word means not only growing a quality crop but bringing it in through many months of the year in quantities that can always be used.

If you can plan for harvesting a salad bowl combining wedges of tomatoes, slices of green peppers and cucumbers and three kinds of lettuce, you have arrived as a vegetable grower.

THE 4 TYPES OF LETTUCE

Crisphead. Also known as Iceberg. If there is only one lettuce in the produce display, this will be it.

'Great Lakes.' 82-90 days to maturity. Slow to bolt. Crisp serrated leaves. May be bitter in hot weather.

'Ithaca.' 72 days. Mild, non-bolting and tipburn resistant all seasons. May break down in late fall weather.

'Imperial 44, and 456.' 84 days. Heads are medium to small. Adapted to spring and summer growing.

'Pennlake.' 70 days. Best in spring. Large and tender.

'Oswego.' 70 days. 'Fulton' 80 days. Similar to 'Ithaca.'

Most frequently recommended for the North and Northeast: 'Great Lakes,' 'Fulton,' 'Ithaca,' 'Pennlake.'

Butterhead. A heading type in which the leaves are loosely folded. Outer leaves may be green or brownish. Inner leaves are cream or butter colored. Butterhead types are not favored commercially because they bruise and tear easily. It's no problem in the home garden.

'Big Boston.' 75 days. Medium size. Leaves are broad, smooth, thick, crisp. Bolts easily, needs cool weather.

'Dark Green Boston.' 73-80 days. Loosely folded. Thick, substantial leaves.

'Deer Tongue' or 'Matchless.' 80 days. Thick green leaves with succulent midribs. Tightly folded.

'Bibb.' 75 days. A small head, 3½ inches across. Small dark green leaves loosely folded. Bolts in warm weather.

'Summer Bibb.' 77 days. Quality of 'Bibb' but slow to bolt.

'Buttercrunch.' 75 days. Thick leaves, more vigorous than 'Bibb.' Heat resistant and slow to bolt.

'Butter King.' 70 days. Large and vigorous. Slow bolting.

'Tom Thumb' 65 days. A miniature butter-head type. Tennis-ball-sized heads.

Recommended varieties for the North and Northeast are: 'Buttercrunch,' 'Summer Bibb,' 'Dark Green Boston.'

Leaf Lettuce or Bunching. More or less open in growth. Many variations in outer leaves; some frilled and crumpled, some deeply lobed. Leaf color varies from light green to red and brownish red.

'Black Seeded Simpson.' 44 days. Light green, moderately crinkled leaves.

'Prizehead' or 'Bronze Leaf.' 45 days. Large, broad bronze-tinted leaves. Mild in flavor. Vigorous.

'Salad Bowl.' 40 days. Crinkly leaves in a broad clump. Tender. Heat resistant and slow to bolt.

'Oakleaf.' 40 days. Medium size. Withstands heat.

'Grand Rapids.' 45 days. Frilled and crinkled.

'Slobolt.' 45 days. 'Grand Rapids' type stands more heat.

'Ruby.' 50 days. Give it high marks for color.

Most frequently recommended varieties are:

'Salad Bowl,' 'Oakleaf' and 'Prizehead.'

Cos or Romaine: Grows upright 8-9 inches tall with tightly folded leaves. Medium green outer leaves and greenish white interior.

'Dark Green Cos' and 'Paris Island Cos' are widely adapted and available.

TIME TO SOW SEEDS IN PLACE
(Can be started in pots indoors 3-5 weeks earlier.)

ZONE	JAN.	FEB.	MAR.	APR.	MAY	JUNE	JULY	AUG.	SEPT.	OCT.	NOV.	DEC.
1			━━	━				━━				
2			━━	━								
3			━━				━━					
4				━━	━		━━					
5						━━	━					
6							━━	━				

Lettuce is a cool season vegetable. The longer days and warmer nights of summer encourage flowering—"bolting to seed." By carefully choosing slow bolting varieties you may bring some lettuce through the summer.

Extend the harvest by a succession of small plantings. If sunlight in your garden is clear-sky intense sunlight, plant the summer lettuce in partial shade.

A little protection will stretch harvests months beyond the normal season. See page 27 .

How to grow: Head Lettuce: Sow seed ¼-½ inch deep. Thin to 12-14 inches between plants in rows 18-24 inches apart. Thinnings can be transplanted for a somewhat later harvest. Or, buy transplants at your garden center. Or grow your own transplants indoors.

Leaf Lettuce. Sow seed ¼-½ inch deep. Thin to 4-6 inches between plants in the first thinning and 6 to 10 on the final thinning, depending on size of variety.

Fertilizing and watering. Lettuce occupies the soil for a relatively short time, but every day must be a growing day with an adequate supply of nutrients and moisture.

Fertilize soil before planting with 3 to 4 pounds of 5-10-10 per 100 square feet. (See page 12). If the growth of a young plant is checked by lack of nutrients, it never fully recovers.

Never let the plant suffer from lack of moisture. The most critical period of water need is when the heads begin to develop.

Mistakes beginners make. Most gardeners find it difficult to be ruthless in thinning any vegetable, but with lettuce they rationalize their reluctance with the thought that they will eat the leaves as the plants grow.

Actually, when you leave two plants of head lettuce in the space where only one should grow, all you get is two poor heads or no heads at all.

Some open leaf lettuce varieties can be harvested a leaf at a time, but with most the best part is the tender light green material in the center of the almost mature plant. If you leave the row crowded with plants all you get is a bunch of little bitter outside leaves.

Salad-Bowl

Cos — Romaine

Ruby

Bibb type

Romaine and Salad-Bowl

Ruby and Butter

Melons pictured (back to front):
Muskmelon, Crenshaw, Casaba, Honey Dew,
Watermelon, Christmas melon, Casaba

Melons

Cantaloupes

All of the melon types can't be grown in every home garden. But with the new introductions of early-maturing varieties of the famous crenshaw and the honeydews, and early varieties of cantaloupes, the choice might be wider than you think.

How to grow. The prescription for success with melons goes like this:

1. Give preference to disease resistant varieties whenever possible.
2. Start seed indoors in containers. See page 14.
3. Set out transplants when weather warms in a black plastic film mulch. See page 26.
4. Cover young plants with hot-caps or clear plastic film.

Melons need space to grow. Space them 12 inches apart in rows 4 to 6 feet apart.

TIME TO SOW SEEDS IN PLACE
(Can be started in pots indoors 3-4 weeks earlier.)

ZONE	JAN.	FEB.	MAR.	APR.	MAY	JUNE	JULY	AUG.	SEPT.	OCT.	NOV.	DEC.
1				—	——							
2				—	——							
3					—	—						
4				—								
5				—								
6												

Fertilizing-Watering. Before planting, work 5-10-10 into the soil at the rate of 4 pounds per 100 feet of row. Make a second application of the same amount when the runners are 12 to 18 inches, spreading the fertilizer 8 inches away from the plants. Make the third application after the first melons are set.

Vines require plenty of moisture when growing vigorously and up to the time they are full grown. But hold back on watering in the ripening period.

Harvesting Muskmelons. 'Full slip' is the guide for ripeness of melons that are shipped to market. It means that the stem breaks away cleanly with slight pressure. That's not "vine ripe." Wait until the stem breaks away when you just lift the melon.

VARIETIES

The varieties most frequently recommended are (Disease resistance is indicated): (PM) Powdery Mildew, (F) Fusarium Wilt).
'Burpee Hybrid' (85 days to maturity). Good medium musky flavor. 3¾ pound fruit. Small seed cavity. Outstanding in all trials.
'Harper's Hybrid' (86) (F). Mild flavor with high sugar content. Thick fleshed 3½ pound fruit, small cavity. Holds its quality after picking.
'Gold Star' (87 days) (F). Bright orange color, strong musky flavor, 3 pound fruit.
'Saticoy Hybrid' (90) (F) (PM). Medium musky flavor. 3½ pound thick fleshed fruit. Quality holds well after picking.

The early varieties of crenshaw and honeydew are being successfully grown wherever the above varieties are successful.

'Early Crenshaw' (90 days). Thick salmon-pink flesh. Oval fruits to 14 pounds. Dark green skins turns yellowish-green when ripe. Traditional crenshaw flavor. Seed source: (5).
'Honey Mist' (92 days). High sugar. Greenish-white flesh. Compares with finest honeydews. Seed sources: (5), (19).

A number of extra early varieties of muskmelons adapted to short season areas are listed in the catalogs. The midget variety 'Minnesota Midget' is in that class. Matures in 60 days. Produces 4-inch melons on 3-foot vines; from University of Minnesota.

One of the most popular novelties in our test garden was a golden, egg-shaped Japanese melon not much larger than a lemon. It can be eaten like a pear, crisp rind, white flesh and all. Sources: Catalogs (9), (19).
'Honey Gold No. 9'; Catalog (30) 'Golden Crispy Hybrid.' Description is the same for both varieties.

Watermelon

The watermelon requires more summer heat than muskmelons. However, in areas where muskmelons are grown, the icebox sized watermelons rather than the 25 and 30 pound varieties, are a good bet.

VARIETIES

'Charleston Gray' (85 days). Cylindrical with greenish-white rind. It is frequently recommended because of its resistance to fusarium wilt and anthracnose.

'Crimson Sweet' (85 days). Green striped oval fruits weighing from 15 to 25 pounds. Flesh is firm and averages about 11% sugar. It is resistant to fusarium wilt and anthracnose.

'Kleckley Sweet Improved' (88 days). Long, dark green, to 30 pounds. Resistant to fusarium wilt.
'Golden Midget' (65 days). 6-inch fruit turns yellow when ripe.
'New Hampshire Midget' (70 days). 6-inch fruit of good quality.
'Sugar Baby' (75 days). 8-inch, dark green. Sweet.
'Red Lollipop' (70 days). 3 pound fruit.
'Yellow Lollipop' (70 days). Yellow flesh.

Harvesting. Picking a watermelon when it's neither too green nor too ripe is not easy.

Some gardeners claim that you can tell the fruit is ripe when the little "pigs tail" curl at the point of attachment to the vine turns brown and dries up. The trouble with this sign is that in some varieties the tendril dries up 7 to 10 days before the fruit is fully ripe.

The sound of a thump — a ringing sound when the fruit is green or a dull or dead sound when the fruit is ripe — is not reliable because the dull-dead sound is also the sign of over-ripeness.

The surest sign of ripeness of most varieties is the color of the bottom surface. As the melon matures the "ground spot" turns from light straw color to a richer yellow.

All fruits when ripe, tend to lose the powdery or slick appearance of the top surface and take on a dull look.

BITTERNESS IS A SOMETIMES THING

"I planted cucumbers near the melons and they must have crossed. My melons taste like gourds." This is one that can be answered with all the backing of scientific research. "Cucumbers will not cross with melons." (See page 69.) But that doesn't satisfy the gardener with bitter melons.

If the cucumbers didn't foul them up, what did?

The reason might be the way they were watered or more likely a spell of cloudy rainy weather as the fruits were ripening.

Sometimes there seems to be a conspiracy between soil, water, temperature to produce bitterness.

The Onion Family

Onions

The onion and its pungent relatives have been highly regarded since antiquity. Onions fed the sweating pyramid builders and the conquering troops of Alexander the Great. General Grant in a dispatch to the War Department wrote, "I will not move my armies without onions."

Emperor Nero earned the nickname "leek-throated" because of his frequent munching on leeks to "clear his throat."

An enthusiastic 19th century gourmet said it all for onion lovers everywhere: "Without onions there would be no gastronomic art. Banish it from the kitchen and all pleasure of eating flies with it . . . its absence reduces the rarest dainty to insipidity, and the diner to despair."

The familiar dry onion is a weather-wise plant.

The nature of the onion is to grow tops in cool weather and form bulbs in warm weather. But the timing of the bulbing is controlled by both temperatures and day length. Varieties are classed by long-day and short-day.

Most varieties grown in the North require 14 to 16 hours of daylight. Onion varieties designed to grow through the cool fall and winter months of the South are triggered to bulb at about 12 hours as the weather warms in early summer.

'Yellow Bermuda' and 'Excel' are standard short-day varieties. Because of early bulbing they make a small bulb in the North. However, good sized transplants, planted early, will make a larger bulb. To get the very small "Pearl" or pickling onions in the North the short day variety 'Eclipse' is planted thickly in late April to May. When grown in winter in the South it develops normal sized bulbs.

Onions are heavy feeders. Work manure and fertilizer into the soil before planting. A pound of manure to each square foot of ground and 4-5 pounds of 5-10-10 fertilizer per 100 square foot will do the job.

A constant supply of moisture is essential. It is especially important during the bulb enlargement. New growth stops from the center when bulbing starts.

How to grow. Start from seeds, transplants or sets. Growing from sets is the easy way but the varieties available as sets are limited. Seedlings are available at garden centers and through mail order seed companies.

When starting from seed, sow ½ inch deep, and thin to 2-3 inches in rows 12-24 inches apart.

Harvesting. When bulbs are ripe, the tops begin to yellow and fall over. When about ¾ have fallen, use a rake to break over those still standing. When all the tops are dead, pull up the plants and spread them in the sun for 3 or 4 days. Place the tops over the bulbs. Then cut the tops off about an inch from the bulb. Store in mesh bags.

TIME TO SOW SEEDS IN PLACE

(Can be started in pots indoors 8 weeks earlier.)

ZONE	JAN.	FEB.	MAR.	APR.	MAY	JUNE	JULY	AUG.	SEPT.	OCT.	NOV.	DEC.
1			▬	▬								
2			▬									
3				▬	▬							
4					▬							
5				▬	▬							
6					▬							

VARIETIES

'Yellow Sweet Spanish' (Utah) (115 days). Large, yellow bulb. Mild, sweet flesh. Medium keeper. Good slicer. Thrips resistant. Plants generally available.

'White Sweet Spanish' (Utah) (110 days). Largest white. Firm. Mild, sweet flesh. Medium keeper. Plants available.

'Early Yellow Globe' (110 days). Medium sized globe. Firm flesh. Pungent taste. Good keeper.

'Southport White Globe' (110 days). Medium sized globes. Firm and pungent. Good keeper.

'Yellow Globe Danvers' (110 days). Medium sized. Flat-

Leeks

Root View of Onions

Chives

tened globe shape. Firm and pungent. Plants available.

'Ebenezer' (105 days). Large bulb. Firm flesh. Pungent.

Serving ideas:

Yellow onions are a staple in most kitchens, and their delicate cousins — the sweet red, big Bermuda, and tiny white boiling onions — play a big role, too.

Use the sweet onions fresh in salads. Mince the yellow onions to add to stews and soups. Use the little boiling onions whole in stews.

Green onions

Any of the standard onion varieties can be used as "green bunching" if harvested at the proper stage.

'Evergreen Bunching' (Nebuka) and 'Beltsville Bunching' do not form bulbs. They produce clusters of 4 to 8 slender white stalks.

The easy way is to start with sets. Plant them 1-2 inches deep, 2-3 inches apart. You can begin pulling them in about a month.

Garlic

Two types of garlic are available. The type you buy at the market—a bulb containing about 10 small cloves, and 'Elephant Garlic,' which is about 6 times larger and may weigh a pound. 'Elephant Garlic' has a slightly milder flavor than the standard garlic.

Both are grown in the same way.

In all but the coldest areas, set out cloves in the fall an inch deep, 2-4 inches apart in rows 12-18 inches apart. Harvest when tops fall over; braid into strings or tie in bunches and hang in a cool dry place.

Sources for 'Elephant Garlic' are seed houses: (4), (19).

Serving ideas:

This potent bulb is indispensable to the cuisines of many lands. The aromatic cloves lend pungency to a range of dishes.

Mince garlic and add to melted butter as a sauce for lobster, snails, mushrooms, broccoli, and green beans, and as a spread for French bread. Brown nuggets of garlic in butter as a finish on veal or pork scallopini or chicken breasts. Mince garlic for meatballs and slow-cooking meat sauce. Sliver garlic to poke into lamb or beef roasts and lamb shanks.

Steep a garlic clove in red or white wine vinegar to imbue it with flavor for salads.

Use garlic in the Provencal mayonnaise called *Aioli* (see page 82) and the Greek almond mayonnaise called *Skordalia*. Include it in the Spanish cold gazpacho soups and hot garlic soups floating crusty bread and poached eggs.

Leeks

Leeks take a good 80 days to grow from transplants and 140 days from seed. When growing from seed, sow in late winter and thin to about 3 inches between plants.

Leeks do not bulb as onions do. The thickened stems are blanched by hilling soil around them. To get long, white stems, plant in trenches 4 to 6 inches deep and hill soil against the stems after the plants are fairly well grown. The most popular variety is 'Large American Flag.'

Serving ideas:

Wash the stalks thoroughly as the sandy grit burrows deep inside them. To achieve this, trim the ends and slice them lengthwise, then hold under running water. Use in quiches, stews, soups, and prepare as in Vegetables a la Grecque (see page 88).

Shallots

French knights returning from the Crusades are credited with introducing shallots into Europe.

They were introduced into the New World in what is now Louisiana by De Soto in 1532.

The shallot is a multiplier type of onion with the habit of dividing into a clump of smaller bulbs that look like small tulip bulbs. Most varieties set no seed.

How to grow. Plant cloves 1 inch deep, 2-4 inches apart with 12-18 inches between rows. Harvest when tops die down in summer. Shallots are hardy and will over-winter as perennials, but for better results lift the clusters of bulbs at the end of each growing season. Replant the smaller ones in the fall.

Catalogs offering shallots are: (12), (19).

Serving ideas:

This sophisticated, delicate little onion lends superb flavor to a vinaigrette dressing for green salad and innumerable sauces. Stir finely chopped shallots into sour cream for a fast dressing for vegetables, meat loaves, fish dishes.

Chives

Chives have been used for ages. In 812 Emperor Charlemagne included chives on the list of herbs to be grown in his garden. No vegetable gardener today would refuse to give it room.

A hardy perennial, willing to be clipped almost continuously. If not clipped chives produces pompoms of lavender flower heads above their grass-like hollow leaves every spring. A half-dozen pots will supply enough snippings for year around use. Will take kitchen window sill treatment. Frozen chopped chives are almost as good as fresh. Clumps of chives add a gay touch to the flower border.

How to grow. Easy way to a quick harvest is to buy plants. Small clumps spread rapidly. Or grow from seeds started in small pots. Grows best in rich moist soil in full sun but will tolerate filtered shade.

How to use

With scissors you can snip these fine grass-like blades of delicate onion flavor into salads, dips, and various fish, chicken and meat dishes. Chive butter lends a delightful aroma and succulence to steaks and broiled seafood. It is a fine spread for hot egg bread or sour dough rye, as well.

Peas

The garden pea, a legume, came from Middle Asia, the Near East and Ethiopia, where wild relatives and cultivated types can still be found. Our varieties came from types developed in England. Peas are known as "English Peas" in the South to differentiate them from cowpeas.

English peas are a cool season crop. In warm summer areas, they must be up and growing in very early spring to find 60-70 days before summer temperatures stop production.

TIME TO SOW SEEDS IN PLACE

ZONE	JAN.	FEB.	MAR.	APR.	MAY	JUNE	JULY	AUG.	SEPT.	OCT.	NOV.	DEC.
1			▬▬									
2												
3			▬▬▬									
4												
5			▬▬									
6												

How to grow. The low-growing varieties that can be grown without staking are the easiest to handle. They can be planted in rows 18-24 inches apart.

The tall growers trained on chicken wire or trellis need 36 inches between rows, but you can plant in double rows 6 inches apart on either side of the trellis.

The smallest of the varieties is 'Mighty Midget.' Designed for the minigarden it produces 3½-inch pods on 6-inch vines in 60 days.

'Alaska' (55-60 days). Its earliness is its chief virtue. Bush type, 24-28″ vines. Small peas lower in sugar than others listed here, good for canning.

'Little Marvel' (63 days) is a good producer of medium large peas on 18-inch vines. 'Wando' (64 days), a sturdy short grower, is more heat tolerant.

Edible-podded Sugar Peas (snow peas). The low grower (24 inches), 'Dwarf Gray Sugar' (63 days) can be grown without staking. The tall growers are 'Mammoth Melting Sugar' (72 days) and 'Burpee Sweet Pod' (68 days). Pick when very young. Just as the peas start to form. If you miss that stage, the peas can be shelled and eaten but the pods will be too tough.

Harvesting. Repeated pickings, taking only the plump lower pods from the plant will give the best yield. You can do a better job of picking if the peas are grown on a trellis. Harvest peas in the cool of the morning rather than in the heat of the afternoon. Shell and rinse the peas in cool water as soon as possible after picking and refrigerate for later use.

Cowpeas — Southern table peas. Middle Asia was the home of the cowpea but it migrated to Asia Minor and Africa before being brought to Jamaica by the slave traders. It was sailed to the warm climates of the West Indies and became an important food there.

Cowpeas have a more distinctive flavor than garden peas. They require heat — warm days and warm nights. They are grown in zones 1-3.

Plant when soil is warmed up. Germination is better in warm soil. Sow seed ½-1″ deep, 5-8 seeds per foot of row. Thin to 3-4″ between plants. Leave 24-36″ between row. Go easy on nitrogen fertilizer. A side dressing 5-10-10 fertilizer at 3 lbs. per 100 feet of row after the plants are up, is adequate.

Cowpeas are usually picked in the green-shell stage, when the seeds are fully developed but not yet hard; or they can be allowed to ripen and stored as dried peas.

Several mail order seed companies offer varieties of the various types of cowpeas. Check numbers (3), (5), (21), (26), (28) on page 111.

Recommended varieties are:

'Brown Sugar Crowder.' Large green peas in 85-90 days.
'Mississippi Silver.' A crowder type. Widely adapted.

'Purple Hull Pink Eye.' When young the peas are white with a small pink eye.

'Early Ramshorn Black Eye.' Green peas in 60 days. Resistant to wilt and nematodes.

Yardlong Bean or Asparagus Bean. Listed in catalogs as a heavy producer of 24-inch long beans this plant is actually a tall-growing variety of cowpeas. It is a vigorous climber and is trained on wire or trellis. Pods of yardlong, picked when young, are used in the same way as snap beans.

Peppers

Columbus searching for a new route to the spice laden Indies had a different pepper in mind than those he found in the New World. The black and white pepper of the salt-and-pepper set comes from the berries and seeds of *Piper nigrum* which is in no way related to the peppers of the genus *Capsicum* Columbus found growing in the Indian gardens in the Caribbean. His find was described upon his return to Spain as "pepper more pungent than that of the Caucasus." Spice-hungry Europeans immediately adopted the new vegetable. Within 50 years peppers were found growing in England, in less than a century on Austrian crownlands. They became so common in India that some botanists thought peppers were native there.

Peppers are classed as a hot weather vegetable but their requirements are not so high as generally supposed. Fruit set occurs in a rather limited range of night temperatures. Blossoms drop when night temperatures are much below 60° and when they go above 75°. Peppers thrive in areas with daytime temperatures around 75° and nights of 62°. High daytime temperature, above 90°, will cause excessive blossom drop but fruit setting will resume with the return to normal weather. Small fruited varieties are more tolerant to high temperatures than the large ones.

Peppers seem to protect themselves from overloading the plant. When the plant has a full quota of fruit underway, new blossoms drop. When some of the peppers are harvested the plant will again set fruit—if the weather is right.

How to grow. The easiest way to start is to buy transplants at your garden store. The varieties of the sweet peppers adapted to your area are generally available. Growing your own transplants from seed is not difficult —see "Seeds and Transplants" page 14.

Don't set out transplants until the weather has definitely warmed. When night time temperatures fall below 55° the small plants will just sit, turn yellow and become stunted.

Peppers pictured below: Hungarian Yellow Wax, Serrano Chile, Sante Fe Grande, Anaheim, Jalapeno, Mercury, Floral Gem

Some gardeners set out more plants than are needed and after a few weeks of growth, pull out the weaklings. Give them space to grow. Set plants 24 inches apart in rows 30-36 inches apart.

When the first blossoms open, give the plants a light application of fertilizer. Water it in well. Any stress from lack of moisture at flowering time may cause blossom drop. Add a mulch to conserve moisture and stop weeds.

When it's time to pick the peppers, use pruning shears or a sharp knife.

TIME TO SET OUT PLANTS
(Sow seed indoors 7-9 weeks earlier)

ZONE	JAN.	FEB.	MAR.	APR.	MAY	JUNE	JULY	AUG.	SEPT.	OCT.	NOV.	DEC.
1					—							
2				—								
3					—							
4					—							
5					—							
6					—							

The shorter the growing season the more reason to chose the "extra early" varieties. Adaptation varies by area. See "Varieties" below.

Decorative in containers. Shiny green leaves, small white flowers, fruits in many shapes and colors—green, yellow, red—favor the peppers as container plants (in tubs, boxes or large pots) for patio, porch or terrace; or as ornamentals in the flower border. The small bushy peppers and basil are good companion plants.

Some of the hot varieties that are especially attractive in containers are:

'Red Chili.' A well-behaved plant growing to 18 inches tall, carries its 2-inch long, tapered fruits upright on its branches. These peppers are really hot and used extensively for pepper sauces.

'Fresno Chili.' Similar in growth habit to 'Red Chili,' but somewhat taller. Fruits are 3 inches long and taper to a point. A prolific bearer of very hot peppers.

'Long Red Cayenne.' A vigorous grower to 24-30 inches tall. Fruits are 4-5 inches long and conical or finger shaped. An early maturing variety, it is adapted to a wide growing range. Used in pickle making and for drying.

The big bells. The large, blocky sweet peppers—ideally shaped for stuffing—are used most often when green but will turn red (sweeter and more mellow) if grown for a longer period. Varieties that represent this group are 'Bell Boy,' 'Keystone Resistant Giant,' 'Pennwonder' and 'Yolo Wonder.' All mature in about 75-80 days. 'Early Calwonder' is ready for use in 65-70 days. The variety 'Golden Calwonder' turns a rich golden yellow at maturity.

Early season bells. There are a number of early varieties that bear smaller less blocky peppers but produce them from 2 weeks to a month earlier than such standard bells as Yolo Wonder.

'Early Bountiful.' High yield in small space. Ripens red fruit a full month earlier than most large-fruited varieties.

'Vinette.' Dwarf plants about 14 inches tall. Will bear 8-10 fruits, moderate blocky but tapered in 65 days. 'Vinedale' and 'Stokes Early Hybrid' are in this "early" class.

In a class by themselves. 'Anaheim Chili.' A vigorous, erect grower to 20-24 inches tall. Fruits are 6-8 inches long, tapering to a point. Medium hot. When boiled, skinned and stuffed with cheese or meat you have *chili rellenos*.

'Sweet Bananna.' Plant grows to 20-24 inches with good foliage cover. Thick-walled fruits $3^{1}/_{2}$-$4^{1}/_{2}$ inches long turn from yellow to red.

Drying peppers. Both sweet and hot peppers are dried for winter use. In Mexico where all peppers are "chiles" the dried peppers are ground in a mortar daily for a supply of chili powder. A pinch will add flavor to almost any dish. The flavor is varied by adding varying amounts of powdered hot peppers.

Serving ideas:

The many decorative hot peppers lend zing to many international dishes: Mexican salsas, Indian curries, African stews, and Spanish and Portuguese dishes.

The large red and green sweet bell peppers are more commonly utilized in the States. Serve them raw, cut in strips, on relish platters. Or serve in rings, strips, or diced in salads. Stuff them when hollowed out, with lamb, beef, chicken, or shrimp mixtures and bake. Use in Chinese beef pepper steak or the French *ratatouille* (see page 84).

California Wonder

Burpee Fordhook

Sweet Banana

'Golden Nugget'

Zucchini squash

Crookneck

Cushaw type pumpkins

Spaghetti squash

French pumpkin

A gourd appeared in the pumpkin patch

Squash and pumpkins

This group includes members of four species of the Gourd Family (see chart, page 69). All of them are native to the Americas. Most of our pumpkins and squashes originated in Mexico and Central America and were used all over North America by the American Indians. Most of our winter squashes originated in or near the Andes in northern Argentina.

How to grow. Squashes and pumpkins, except for bush forms, are space users, not to be grown by the mini-gardener unless he has a way of using vertical space, such as a fence, a wall, or a stout trellis. Even a compost pile can serve as a place for a vine to ramble. They are sometimes grown with corn, but should be sparsely spaced.

On the ground, the vining types need 10 feet or more between rows, but can be grown in less space by training the vines or pruning. The long runners may be cut off after some fruit are set, if a good supply of leaves remain to feed the developing fruit. Leave 2-4 feet between plants, depending on the vigor of the variety. Bush types do best in rows 5 or 6 feet apart, but can be grown with less space. Plants can be 16-24 inches apart.

Direct seeding is best but in short-season areas some gain can be made by starting in individual pots, as with melons. Fertilizing and watering requirements are the same as cucumbers and melons. Summer squashes, like cucumbers, should be kept picked continuously for a steady supply of young fruit.

TIME TO SOW SEEDS IN PLACE

(Can be started in pots indoors 3-4 weeks earlier.)

ZONE	JAN.	FEB.	MAR.	APR.	MAY	JUNE	JULY	AUG.	SEPT.	OCT.	NOV.	DEC.
1				——	——							
2					——	—						
3					——							
4				—	—							
5					——	—						
6					—							

Harvest and use. Summer squashes are picked when they are young and tender. The seeds should be undeveloped and the rind soft. Zucchini and crookneck types are usually taken at 1½-2 inches in diameter, and bush scallops at 3-4 inches across.

Winter squashes must be thoroughly mature to have good quality. When picked immature they are watery and poor in flavor. Flavor is usually better after some cold weather increases the sugar content. Learn to judge your varieties by color. Most green varieties get some brown or bronze, and 'Butternut' must lose all its green and turn to a distinct tan.

Don't worry when the first blossoms fail to set fruit. Some female flowers will bloom before there are male flowers for pollen and dry up or produce small fruits that abort and subsequently rot. This is a natural behavior, not a disease. The same thing happens when a good load of fruit is set and the plant is using all its resources to develop them. The aborting of young fruits is a self-pruning process.

VARIETIES
Squash
From a multiple list of 30 or more acceptable varieties the following can stand as good representations of their class:

Winter squash: 'Gold Nugget' (85 days). Bush variety. Very early. 'Butternut' (95 days). Mild flavor. 'Buttercup' (100 days). Sweet, strong flavor. 'Table Queen' (85 days). Acorn type, early baking squash. 'Hubbard' (110 days). Large, good keeper. 'Banana' (110 days). Long, pink, grey. Jumbo strains available.

Summer squash: *Green:* 'Burpee Hybrid Zucchini' (50 days); 'Cocozelle (60 days). *Yellow:* 'Seneca Butterbar' (51 days); 'Early Golden Summer Crookneck' (53 days). *Scallop:* 'Early White Bush Scallop' (60 days).

Pumpkin
'Cheyenne Bush' (75 days). Small early *bush*, for pie.
'Cinderella' (95 days). Bush, medium size jack-o-lantern.
'Small Sugar' (New England Pie). (100 days).
'Jack-O-Lantern' (110 days). Medium size.
'Connecticut Field' (Big Tom). (120 days). Large jack-o-lantern type.
'Big Max' (120 days). Contest winner for size, not table quality.

Serving ideas:
The summer squashes — yellow crookneck, zucchini, and pattypan or scallop — play a role in most cuisines. They cook relatively swiftly, compared to the winter squash varieties.

Zucchini is excellent grated and steamed quickly in a little butter. Or thinly slice it and arrange in overlapping rows in a large frying pan. Drizzle with olive oil and steam until crisp tender. Sprinkle with grated Parmesan cheese and slip the pan under the broiler until the cheese is crusty.

Slice zucchini to cook in Oriental stir-fries or Italian frittatas. Split and stuff the squash with ground beef, crumbs, and cheese, and bake.
The yellow crookneck looks festive simply halved, steamed in butter, and dusted with nutmeg. The pattypan takes well to stuffing.

Winter squash are good to steam. Drizzle halves of hot, tender acorn or butternut squash with honey or brown sugar and butter. Or fill with browned sausage links. Children delight in steamed Hubbard squash, mashed and topped with marshmallows, then baked until toasty.

South Americans favor pumpkin in soups, while Greeks bake it between fila layers for a honey-drenched dessert.

Tomatoes

Of the vegetable gifts from the New World to the Old World none took as long to be appreciated as the tomato.

Centuries old in use in South America and Mexico, recorded as being cultivated in France, Spain and Italy in 1544, tomatoes were grown only as a curiosity in England a century later. Seemingly the first seeds to reach Europe were of the yellow variety. They were the "apples of gold" *(pomi d'oro)* in Italy. And a few years later as the "apples of love" *(pommes d'amours)* in France.

In pioneering America only a few brave souls ventured to eat the fruit. New Englanders in Salem in 1802 wouldn't even taste them. By 1835 they were recognized as "a useful article of diet and should be found on everyman's table" by the editor of *Maine Farmer.*

TIME TO SET OUT PLANTS
(Sow seed indoors 5-7 weeks earlier)

ZONE	JAN.	FEB.	MAR.	APR.	MAY	JUNE	JULY	AUG.	SEPT.	OCT.	NOV.	DEC.
1				—								
2				—								
3					—							
4					—							
5					—							
6						—						

Starting from seed. The usual method of growing from seed, starting 5 to 7 weeks before time to set out plants, is described on page 16. How to grow from seed without transplanting is shown on page 14.

Planting. When growing or buying transplants the ideal is a stocky bushy plant.

Unlike other plants, tomatoes are set deep in the soil. Set them so that the first leaves are just above soil level. Leggy plants are planted horizontally. See sketch. Roots will form along the buried stem.

Good transplant   Leggy transplant   . . . Both should be planted deep. Roots will develop along the buried stem.

Mistakes beginners make. Failure to fit the variety to the climate is one way to a disappointing crop.

Failure to choose disease resistant varieties may or may not be a cause of failure—see page 22.

Plant too early in the season.

Try to grow in a shady location. The tomato requires at least 6 hours of direct sunlight.

VARIETIES

Tomatoes come in a wide variety of sizes, shapes and colors. The fruit may be yellow, orange, pink or red. Its shape may be round, slightly flattened, globe or pear-like.

Listed below are varieties recommended by 5 or more State Universities in the North. Check your County Extension Agent for the latest list for your state.

Remember, there's more to choosing a variety than size and color of fruit.

Pay attention to the "season" indicated in the number of days from setting out plants to harvest. Where growing season is long you can stretch the harvest season by planting all three kinds—early, main season and late.

In the short-season areas you may have to limit your choices to the "early" and "midseason" varieties but even then the choice is wide. *If you have had* trouble with diseases, look for varieties resistant to the wilts. Both Fusarium and Verticillium wilt can cause death of the vines. The plant will wilt even with good soil moisture. Both wilts live over in the soil and also infect peppers, eggplants, and melon.

If your soil is infested, the only solution, other than sterilizing the soil, is to use resistant varieties. Where nematodes make tomato growing difficult, look for varieties resistant to these root destroyers.

In the list of varieties below, their resistance is indicated by the initials "V"— Verticillium; "F"— Fusarium; "N"— Nematode.

The initial "H" says that it is a hybrid variety.

The number of days indicates the approximate time from setting out transplants to harvest.

The growth habit of the variety is indicated by the words "determinate" and "indeterminate." (In text as "Det." and "Ind."). The determinates are the self-topping bush type, generally 3 feet or less. The indeterminates are the tall growers and are generally grown on stakes or trellis.

Red-Early
'Springset.' (H.V.F.) 65 days. Open-growing Det. High yield of medium sized fruit. Concentrated set.

'Spring Giant.' (H.V.F.) 65 days. Vigorous Det. 1969 All American. Good yield of 1½ pound fruits if you're lucky.

Red Main Season
'Moreton Hybrid.' 70 days. Large fruit. Ind. Stake or train.

'Fantastic.' (H.) 70 days. Medium to large fruit. Ind. Stake or train.

'Jetstar.' (H.V.F.) 72 days. Medium fruit. Ind. Stake or train.

'Better Boy.' (H.V.F.N.) 72 days. Medium to large fruit. Ind. Stake or train.

'Cardinal.' (H.) 74 days. Large, crack-resistant fruit. Vigorous Ind. growth. Stake or trellis.

'Glamour.' 77 days. Medium to large. Crack-free, meaty, fruit of mild flavor. Ind. Stake.

'Campbell 1327.' (V.F.) 69 days. Vigorous semi-Det. Extra large fruit.

'Heinz 1350.' (V.F.) 75 days. Compact semi-Det. Heavy yielder.

Red Late
'Supersonic.' (H.V.F.) 79 days. Large fruit. Strong-growing, large, Ind. vine.. Stake.

'Big Boy.' (H.) 80 days. Strong grower; heavy producer of 1 to 2-pound fruits. Stake.

Tomatillo Husk Tomato

Pear-Shaped 'San Marzano' Tomato

Yellow Pear

'Snowball'

'Golden Boy' Hybrid

More than a pailful

'Beefmaster.' (V.F.N.) 80 days. Ind.; large 1 to 2-pound fruits. Stake.

'Ramapo.' (H.V.F.) 85 days. Strong-growing Ind. Stake. Large fruit.

Orange

Generally the non-red fruit are considered to be less acid but this is not always true. Vitamin C content of these varieties is not significantly different from standard reds. All about 75 days to maturity.

'Caro-Red.' Round, medium fruit; has 10 times the pro-vitamin A of the standard red varieties.

'Jubilee,' (72 days) and 'Sunray,' (72 days) and 'Golden Boy,' (65 days). Large fruit; has lower (1/3) provitamin A than standard red varieties.

TOMATOES IN CONTAINERS

Tomatoes are well adapted to growing in containers. And there is a variety to fit every size of a container. Even the large growers will produce good crops when grown in as little as 2 gallons of "soil." You compensate for the restricted root space by light but frequent applications of fertilizers.

In the last few years a number of varieties have been introduced that have been bred for growing in contain-ers on deck or patio. The smallest is 'Tiny Tim,' a 12-inch plant with cherry-sized fruit. 'Burpee Pixie Hybrid' bears clusters of 1¾-inch fruit on an 18-inch plant. 'Presto Hybrid,' a 24-inch plant, yields half-dollar sized fruit early and late. 'Early Salad Hybrid' produces hun-dreds of 1½-inch fruits on compact vines 6-8 inches high with 24-inch spread. 'Patio Hybrid' grows as a sturdy, compact vine to 30 inches with 2-inch fruits. 'Small Fry' is the most vigorous grower of this group and is best when trained on a trellis. Vines 3 feet or more tall; producing hundreds of 1-inch fruits—8 to 10 in a cluster.

Any tomato that can be grown in a vegetable garden can also be grown in a container.

Gardeners with unfavorable soil or facing the possibility of soil diseases or nematodes, find container growing the way to success with tomatoes.

The "soil" may be sawdust, wood chips, shavings, per-lite, vermiculite or any of the sterile planter mixes. See page 8.

The container may be a bushel basket, a 5 gallon can, a plastic bag or what have you. Be sure to provide drainage. When using materials containing no fertilizer, follow the feeding methods of water culture or hydroponics. The material in the container must be kept moist. You water the plant with a nutrient solution (a diluted liquid fer-tilizer).

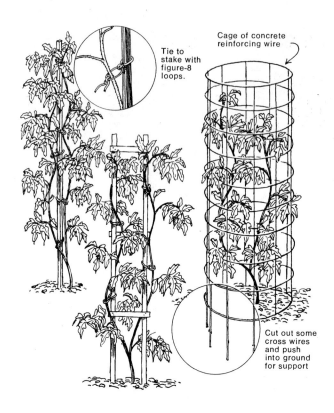

Tie to stake with figure-8 loops.

Cage of concrete reinforcing wire

Cut out some cross wires and push into ground for support

STAKING – TRAINING

If you consider staking and training as a means of keep-ing tomatoes from touching the soil, you have many ways to accomplish it. Every other gardener we have worked with has given us the "best way" to train toma-toes. Some of them are illustrated here and more can be

Pixie

Patio

Pixie

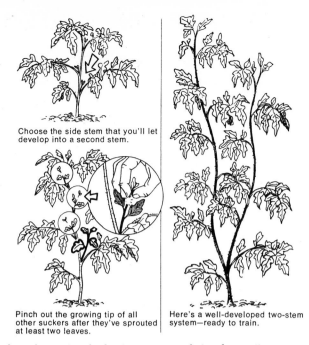

Choose the side stem that you'll let develop into a second stem.

Pinch out the growing tip of all other suckers after they've sprouted at least two leaves.

Here's a well-developed two-stem system—ready to train.

found in "Good Ideas From Good Gardeners" on pages 108-111.

Probably the favorite way to train large growing tomatoes is the circular cage made from a 5-foot length of concrete reinforcing wire. The 6-inch mesh allows for easy picking within the cage. No pruning of the vine is necessary.

Training to a single stake with all suckers removed, as illustrated, is not the best way to train tomatoes for an all-season crop. If getting tomatoes a week or two early is important, the single stem pruning makes sense. But a 2-stem plant will produce more tomatoes and with better foliage protection from sunburn than the single stem plant.

The low growing, bushy types may be staked or allowed to sprawl. To protect the sprawlers, mulch the soil around them with straw or other organic mulch or with black plastic.

PROTECTION FROM THE ELEMENTS

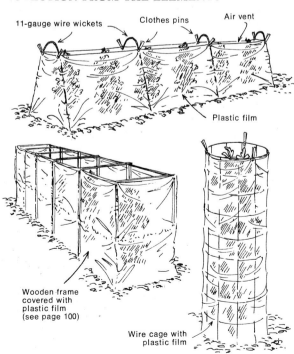

11-gauge wire wickets

Clothes pins

Air vent

Plastic film

Wooden frame covered with plastic film (see page 100)

Wire cage with plastic film

Early planting calls for some kind of help to increase temperatures. If you use the wire cage, a cover of polyethylene film in the early stages of growth will boost temperatures.

The covering of a row of 4 or 5 plants with polyethylene film, as illustrated, may be used for early planting with a row tent only 2 feet high or for later protection against rain with a tent as high as the mature plant.

FAILURE TO SET FRUIT

The failure of a tomato plant to set fruit may be caused by several conditions.

The tomato sets fruit within a very narrow temperature range. You get maximum fruit set when *night* temperatures (at least for a part of the night) are in the 60°-70° range. Day temperature is not the controlling factor of tomato growth. Set a plant out before there are a few hours of darkness with temperatures above 55° and the plant just sits and sulks.

Generally the early varieties will set fruit at lower *night* temperatures than midseason varieties but rushing the season — setting plants out while the nights are still cold — is the most frequent cause of blossom drop in the spring.

In the summer the high night temperatures (above 75°) will stop the setting of fruit. High daytime temperatures, and hot dry winds will also cause blossom drop.

Rain or prolonged humid conditions hamper fruit set. Growers in cool, humid situations have found that fruit set can be increased by shaking the plant. Or vibrating it with a battery-powered electric tooth brush. When plants are trained on stakes, hitting the top of the stakes will increase pollination by releasing pollen. Best time to shake the plants is in midday when it's warm and the humidity is low.

ALL VINE AND NO FRUIT

The failure of the tomato to set fruit is also blamed on too much water, too little water and too much fertilizer.

The tomato plant may fail to change gears from the vegetative stage to the fruiting stage of growth. Too much nitrogen fertilizer and too much water in the first stage of growth is one cause of the failure. Too much shade is another. You can help the plant switch over to the fruiting stage by plucking out the terminal shoots, or by withholding water to check growth, or even by root pruning. And by following the fertilizing schedule suggested here.

FERTILIZING

Before planting, mix into the soil a fertilizer high in phosphorus. (See page 12). This application will take care of the plant until the first fruits are set. Feed then and every month while the fruit is developing. Stop fertilizing when tomatoes near mature size.

BLOSSOM-END ROT

Symptoms of this disease appear as a leathery scar or rot on the blossom end of fruits. It can occur at any stage of development. It is usually caused by sudden changes in moisture in the soil. Blossom-end rot is most serious when plants growing rapidly with high soil moisture hit a hot dry spell. Lack of calcium in the plant is another cause of blossom-end rot. If you have had trouble with this disorder, do this: Before planting, add 5 pounds of pulverized limestone (adds calcium), to 100 square feet. Mix thoroughly throughout the top 8 to 12 inches of soil. Mulch plants with black plastic or organic material to reduce fluctuations in soil moisture and temperature. Do not plant in poorly drained soil.

If you have room

We find it difficult to say what should and shouldn't be given space in a vegetable garden. It's probably none of our business. It's your garden. From the point of view of maximum yield of food from a relatively small space it doesn't make good sense to plant such as potatoes, pumpkins and peanuts if they crowd out lettuce, beets, carrots and snap beans.

However, when you consider the fun of growing something you have never grown before, it seems worthwhile to look for odd spaces to at least sample any vegetable. In the next 6 pages we discuss both the common and unusual vegetables which are generally in the 'try them if you have room' class.

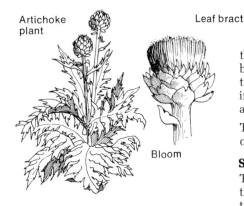

Artichoke plant

Leaf bract

Bloom

ARTICHOKE

Centuries before Christ the Romans were paying top prices for this thistle-like vegetable and preserving it for year-'round use. It disappeared with the decline and fall of the Roman empire and did not come to light again until a thousand years later in southern Italy. Catherine de Medici found artichokes in Florentine gardens and introduced them to France as gourmet delicacies. French and Spanish explorers brought artichokes to this country.

This perennial vegetable is handsome enough in the landscape to cause Northern gardeners to take unusual pains in adapting it to their gardens.

The globe artichoke grows to a height of 4 feet with a 6 foot spread. Somewhat fountain-like in growth with silvery green foliage bearing fleshy tight buds in late spring followed by 6 inch purple-blue flower heads if the buds are not cut.

Starting from seed, sow indoors in peat pots, 4 to 6 weeks before time to set out in the garden — when danger of heavy frost is passed.

Give it space to grow to its 3 to 4 feet in height and 5 to 6 foot spread.

The production of edible buds will depend upon spring and early summer weather. If summer heat comes early, buds will open rapidly and become tough and leathery.

Some artichoke enthusiasts cut back the tops in late fall and store the roots in a cold frame over winter. In

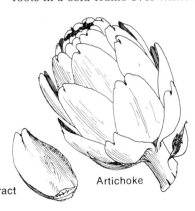

Artichoke

the mild winter zones the plant can be carried through the winter by cutting back tops to about 12 inches, tying the leaves over the root crown and mulching heavily.

The variety is 'Green Globe.' Sources of seed are: (3), (14), (25), (26), (31).

Serving ideas:

This beautiful thistle is beloved by the Mediterranean people. Serve the tiny cooked hearts in a lemon, oil, and herb sauce or stuff the large ones with ground lamb. Or serve the large chokes hot, Roman style — with long stems pointing upward and the flower ends down. Hollandaise sauce enhances them. Cold, cooked artichokes are good marinated in a vinaigrette dressing (see page 74).

CHAYOTE

This member of the gourd family (See chart on page 69) is native to Mexico and Central America. As a fresh fruit it appears in the specialty produce markets of the U.S. in late fall and winter as Chayote (chy-oh-tee) or Vegetable Pear. It's also known as the One-Seeded Cucumber, and to the Creoles as Merliton.

It's an evergreen perennial in the frost-free areas of the South. In the mild winter areas frost kills the tops each winter but the vine renews itself each spring.

Reportedly it can be grown as an annual in the North wherever there's summer heat enough for gourds.

It's a fast growing vine and will cover a pergola, a wall, or a 10-15 foot section of a fence with large, lobed leaves by midsummer.

Flowering begins when the days shorten in late summer. Harvest starts about a month after flowering and continues until the vine is stopped by frost. A strong healthy vine in a favorable climate will produce as many as 100 fruits.

The fruit will weigh $\frac{1}{2}$ to 1 pound. It's somewhat pear-shaped and furrowed. Color varies from very light to dark green.

The whole fruit is used as "seed." Plant it with the large end sloping downward into the soil, and with the small end slightly exposed.

You get a start by knowing someone who grows them or by buying the fresh fruit when it's available in produce markets and storing it in a cool place until soil warms up in the spring. The fruits may send out long shoots in storage. If they do, cut shoots back to 2 inches when you plant.

Chayote can be used in as many ways as you would prepare squash — and more.

OKRA-GUMBO

There are two types of okra. Tall growers to 4-7 feet and the so called dwarf which grows 2-4 feet tall. Its botanical name *Hibiscus esculentus* says that it is an edible hibiscus, and you can plant it in the flower border as an annual hibiscus with hollyhock-like flowers.

A half dozen plants will give you more than enough over a long season for the cupful you'll need now and then for chicken gumbo, stews, and to add body and flavor to soups.

Okra is a warm season vegetable and the planting dates, fertilizing and watering schedule for corn will take care of it very well.

Give it space to grow—36-48 inches between rows and thin to 8 to 10 inches apart in the row.

In short season areas start seeds in small pots about 5 weeks before you would plant corn or beans and set out when soil is thoroughly warm.

Varieties. 'Clemson Spineless' grows to 4-5 feet tall and is a heavy yielder. 'Perkins Spineless' is a dwarf to $2\frac{1}{2}$-3 feet.

Special handling. To keep the plant producing, no pod should be allowed to ripen on the stalk. Young pods are more tender and more nutritious.

GARDEN HUCKLEBERRY

If you happen to read that "this is the cultivated form of the poisonous black nightshade" change it to read "edible form." It's a relative of the potato and eggplant, growing to about 2½ feet.

The fruits of the Garden Huckleberry should not be used until they turn thoroughly black. They are not harmed by light frosts; the flavor is improved by it. The fruits sometimes have a bitter taste which can be removed by parboiling for 10 minutes in water containing a pinch of baking soda. When combined with lemons, apples or grapes, it makes excellent jellies and preserves. Available from (4), (9), (12), (16), (20), (26), (27). (See page 111.)

HUSK TOMATO

Also called Ground Cherry, Poha Berry and Strawberry Tomato. It is grown in the same way as tomatoes and is about the same size as the cherry tomato. The ornamental Chinese Paper Plant is a close relative. The fruits are produced inside a paper-like husk. When ripe, the husks turn brown and the fruits drop from the plant. If left in the husks they will keep for several weeks. The fruit is sweeter than the small-fruited tomatoes and is used in pies, jams or may be dried in sugar and used like raisins. Hawaii's *Poha* jam is Husk Tomato jam.

Here's a recipe for Ground Cherry preserves received from Burgess Seed & Plant Company:

Remove husks from Ground Cherries. Make a syrup of 1½ cups sugar, 3 cups water and juice of 2 lemons: boil 5 minutes; add enough cherries to come to top of syrup. Boil slowly until cherries are tender and clear, and, if desired, can and seal in sterilized jars as other fruit.

Or, in place of the lemon, add 1/3 as many sliced tart apples and cook until apples and ground cherries are thick and clear.

Tomatilla or Jamberry. Very similar to the Husk Tomato in growth habit but the fruit is larger, and fills the husk completely.

SOYBEANS

Soybeans were cultivated in China in 3000 B.C. and since earliest times have been an all important food in Manchuria, Korea and Japan. They were first taken to the United States in 1804 but were used mainly as a forage crop until 1920. The big boom in commercial planting for seed began in 1942 as a result of the wartime demand for edible oils and fats.

Soybeans are now being recognized as a superior home garden vegetable. As a fresh vegetable the beans are picked in the immature or green-shelled stage.

One characteristic of the soybean that sets it apart from all other beans is its time clock. It gets its signal for flowering from the sky. Short nights (long days) delay flowering; long nights (short days) speed up flowering.

Most varieties have a narrow range in which they will mature properly and produce a satisfactory crop.

The United States and Canadian researchers classify 9 maturity groups in the United States, each with a narrow range of latitude, ranging from early varieties adapted to the short summers and long days of Southern Canada and Northern states (group 0 to 1) to late-maturing varieties of the Gulf Coast (Group VIII).

Varieties

The varieties available through mail-order seed companies are grouped as follows: (numbers in parenthesis following each variety indicate seed company offering it. See page 111).

Group 0 and 1 — 'Disoy' (10) (12), 'Early Hakucho' (19), (25), 'Okuhara Early' (19), 'Giant Green' (9).

Group II — 'Verde' (21).
Group III — 'Kanrich' (3), (4), (5), (7), (14), (19), (29), 'Sodefuri' (19).

These groupings are based on full season crops (May planted, 120-130 days to ripen). When grown south of their adapted area they mature earlier. In other words, all varieties listed will grow in the South and mature early.

How to grow. Soybeans are as easy to grow as snap beans and are treated in the same way. Sow 6 to 8 seeds to foot of row 1½-2 inches deep. Thin to 2-3 inches between plants in rows 24-30 inches apart. Early varieties can be planted as close as 2 feet. Later maturing varieties require 3 feet.

Avoid cultivating or working around beans when they are wet from rain as the plants are easily bruised and broken.

Inoculation. Soybeans need inoculation with a commercial culture of nitrogen-fixing bacteria unless the bacteria are known to be in the soil. Soybean bacteria live in the soil a number of years. Some farmers do not inoculate if a nodulated crop of soybeans has been grown on the field in the past 4 or 5 years. Others inoculate even though soybeans recently have been grown on the field.

Use inoculant prepared specifically for soybeans; inoculant containing bacteria from other legumes is not effective on soybeans. Follow the directions on the container.

In the absence of nodulation, soybeans require nitrogen fertilizer for maximum yields.

When to harvest. Green beans are ready to use as soon as the pods are plump and the seeds are nearly full size but still green. All of the beans on the plant ripen about the same time so you might as well pull the plant and find a shady spot to pick the pods.

Serving ideas

Soybeans are not shelled like peas or lima beans. The best method is to pour boiling water over the pods and leave them in the hot water for 5 minutes and then drain and cool.

After this treatment it is easy to break the pods crosswise and squeeze out the beans.

Instead of shelling before cooking a much easier way (easier on the cook) is to cook in salted boiling water and serve in the pod. You then squeeze out the seeds as you eat them. This is commonly done in Japan and adds to the enjoyment, especially among the younger set.

VEGETABLE SPAGHETTI OR SPAGHETTI SQUASH

This novel squash has the same strong vining growth habit as other winter squashes and is grown in the same way. Two plants will produce more fruits than a family can use.

First fruits will be ripe in about 90 days from seeding. Do not pick until fully ripe — when the rind turns a deep yellow.

Flesh of the squash is made up of crisp spaghetti-like strands that can be pulled apart after the squash is cooked. An easy way to handle the squash is to bake it whole. Seed sources are: (4), (14), (25), (26), (27). See page 111.

Serving ideas:

Place the squash in a shallow baking pan and bake in a 350° oven for 1½ hours, turning once, or until the squash yields to gentle pressure. Then cut the squash horizontally and remove seeds. With a fork, fluff up the strands. Mix with 3 tablespoons soft butter, ¾ cup shredded Parmesan cheese, and 6 to 8 slices crisp, cooked diced bacon. Return the half shells to the 350° oven and heat 10 to 15 minutes longer, or until hot through. Makes about 4 servings.

Gourds

Ornamental gourds

Three different happenings brought about these pages on gourds:

First, the gardeners coming up with a strange vegetable creation from their supposedly sincere vegetable patch, asking for identification.

Second, the increasing number of "edible" gourds finding their way into the vegetable seed catalogs.

Third, the letters from irate gardeners claiming that we were misleading gardeners by telling them that they need not worry about cucumbers crossing with melons.

These happenings convinced us that a botanist had to be brought into the picture to find where in the gourd family the *edible* and *inedible* varieties belonged and to set us straight on the question of crossing.

The chart on the following page is the result. In some ways it's a shocking piece of information. We will never have the same confidence in the common names of Squash and Pumpkin as we had before reading the chart. It's obvious, too, that we must deal with most of this great family elsewhere in this book.

If you look down the "genus" column in the chart you will come upon *Lagenaria* and its one species *siceraria*. These are the larger gourds, often listed in seed catalogs as separate varieties, such as bottle, dipper, and 'Hercules Club.' In many regions of the world, Lagenarias made up the total of domestic utensils before the invention of pottery. They were made into bottles, bowls, ladles, spoons, churns, and many types of containers. They are used to make musical instruments, pipes and floats for fishing nets.

The individual shapes and colorings of these ornamental gourds have been maintained over the years by seed growers through isolating the growing area for each.

The varieties in the species cross easily and if all were grown together, many of the present forms would be altered and new forms would appear.

All types of gourds are fast growers if they have their quota of heat, especially warm nights.

Planting should be delayed until soil is warm. Gardeners in short-season areas start seed indoors in pots 3 to 4 weeks earlier.

Set out transplants (or thin plants in the row) 2 feet apart.

About the edible Lagenaria. Three edible gourds are offered by the seed companies that we believe to be the same vegetable. It belongs in the *Lagenaria siceraria* species.

Catalog (4) calls it New Guinea Butter Vine and describes it this way: "(Italian Edible Gourd) Will grow to enormous size — often 3-5 feet long and weighing 15 lbs. Similar to squash in growth, or can be trellised. Fruits should be eaten when small while the fuzz is still on them. Cook like squash or fry like eggplant.

Catalog (7) calls it 'Italian Climbing Squash' *(Cucuzzi caravaci).* "An edible species of running gourd."

Catalog (19) calls it *Lagenaria longissima* and describes it as follows: "Italian vegetable used like summer squash if picked half-ripe. Has a rich, full flavor. Delicious baked with fresh tomatoes, sprinkled with basil and olive oil. One customer from Boston wrote. "They are so good, I eat them for breakfast."

Some forms of Lagenaria gourds

Luffa cylindrica. Vegetable sponge, Dishrag Gourd. A fast growing vine climbing to 10 to 15 feet, carrying cylindrical fruits 12 to 24 inches long.

Luffas' origin is thought to be tropical Asia. It reached China about 600 A.D. It is now cultivated throughout the tropics. Although it is a tropical, the best Luffas are grown in Japan.

To get the "sponge" — the fibrous interior—the ripe gourds are immersed in a tank of running water until the outer wall disintegrates. They are then bleached and dried in the sun.

Luffa is grown commercially for use as sponges and in the manufacture of many products — filters in marine and diesel engines, bath mats, table mats, sandals and gloves.

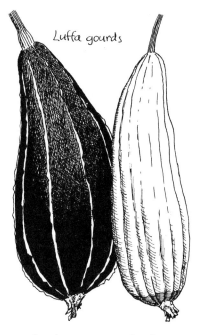

Luffa gourds

In India the young tender fruits, not more than 4 inches long, are eaten like cucumbers or cooked as a vegetable. According to *The Gourd* magazine, in Hawaii and China the small pods are used to replace edible podded peas in chop suey.

Seeds of Luffa can be obtained from the following seed companies:
See page 111 for (19), (21), (25), (26), (31).

The 'Turks Turban' squash appears in both the decorative gourd section of the catalogs and in the winter squash varieties.

Turk's Turban gourd

Vegetable gourd

The 'Vegetable Gourd' seems to be properly included in the *pepo* species along with a mixture of squash and pumpkin. A vigorous growing vine, attractive in foliage and fruits when trained on a trellis. Fruits are roundish, 3-5 inches across, weighing about ½ pound. When mature the gourd is striped a creamy white mottled with dark green. Flesh is like a sweet winter squash. A favorite way to prepare: stuff and bake like bell peppers with meal and rice.

The 'Vegetable Gourd' is available from catalogs (19), (21).

Except for perhaps the mustard family, the gourd family has the greatest diversity in its edible forms, and certainly the widest variation in color and form of fruit among the vegetables. Cross two varieties of summer squash, such as Zucchini or Yellow Crookneck with White Bush Scallop and the second generation will produce an unbelievable array of color, shape, texture, and size of fruit. If a large enough population is grown there can be hundreds of which no two are alike.

The seeds of pumpkins and squash you buy are from seeds of the variety grown in isolated blocks free from pollen of any other variety. However, Nature has a way of sneaking in a cross or two. These will show up as occasional strange plants when commercial seed is planted in the garden. Seeds saved from the odd ones will produce many different forms the next year.

Possibilities for crossing can be summarized as follows:

Any two or more varieties *of the same species* will cross freely. For example, 'Hubbard' and 'Buttercup' squash will cross, as will 'Harper Hybrid,' 'Hales Best,' and 'Crenshaw' melons.

The only crossing which occurs *between species* is in the genus *Cucurbita*. *Pepo* will cross with *moschata*. *Maxima* will cross with *moschata*. *Pepo* will not cross with *maxima*. An additional cross, *pepo* with *mixta* will also occur. Therefore we know that 'Acorn' squash will cross with 'Butternut' squash, but Acorn will not cross with 'Hubbard' squash.

Other crosses between species, such as muskmelon with cucumber (Cucumis melo x C. sativus) do not occur. Nor do any crosses between one genus and another.

The cultivated members of the gourd family

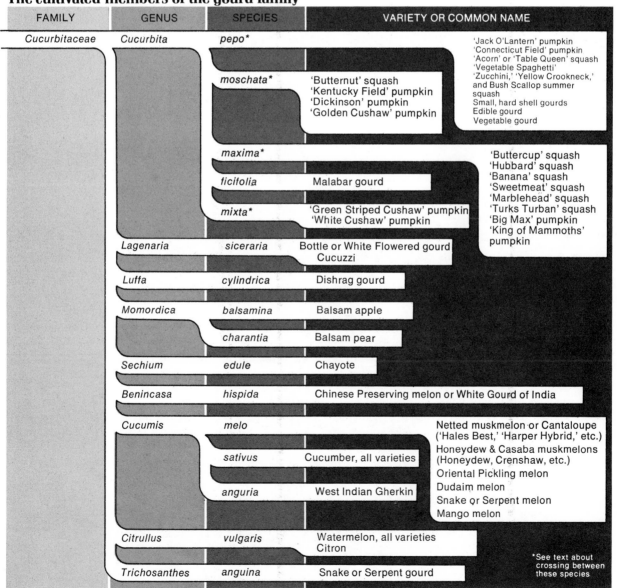

FAMILY	GENUS	SPECIES	VARIETY OR COMMON NAME	
Cucurbitaceae	Cucurbita	pepo*		'Jack O'Lantern' pumpkin 'Connecticut Field' pumpkin 'Acorn' or 'Table Queen' squash 'Vegetable Spaghetti' 'Zucchini,' 'Yellow Crookneck,' and Bush Scallop summer squash Small, hard shell gourds Edible gourd Vegetable gourd
		moschata*	'Butternut' squash 'Kentucky Field' pumpkin 'Dickinson' pumpkin 'Golden Cushaw' pumpkin	
		maxima*		'Buttercup' squash 'Hubbard' squash 'Banana' squash 'Sweetmeat' squash 'Marblehead' squash 'Turks Turban' squash 'Big Max' pumpkin 'King of Mammoths' pumpkin
		ficifolia	Malabar gourd	
		mixta*	'Green Striped Cushaw' pumpkin 'White Cushaw' pumpkin	
	Lagenaria	siceraria	Bottle or White Flowered gourd Cucuzzi	
	Luffa	cylindrica	Dishrag gourd	
	Momordica	balsamina	Balsam apple	
		charantia	Balsam pear	
	Sechium	edule	Chayote	
	Benincasa	hispida	Chinese Preserving melon or White Gourd of India	
	Cucumis	melo		Netted muskmelon or Cantaloupe ('Hales Best,' 'Harper Hybrid,' etc.) Honeydew & Casaba muskmelons (Honeydew, Crenshaw, etc.) Oriental Pickling melon Dudaim melon Snake or Serpent melon Mango melon
		sativus	Cucumber, all varieties	
		anguria	West Indian Gherkin	
	Citrullus	vulgaris	Watermelon, all varieties Citron	
	Trichosanthes	anguina	Snake or Serpent gourd	

*See text about crossing between these species

The tubers

SWEET POTATO

This member of the morning glory family was taken from Central and South America to Spain by Columbus. After the conquest of Mexico the Spaniards took them to the Philippines and the Chinese picked them up there. Portuguese ships carried them to Africa and Asia. Records show that sweet potatoes were cultivated in Virginia in 1648.

No vegetable commonly grown in the United States will withstand more summer heat and very few require as much heat as the sweet potato.

Most of the commercial production in the North is New Jersey, Virginia, Missouri, and Kansas.

How to grow. There are plenty of reasons why most small-space gardeners in the North should not give garden space to sweet potatoes. (But home gardeners grow them as far North as southern Michigan.)

They take 140-150 warm days and nights from setting out transplants to harvest.

They need a light sandy soil. When grown in heavy soils, the enlarged roots are apt to be long and stringy.

Too much water tends to make the roots more elongated and less blocky. Excess moisture during the 3 weeks before harvest will cause the roots to crack.

Too much nitrogen will develop more vines than roots. However, it's not a poor soil crop. One method of fertilizing: Make a furrow 4 to 5 inches deep and spread 4 pounds of 5-10-10 in the furrow per 100 feet. Cover the fertilizer with enough soil to make a ridge 6 to 8 inches high. Do this 2 weeks before setting out plants in the ridge 9 to 12 inches between plants.

Sweet potatoes are started from slips (rooted cuttings).

They are available at garden centers in warm summer areas. For sources of slips from seed companies see (4), (10), (12), on page 111.

Sweet potato in a box. If you would like to just sample sweet potato growing, try growing one in a box or tub that's at least 12 inches deep and 15 inches wide. Use a light porous soil mix. Place a 4 foot stake in the center to support the vine. Or grow as a lush vining houseplant indoors in a bowl or jar. See page 107. (A shoot or cutting from the houseplant can be used as a transplant for the box.)

'Jersey Orange,' 'Nugget' and 'Nemagold' are the popular dry-fleshed varieties. 'Centennial,' 'Porto Rico' and 'Gold Rush' rate high in the list of moist-fleshed varieties.

Serving ideas:

This delectable root plays a role in many cuisines. Include it on a Japanese tempura tray, as it is excellent deep-fat fried. Dice it for a stew or puree it for a pudding.

POTATO

The wild species of potatoes are distributed from the Southern United States to Southern Chile. The first cultivated varieties appeared in South America in the Andes at altitudes above 6500 feet.

Spanish explorers brought the potato home with them. But for more than a century it was regarded mainly as a curiosity in England, France and Germany.

Potatoes became a fairly important crop in America after 1718, when many Irish Presbyterians arrived, and a very significant crop right after 1846 — the year blight wiped out Ireland's potatoes.

Now, in volume and value, the potato exceeds all other crops in the world. The largest producers are the Soviet Union and Germany.

How to grow. Buy certified seed potatoes, or seed pieces, or "eyes" from garden stores or from mail-order seed companies.

Good sized seed pieces increase the chances for a good yield. Cut pieces about 1½ inches square. Be sure that there is at least one good eye in each piece.

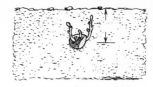
Seed piece sprouting

Tubers forming in soil mounded around stems

Potatoes will form in straw or peat moss, too ... and are easier to harvest

The usual planting method is to set seed pieces, cut side down, 4 inches deep, 12 inches apart in rows 24-36 inches apart. The tubers (what you eat) form on many stems rising from the seed piece. The potatoes do not grow in the roots. They form above the seed piece on underground stems.

When plants are 5 to 6 inches high, scrape soil from between the rows and hill up the plant — cover stems with soil. Potatoes exposed to light, either in the garden or storage, turn green and become inedible.

Apply fertilizer in bands at both sides of seed pieces at time of planting. Best method is to make a 3-inch deep and 6-inch wide trench. Place seed pieces in a row in center and work in fertilizer 1 to 2 inches deep at the edges of the trench.

A steady supply of moisture is necessary. If soil dries out after tubers begin to form, a second growth starts when soil becomes moist. The result is knobby potatoes or multiples.

Alternate wet and dry conditions will also cause "hollow heart" or cavities near the center of the tuber.

The many ways of sweet potatoes.
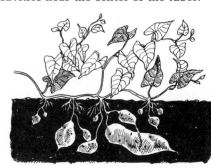

When to plant. Cool nights are needed for good tuber formation. (The complaint of "all tops and few potatoes" comes from gardeners who ignore best planting dates in warm summer areas.)

Mistakes beginners make. You can start potatoes from the potatoes you buy at the market. However the market potatoes may carry plant diseases and might have been treated to prevent sprouting. Freshly dug potatoes won't sprout until they have had a rest period.

Other mistakes are overfertilizing before tubers are formed and ignoring best planting dates, and permitting the tubers to turn green from exposure.

Special handling. An old-time method of growing potatoes that you pick rather than dig is this: Set seeds in a wide trench 3 inches deep and as stems grow build up a covering of straw or pine needles or any material that will protect them from the sun. (Cover the material with 1/2 inch of soil if wind is a problem.) The potatoes will form almost at ground level and can be picked up by pulling back the straw. Early potatoes can be picked when tops begin to flower. They will reach full size when the tops die down.

One potato vine will yield from 6 to 8 pounds of potatoes. We grew a few in the flower border and in boxes with good results.

Varieties
Early: Irish Cobbler, Norgold Russet, Norland, Red Pontiac, Superior, White Rose. Late: Katahdin, Kennebec, Russet Burbank—Netted Gem.

PEANUTS
This tropical from South America was taken by the Portuguese from Brazil to West Africa. The Spanish galleons carried peanuts from South America to the Philippines from where they spread to China, Japan and India. They found a favorable climate in North America early in our history. Jefferson wrote of their culture in Virginia in 1781.

How to grow. There are two types—Virginia with 2 seeds per pod and Spanish with 2 to 6 seeds. Most of the forms of the Virginia type are spreading and the Spanish are bunching. However, bunching varieties of Virginia are available and better adapted to short season areas than the spreading type.

A long warm growing reason of 110 to 120 days is required for most varieties. One seed catalog lists 2 varieties as doing well in South Dakota.

However if summers are cool better forget peanuts as a crop regardless of the length of season.

The strange growth habit of peanuts encourages gardeners to experiment in growing them even when they must be grown in a container with special protection.

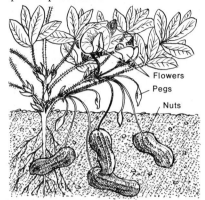

The plant resembles a yellow-flowering sweet pea bush. After the flowers wither, a stalk-like structure known as a "peg" grows from the base of the flowers and turns down to penetrate the soil. When the peg pushes to a depth of 1 to 2 1/2 inches it turns to the horizontal position and the pod begins to form.

The soil should be light and sandy. Peanuts require a generous supply of calcium in the top 3 or 4 inches of soil where the pods develop. Foliage is often dusted with gypsum at the time of flowering.

Sow seeds (shelled) 1 1/2 inches deep, 2 or 3 to the foot and thin to 6 to 10 inches apart in rows 30 inches apart. Make sure plants get regular supply of water up to 2 weeks before harvest. Shallow cultivating is called for to prevent damage to peanuts near top of soil.

When plants are about 12 inches tall, mound soil around base of plants and cover with a mulch.

When plants turn yellow at the end of the season, pull up the whole plant —and there should be a flock of peanuts hanging by their pegs.

Before stripping peanuts from plants let them cure in a warm, airy place for 2 to 3 weeks.

To roast peanuts with no chance of scorching, place unshelled nuts in a colander or wire basket. Preheat over to 500°. Place peanuts in oven. Turn oven off. When peanuts are cool to touch, they're ready to eat.

JERUSALEM ARTICHOKE
This vegetable took its place in colonial American gardens under a very misleading common name and has suffered with that handicap to this day. It is in no way related to the artichoke and the Jerusalem in the name has no connection with the Holy Land.

Jerusalem artichoke is native to eastern North America. Early explorers (1616) found it being used by the Indians and carried it back to the old world under the Italian name *Girasole* which means "turning to the sun." It is thought that some mumbling of that name turned it into "Jerusalem" in non-Italian ears.

European botanists classified it as *Helianthus tuberosus* or a tuberous sunflower.

It's a perennial, growing 6 to 10 feet high with the look of a rough sunflower.

How to grow. Start with tubers in the same way as potatoes. A few seed companies (4), (12), (15), (19), (25) (page 111) will ship them between April and May.

Harvest begins about 100-105 days after planting. They can be left in the ground over winter.

Serving ideas:
Girasole may be prepared in all ways that potatoes are served — but with an important difference. Girasole is delicious raw and never should be overcooked. Use raw slices as a last minute garnish in clear soups. Use lightly boiled tubers in salads with oil and vinegar dressing. Slowly sautée quartered tubers in butter just until they are tender.

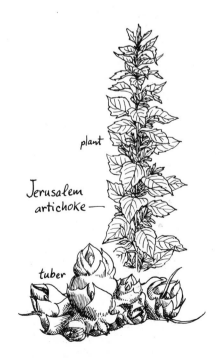

plant

Jerusalem artichoke —

tuber

When the good cook gardens

The good cook looks over the garden space, flower border and all, with menus in her eyes. She (or he) knows what a little touch, a little pinch, of fresh leaves can do for many dishes. She remembers a dish that is never quite right without fresh basil leaves, or a cupful of very young okra or a snipping of chives. Surely she can find space for a plant or two. She pictures a beautiful platter of raw vegetables and looks for space for Florence fennel, celeriac and

The chard's greatest virtue is its ability to take summer temperatures in which spinach and lettuce bolt to seed.

How to grow. It's easy to grow and fool-proof. Sow seeds in rows 18-24 inches apart and then to 4-8 inches. Use thinings for greens.

When to plant. Plant the same time as beets. Since leaves can be cut from plants continuously there is no need for successive sowings. Even when entire plant is cut off an inch or two above the crowns new leaves will be produced.

Varieties

'Rhubarb Chard.' 60 days. Dark green leaves and red stalks. A favorite vegetable for the flower border.

'Lucullus.' 60 days. Light green

ENDIVE, CHICORY, ESCAROLE

When buying these lacy, slightly bitter greens at the market, you can call them "chicory" or "endive" as you please. They are sold under both names. But when you want to plant this "lacy, frilly one," buy Endive *(Cichorium endiva)* (Escarole is a broad-leafed form of Endive).

If you want to try your hand at producing the blanched, tubular French or Belgium Endive, buy seeds of Witloof Chicory *(Cichorium Itybus)* (See description below).

Endive is grown in the same way as lettuce but it is at its best when grown for fall or winter harvest.

The finely cut type is represented by the varieties 'Green Curled,' 'Pancalier' and 'Ruffec.'

The less frilled, broad-leaved type, often called "escarole," is cataloged

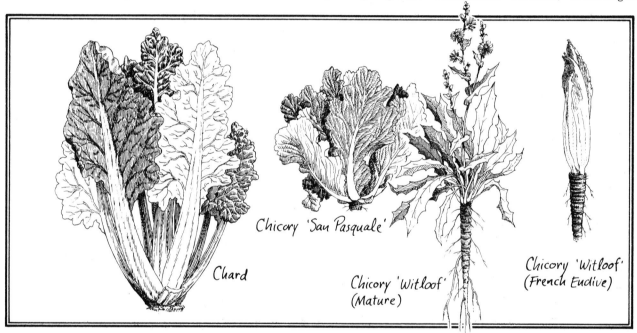

Chard

Chicory 'San Pasquale'

Chicory 'Witloof' (Mature)

Chicory 'Witloof' (French Eudive)

Jerusalem artichoke the wedges of which would elevate the plate to stardom. And there are salads that are not quite right without a mixture of greens — some sharp, some mild.

So in the next 8 pages we touch upon the vegetables that give the good cook the variety she needs in salads, "greens," stalks and roots.

SWISS CHARD

Chard is a beet that produces edible leaves and stalks rather than edible roots. Chard is the beet of the ancients — popular long before Roman times.

One planting can be harvested over many months. The large, crinkly leaves and fleshy stalks can be cut from the plant as it grows.

leaves and broad white stalks. Mild spinach-like taste.

'Fordhook Giant.' 60 days. Produces very broad (2½-inch) thick white stalks and thick, crinkly dark green leaves.

How to serve:

Cut the thick stalks into 2 or 3-inch lengths and simmer in boiling salted water until tender. Serve hot with butter and a touch of wine vinegar. Or chill and spoon over a vinaigrette (see page **74**).

Coarsely chop the leaves and cook quickly in just the water that clings to the leaves; dress with butter and salt. Or serve hot cooked greens in a hot bacon and wine vinegar dressing and sprinkle with shredded hard-cooked egg. Or add coarsely chopped leaves to Italian minestrone.

as 'Full Heart Batavian' and 'Florida Deep Hearted.'

Both types are best for salads when blanched. Draw the outer leaves together and tie with a string. In 2 to 3 weeks the blanching should be complete.

How to serve:

Wash and chill until crisp. Tear into bite-sized pieces and mix with an oil and vinegar dressing. Embellish with blue cheese and garlic croutons.

Try a Greek country salad: a medley of tomato wedges, sliced cucumbers, black olives, anchovy fillets, feta cheese and bites of endive. Or mix endive in an Italian salad of sliced green or red peppers, artichoke hearts, sliced eggs, sardines, Romaine, an oil and vinegar dressing with shredded Parmesan cheese. The French favor chicory and hot sausage in a unique wilted salad arrangement shown on page 84.

Witloof Chicory or French Endive or Belgian Endive

How to grow: Seeds are sown in early summer and require 5 months to produce the roots, which are grown like parsnips. Do not plant too early. A plant that goes to seed is useless for the next step, called forcing. The roots are dug in the fall and the tops cut off 2 inches above the crown to prevent injury to crown buds. The roots are stored in a cool place and subsequently forced at room temperatures of 60° to 70° F. as follows:

The tip of the root is cut so it is uniform in length, about 6 to 9 inches. They are set in an upright position in a trench or box with the crown up. The space between the roots is filled with soil. After thoroughly wetting the soil, the entire vegetable, root and crown, is covered with sand to a depth of 6 to 8 in. The soil should be kept moist. The sand keeps the heads compact and excludes light, to cause blanching. 3 to 4 weeks are required to produce good heads weighing 2 to 3 ounces and measuring 4 to 6 inches tall. Medium-sized roots (1 to 1¾ in. in diameter) produce the largest yield. Small roots produce low yields and large roots produce compound heads.

Varieties

'Large-Rooted Madgeburg'. Grows about 15 inches tall with upright dandelion-like foliage. Root 12 to 14 inches long. Young tender leaves can be harvested for greens at about 65 days; roots are mature at about 120 days.

'Cicoria Catalogna' or 'Radichetta'. 65 days to harvest leaves, which are toothed and curled. Used for early greens. Flower shoots are edible, have a faint asparagus flavor.

'Cicoria San Pasquale'. 70 days to harvest leaves. Light green leaves are broader than Magdeburg, are used for greens.

CORN SALAD OR LAMB'S LETTUCE OR FETTICUS

The only reason for "corn" in its name is that in Europe it frequently sprouts in the fall in harvested corn fields. In this country it comes from the garden when it's too cold for lettuce.

Flavor is very bland and it is favored in salads with strong-flavored leaves such as mustard and endive. Dress the green salad with oil and vinegar, then pour on a hot bacon dressing. Use corn salad alone as a salad base for a medley of cooked vegetables: celery root, beets, green beans, garbanzos and red peppers, all dressed with vinaigrette (see page 74).

How to grow. Same as lettuce. Rows 12 to 18 inches apart, 5 to 6 inches apart in the row.

When to plant. Try for winter crop by planting later than lettuce in the fall. See "Lettuce".

CRESS

There are 4 kinds of cress cultivated in gardens and numerous cresses growing wild, generally gathered in the spring and used as a substitute for watercress. Common names for these are Lamb's Cress, Lady's Smock, Meadow Cress, Marsh Cress, Pennsylvania Bitter Cress and Penny Cress. The 4 cultivated kinds are:

Garden Cress or Pepper Grass. The variety 'Fine Curled', 'Curled' or Burpee's 'Curlycress' has the look of parsley. It is a fast growing annual that is used in the sprout stage, and when leaves form in 7 to 10 days and in all stages up to maturity in 6 weeks. It goes quickly to flower in the long days of summer. Plant early in the season in rows 8 to 12 inches apart and use the thinnings. Make successive sowings in spring and again in fall. Keep soil moist and feed frequently but lightly.

Upland Cress. Resembles watercress, making a dense growth 5-6 inches high and 10-12 inches wide. Sow seed in rows 12-14 inches apart. Thin to 4-8 inches apart and use thinnings. Young tender tips will be ready in about 7 weeks. Will withstand fall frosts. Requires moist soil.

Winter Cress or Belle Isle Cress is a hardy biennial which survives severe winters. Sow in late summer, use in winter and in summer before seed stalks develop.

Endive

Corn Salad (Fetticus)

Watercress. This hardy aquatic perennial has been grown as a food and a medicine for 2000 years. Its health giving qualities, extolled by the ancients, are recognized by modern medicine. Seed was brought from Europe by the earliest explorers. Today it is found in many areas wherever there are springs and small slow-running streams.

Watercress can be grown from either seed or cuttings. You can take cuttings from the watercress you buy at the market. Stick them in sand or planter mix in a pot. Set in a tub of water.

Seed is very small. Sow in small containers and transplant when 2 or 3 inches tall. If you can supply enough water to keep the soil continuously moist — even by a drip method — you can grow watercress in a cold frame, planter box or in a trench.

In sandwiches, watercress lends a sprightly bite. Tuck sprigs into sliced chicken and tomato sandwiches. Or layer with sliced avocado and bacon on toasted egg bread.

In soups, cress goes well in a creamy chicken broth. Or drop shredded leaves into a smooth potato and onion soup.

As a garnish, cress enhances a variety of entree platters with its fresh deep green color and spicy undertones.

DANDELION

The name dandelion is translated "tooth of the lion" because of its jagged, irregular leaves. Native to Europe and Asia, its seeds have traveled far and wide.

As a garden vegetable it tops all other vegetables and fruits in iron and vitamin A.

How to serve.
The young leaves fresh from the garden are tenderest and best. Try them in salads (without stalks) tossed in a vinaigrette dressing (see page 74) or dress the leaves with hot bacon drippings, vinegar and crumbled bacon crisps.

Cook the leaves quickly with a dash of olive oil and serve with lemon wedges and oregano as an accompaniment to fish, in the Greek manner. For an Italian dish, mix the boiled leaves with hot spaghetti and toss with olive oil and freshly shredded Parmesan cheese.

The true French dressing is vinaigrette. Make it as close to serving time as possible — the fresher it is the better:

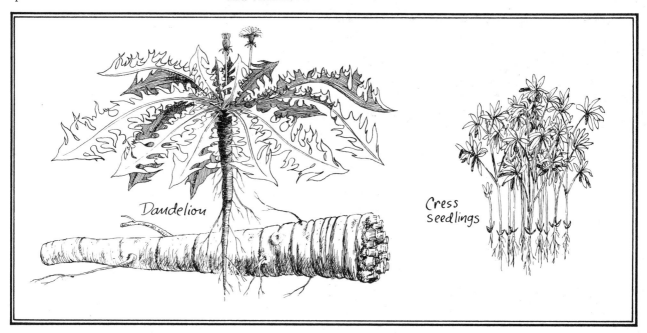

Dandelion

Cress seedlings

If you have a small stream or spring suitable for watercress, you'll find detailed information on growing it by sending 10¢ for *Commercial Growing of Watercress* (Farmers Bulletin No. 2233) to Superintendent of Documents, Wash., D.C. 20402.

How to serve:
Cress is a spicy, fresh addition to salads. Mingle sprigs with raw mushrooms, sliced and marinated in a vinaigrette (see page 74) for a first course salad plate. Mix watercress sprigs with chunks of chicken, toasted almonds and seedless grapes in a sour cream dressing for a luncheon salad. Combine watercress sprigs with butter lettuce and dress with oil and vinegar to serve with the cheese course. Pair cress with sliced hearts of palm and crab or shrimp for a luncheon salad plate.

How to grow. Sow seed and transplant or seed in place in rows 12-16 inches apart and thin to stand about 12 inches apart in the row. Fast growth, with a good supply of moisture and fertilizer, is necessary for a quality product.

When to plant. Plant it the same time as lettuce for an early crop or seed in July-August for a fall crop or a very early spring crop the following year. Dandelion is a perennial; so if allowed to develop and store food all season it will come with a rush of new growth the following spring.

Dandelion tops can be blanched by tying up leaves, or by covering with any material that shuts out light. The popular variety is 'Improved Thick Leaved'.

VINAIGRETTE DRESSING

3 or 4 parts olive oil or
*   other salad oil*
1 part red or white
*   wine vinegar*
Salt and ground pepper
Herbs to taste

Thoroughly combine the oil and vinegar, beating with a fork or whisk. Add salt and pepper to taste. Sample it for the "balance" between oil and vinegar, add to taste. Add fresh or dried herbs appropriate to the dish by blending them in at the last moment. You can store vinaigrette at room temperature but it will complement the dish better if you use it immediately.

MUSTARD

There are many mustards. The species most frequently grown commercially is *Brassica juncea*, native to the Orient. Several varieties are offered in seed packets, differing in shape and texture of leaf (see "Varieties"). Another species *B. campestris* is listed in seed catalogs as Mustard Spinach or Tendergreen Mustard.

How to grow. Treat same as lettuce. Sow seed in place in rows 12 to 18 inches apart and thin as they become crowded to 4-8 inches apart. For tender leaves, give plants plenty of fertilizer and water and harvest before they are full grown. Fast growth in fertile soil — 25 to 40 days from seed to harvest.

When to plant. Mustard is a cool-weather, short-day crop and bolts to

How to serve:

These strong, distinctive greens substitute for the more familiar spinach in an easily prepared Italian omelet or *frittata*. Served as a vegetable dish they are best cooked quickly in a small amount of boiling salted water. Dress them with olive oil and a splash of white wine vinegar or finish them with a bacon and vinegar dressing.

CARDOON

This native of the Mediterranean is closely related to the globe artichoke which it resembles in general appearance. Both are like big ornamental 3-4 foot thistles with deeply cut leaves, a crown which multiplies by sending out sidebranches, and a heavy flower head, complete with the thistle's purple bristles. While the globe artichoke is raised primar-

below the crown and the outside leaves trimmed off. You will have left a blanched heart some 18-24 inches in diameter. The stalks of this heart are cut into sections which require parboiling for an hour and a half before they are tender and lose their bitterness.

Catalogs (7), (19), (25), (26) offer the spineless varieties 'Large Smooth,' 'Ivory White Smooth,' and 'Large Smooth Spanish.'

How to Serve:

The Italians are partial to this vegetable. After blanching the stalks, they dress them with oil and wine vinegar and serve them chilled, or hot topped with a cream sauce and croutons. Sometimes chunks of cardoons are batter-dipped and deep-fried until crispy.

Watercress

Mustard

seed very early in the spring, or in August-September.

Varieties

'Florida Broad Leaf.' About 50 days. Large, thick, green leaves with a whitish midrib.

'Southern Giant Curled.' About 40 days. Upright growth of large, wide leaves, bright green and yellow-tinged with very curly edges.

'Fordhook Fancy.' About 40 days. Dark green leaves are deeply curled, fringed and curved backward like an ostrich plume. Slow to bolt. Mild flavor.

'Tendergreen' or 'Spanish Mustard.' About 40 days. Good heat resistance. Produces a large rosette of thick, smooth, glossy dark green leaves. One of the mildest in flavor.

ily for the fleshy flower bud, cardoon is grown for the young leafstalks which are blanched and eaten like celery in salads and soups.

Plant seeds in late April in the garden, or plant in pots inside in March for setting out in May. The large plants need space — 18 inches between plants with 3-4 feet between rows. They are sometimes planted in the bottom of a 1 foot deep trench. When they are large plants in September the leaves are tied together in a bunch, wrapped with paper or burlap and mounded up with soil to blanch the leafstalks. It takes about a month for adequate blanching.

Keep cardoon well fed and watered to get vigorous growth. Otherwise the leafstalks may get pithy and the plant may go into flowering.

The blanched plants are cut off just

CELERY

This member of the Parsley family probably originated near the Mediterranean, but wild forms grow in wet places all over Europe and across southern Asia. Its use as food started around 1600, but it was used from ancient times as a medicine. When it was first grown for feed, celery had hollow stalks which were fibrous and very strong in flavor and blanching was necessary to make it edible. Modern celery is solid, relatively free from fiber, mild, and can be eaten in its natural green state.

How to grow. Celery demands more time and attention than most vegetables. If you don't start from transplants from the garden store, you have a 10-12 week growing period indoors and 120 days in the garden.

Sow the very small seed 1/8 inch deep. Keep them moist by covering the flats or pots with moist burlap until emergence starts. Use care in transplanting, supplying shade and water to reduce stress on the plants.

Heavy applications of fertilizer are necessary; as much as 16 pounds of 5-10-10 per 100 feet of row. These quantities must be thoroughly mixed into a wide row to avoid burning.

Celery must have an abundant and continuous water supply.

Blanching is not usually necessary with modern varieties, but can be done by wrapping with paper or shading with boards.

Varieties

Celery is a biennial plant which is induced to flower rather easily by exposure of young plants to cold weather.

'Giant Pascal' (125 days). Good storage, large heart, thick stalks.

(Mature celery left to overwinter will produce great quantities of seed that can be harvested and used for flavoring purposes.)

How to Serve:

As a relish, serve it raw spread with blue or cream cheese spreads. Or use on a raw vegetable platter to dip into such spreads as clam dip, guacamole, and onion and sour cream dip. Or include it on a *Bagna Cauda* tray (see page 81). It adds crunch to numerous salads, especially shrimp, crab, chicken, and Waldorf.

Serve it hot adorned with anchovy fillets and wine vinegar. Or braise and chill it, then dress with vinaigrette (see page 74) for Celery Victor. Include diagonal slices in fast stir-

Mingle cooked sliced celery root with cooked shrimp in a mustard-scented vinaigrette on a bed of butter lettuce and watercress. Include celery root in a beef shank soup with leeks for a Bavarian soup. Or add the root to the famous Greek Easter lemon soup, called *Mageritsa*.

CELTUCE

Celtuce is a cultivated variety of lettuce and is grown in the same way. Give it 1½ square feet of growing space.

The big difference between head lettuce and Celtuce is that you expect Celtuce to go to seed. The thickened stem that shoots up from the "lettuce" base is what you are after. The leaves of the young plant may be used as lettuce or as boiled greens. The heart of the stem is used in all

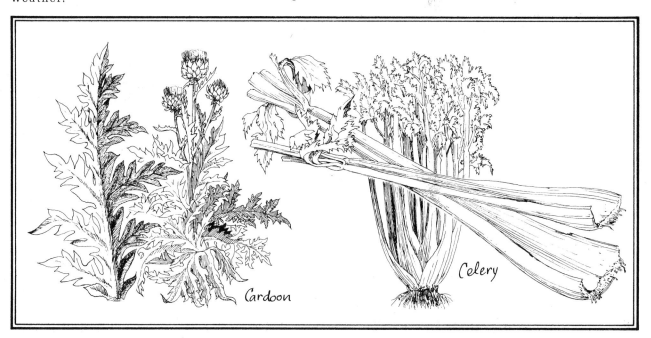

Cardoon

Celery

Therefore choose one of the following slow bolting varieties for early spring planting:

'Summer Pascal' (115 days to maturity). Medium green type, very thick stalks.

'Golden Self Blanching' (115 days). Lighter color, less thick than 'Summer Pascal.'

For late spring or summer planting where bolting would not be a problem:

'Utah 52-70' (125 days). Dark green, thick stalks. The leading variety of this type in the U.S.

fries with shrimp, beef, or pork. Or dice and cook it in soup — either a creamed version or a mixed vegetable in clear broth with beef.

CELERIAC

A form of celery grown for its swollen root. The plant is more dwarf than celery and the foliage is a very dark green.

Grow in the same way as celery. It is just as demanding of high fertilizing and a continuous supply of water.

How to Serve:

Mix raw julienne strips of celery root with apple, tongue, and chicken for a Dutch-style luncheon salad. Dress with vinaigrette (see page 74) and garnish with tomato wedges and egg slices. Or shred the raw root and toss it in an oil and vinegar dressing and garnish with watercress and olives.

the ways   you would prepare celery. Harvest when the stalk is about an inch thick at the base. It remains flavorful until the flower buds. Available from (5), (9). (See page 111.)

FLORENCE FENNEL—FINOCCHIO

Florence Fennel was described as 'Azorian Dwarf' or 'Finocchio' in 1778. It was planted in American gardens in 1800.

Florence Fennel is a variety of the Common Fennel (see page 92) grown for its bulb-like base formed by overlapping leaf-stalks. Sow seed indoors in peat pots and set out in early spring 8-12 inches apart in rows 24 inches apart. Give it a well fertilized soil and plenty of water. As the plants develop the thickened bases, pull up soil to cover and blanch them. Cool weather is almost essential for successful growth. Where spring is short and summers hot, sow seed in summer for a fall crop.

Leaves can be used in the same ways as common fennel. In fact, some seed catalogs list this variety as Common Fennel. In produce markets you may find Florence Fennel labeled as "Anise."

Ways to use: This important vegetable in Italian cooking is used in many ways. The stalks are braised or steamed and treated in all the ways appropriate to celery. The bulbous base is eaten raw or briefly blanched and chilled for a flavorful addition to salads. Braised fennel goes well with pasta or risotto dishes.

NASTURTIUM

This old timer in the flower border

usable foilage. This is a day-length controlled change and is highly related to variety. Long days hasten flowering, and the effect is increased by low temperature early in the life of plants, and by high temperature in the later stage. This combination of effects makes spring culture of a bolting susceptible variety almost sure to fail. Bolting resistant (long standing) varieties must therefore be used in spring, but some of the quick bolting varieties which are otherwise good can be used in the fall, and in winter in mild areas. Spring plantings in northern areas should be made as early as possible; fall plantings about a month from the average frost date. In mild winter areas plant anytime from about October 1 to March 1.

In addition to bolting tendency, you may need to consider varietal resis-

'Dixie Market' (40 days). Savoy, resistance to downy mildew.
'Early Hybrid No. 8' Semi-savoy; resistance to downy mildew, blight.

Summer "Spinach"

In the summer months when the cool-season spinach fails the gardener, a trio of tropicals offer fresh "greens" as rich in vitamins and comparable in flavor to the true spinach. They are:

Malabar spinach *(Basella alba)*. An attractive, glossy-leaved vine that grows rapidly when weather warms to produce edible shoots in 70 days. Train it against a fence or wall. Young leaves and growing tips can be cut throughout the summer. Use cooked or fresh in salads. Seed sources are: (5), (25), (31). See page 111.

New Zealand Spinach *(Tetragonia*

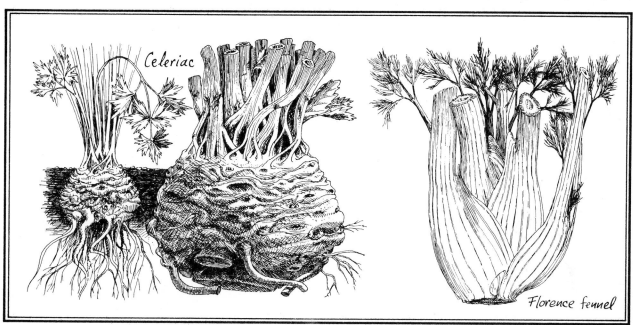

Celeriac

Florence fennel

and rock garden, used to cover fences and banks, is a fast grower in full sun or part shade. For a supply of leaves plant one of the dwarf type in containers if there's no place in the landscape for the trailing types.

SPINACH

Spinach comes from Iran and adjacent areas. It spread to China by 647 A.D., Spain by 1100 A.D., and to America with the first colonists.

How to grow. Spinach is a problem in the home garden. The plant has a short life before going to seed and is choosey as to temperatures.

Excellent substitutes for spinach are Swiss Chard, New Zealand spinach and Malabar spinach.

The big problem with spinach is its tendency to hurry on into its flowering phase, which stops production of

tance to two important diseases, downy mildew or blue mold, and spinach blight or yellows. Varieties also differ in being savoyed or smooth. Savoy types are harder to clean but are thick, dark green and usually preferred.

Long standing varieties — for spring planting include:

'Long Standing Bloomsdale' (48 days). Savoy, dark green.
'America' (50 days). Savoy, dark green.
'Winter Bloomsdale' (45 days). Smooth leaf, dark green, early.

Other varieties: for fall and winter only:

'Virginia Savoy' (42 days). Savoy.
'Hybrid No. 7 (42 days). Semi-savoyed; resistance to downy mildew and blight.

expansa). A low growing ground cover type plant spreading to 3 or 4 feet across. The young tender stems and leaves can be cut repeatedly through the summer. Seeds are really bundles of seeds, like beet seeds, and are slow to germinate. Start indoors in peat pots and set out after frost in spring. Seeds are widely available.

Tampala. This tropical is a cultivated variety of *Amaranthus gangeticus.* A close relative of the amaranthus of the flower garden. In the opinion of those who grow it, it is sweeter and more tasty than spinach. Tender young leaves need only a few minutes to cook. Seed sources are: (4), (5), (21). See page 111.

How to Serve:

Cut the greens into 2 or 3-inch lengths and stir-fry with beef, garlic, and soy for a fast Oriental dish.

PARSNIPS

Native to the Mediterranean. The Romans collected wild parsnips from the fields but the first century Emperor Tiberius imported them from Germany.

By the 16th Century they had become common in Europe and the early Colonists brought parsnips with them to North America. The Indians enjoyed the sweet nutty flavor of parsnips and grew them in their gardens.

How to grow. Roots develop to a length of 12 to 18 inches and become distorted in a heavy rough soil. The parsnip therefore is best when grouped with carrots and salsify in deeply dug soil to which generous amounts of organic matter has been added, or in a raised bed. (Comment from gardeners: "Hard digging is

vest. U.S.D.A. Leaflet No. 545 "Growing Parsnips" states: "there is no basis for the belief that parsnips that remain in the ground over winter are poisonous. All reported cases of poisoning from eating so called wild parsnips have been traced to Water Hemlock (*Cicuta*) which belongs to the same family and resembles the parsnip somewhat. Avoid gathering wild plants that look like the parsnips."

Varieties.

'All American,' 'Model' and 'Hollow Crown' are the standard varieties.

How to Serve:

Parsnips should be parboiled or steamed in their skins and then peeled and sliced lengthwise. If a large core has developed, cut it out.

use through the winter or left in the ground if it is well drained. Salsify, like carrots and parsnips, is at its best in a raised bed filled with a special mix of organic matter and fine sand, vermiculite, or perlite.

The plant is usually a biennial, growing 2-3 feet high. It produces long-stemmed purplish flower heads the second year.

How to Serve:

Oyster plant is good both raw with dips and cooked and masked with sauces such as Hollandaise, Mornay, and bechamel. To accompany fish, try it parboiled, then browned in butter. Its delicate flavor goes well with almost any meat.

Scorzonera (Black Salsify) is a relative of Salsify. The skin of the long cylindrical roots is black but the flesh is white.

Nasturtium

Spinach

probably more of a problem than distortion. Extracting them from mud in winter is hard going.")

Seeds are slow to germinate, 15 to 25 days. Sow 8 to 12 or more seeds per foot, $1/2$ inch deep and cover the row with white plastic. (See page 14 about plastic covering.) Remove plastic when seeds germinate. Later thin to 3-4 inches between plants in rows 16-24 inches apart.

Roots will take from 100 to 120 days to mature and must be subjected to winter cold near the freezing point to change the starch to sugar and give it the sweet nut-like flavor it's famous for.

Parsnip roots may be left in the ground all winter or dug out in the late fall and stored in moist sand. They can stand alternate freezing and thawing in the soil but are definitely damaged if frozen after har-

It's ready then to pan glaze with butter and a touch of brown sugar and nutmeg. (The best candied sweet potatoes you have ever tasted.) Or puree the boiled vegetables and blend in butter and cream and top with buttered crumbs.

SALSIFY—OYSTER PLANT

The flavor of the Salsify root earned it the names of "Vegetable Oyster" and "Oyster Plant."

Here's a plant that will repay you for creating a deep crumbly soil by producing longer straighter roots with fewer side roots.

Sow seed $1/2$ inch deep in rows 16-18 inches apart. When seedlings are 2 inches high, thin to 2-3 inches apart. Sow seed as soon as ground can be worked. Roots will be ready to harvest in the fall. They can also be lifted and stored in damp sand for

The roots can be left in the ground over winter and will increase in size the second year. It bears dandelion-like yellow flowers on stems 2 to 3 feet high.

Scorzonera may be prepared in the same manner as Salsify.

HORSERADISH

This old plant has been able to take care of itself through the centuries. Native to eastern Europe from the Caspian through Russia and Poland to Finland. It was planted in colonial American gardens and escaped to flourish as a wild plant.

Horseradish rarely produces seed and is generally grown from root cuttings. If cuttings are not available locally check catalogs (4), (5), (10), (12), (15). Set the cuttings small end down and large end 2-3 inches below soil surface. Plant 12 inches apart. Roots set out in spring will be harvest size in the fall.

Some growers set the cuttings on a slant rather than vertically. When the leaves are about a foot high the root is partially exposed and the small branched roots at the base are not removed. Roots are then recovered. This operation, aimed to get a quality root, is repeated about a month later.

Since it makes its greatest growth in late summer and early fall, delay harvesting until October or November.

How to use:

Beloved for its hotness, this root plays a role in cuisines throughout the world.

Peel and grate the root and blend with heavy whipped cream or sour cream to accompany sauerbrauten or roast pork.

velop much more slowly, are more solid, and have a long storage life. Rutabaga roots are much higher in Vitamin A and higher in most other food components. The tops of both are outstanding sources of Vitamins A and C.

Climate and Season. Cool seasons are preferred by both. Turnips do well in both spring and fall planting, maturing in 60 days, or less. Spring seems to be preferred in the northern areas, but spring planting should be as early as possible. However, too much exposure to 40° temperature will cause bolting. In warmer climates fall and winter is preferred because the ripening period comes at the cool end of the season. The short season of the turnip permits it to be grown, at some time, everywhere in the U.S. Rutabagas, taking 90- over 100 days to mature, are grown in the northern

der ideal conditions they can be 3 or 4 inches thick and still mild and solid). For turnip greens, use them when they are young and tender as thinned plants, or grow special greens varieties such as 'Seven Top.' These can be pulled and cooked whole or the plants left for several harvests of the younger leaves.

Rutabagas are usually harvested after they are 3 or more inches thick. They have a long keeping quality and can be left in the ground after they reach usable size, or dug and stored in a cellar.

Varieties

The standard rutabaga variety is 'American Purple Top Yellow,' matures in about 88 days. Some of the leading turnip varieties are:

'Purple Top White Globe' (58 days). Standard variety for roots.

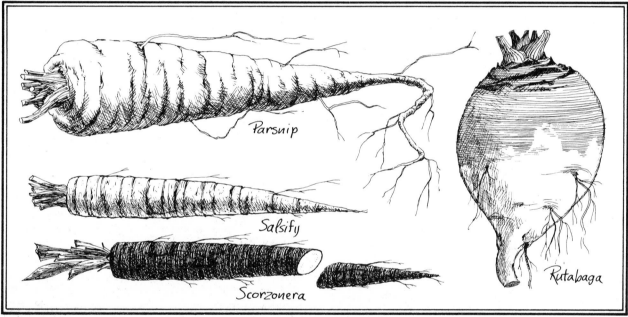

Parsnip

Salsify

Scorzonera

Rutabaga

Serve freshly grated horseradish as a side dish to pot-au-feu (see page 86).

Add the grated root to a white sauce to accompany roast beef or tongue.

TURNIPS AND RUTABAGAS

Turnips originated in Western Asia and the Mediterranean in prehistoric times. Rutabagas are more recent, apparently originating in the Middle Ages from a cross of turnip and cabbage.

Though these two crops are often considered together, as they are here, there are distinct differences. Though there are white and yellow forms of each, most turnips are white-fleshed and most rutabagas yellow. Turnips have rough, hairy leaves, are fast growing and get pithy in a short time. Rutabagas have smooth waxy leaves, emerge and de-

areas where summer average temperatures do not exceed 75°. Only one crop a year is possible and it should be planted to mature after hot weather is over.

How to grow. General soil and nutrient requirements are about the same as beets, though perhaps these crops need slightly less nitrogen. The seed bed need not be extremely fine because seedlings come quickly and easily and the enlarged roots are borne partly out of the ground.

Direct seed about 1/2 inch deep in rows as close as 15 or 18 inches. Thin in stages to 1-2 inches apart, using the last thinnings for greens. Keep the crop well watered and growing fast for best quality.

Harvest. Turnip roots must be used before they get pithy, fibrous, and bitter. Usually they can be 2 inches in diameter (but this varies and un-

'Just Right' (37 days). White hybrid for greens or roots.

'Seven Top.' Primarily for greens in late fall and early spring.

'Shogoin' (30 days). Primarily for greens. Will grow in hot weather better than other varieties.

How to Serve:

Turnip greens, simply boiled, are popular in the South, China, Japan. The root is good sliced and served on a relish tray with dips. Or slice and boil it and finish off with butter; or mash and season it with dill weed or basil. Add it to souffles or stews. It especially complements duck, goose, or lamb.

Serve thin slices of rutabagas raw with a dunking sauce. Or boil the vegetable and mash to accompany goose, duck, or turkey. Dill weed and fennel complement it.

The international garden deserves an international cook

The vegetables we grow have traveled far and wide over the centuries. And wherever in the world they could be grown, they have found special treatment in the kitchen. Today's good cook realizes that cooks of Italy, France, Greece, China, Japan—every country in the world—have worked out their own ways to prepare and serve vegetables, fascinating ways she (or he) can borrow.

Thus, with an international garden just beyond the kitchen door, the international cook is free to travel—with a palate without prejudice. She sharpens a relish plate with chunks of anise-flavored fennel spread with Roquefort, punctuates an Italian salad with the pleasing bitter bite of freshly cut endive, or whets the French *Aioli* sauce with an abundance of garlic from prize heads pulled from the garden. This adventurer gilds a Spanish paella with golden saffron (at a fraction of the market cost), adorns a Moroccan stew with tangerine-hued nasturtium blossoms plucked minutes before from Mexican patio pots, snips chives to blend into a herb butter for sour dough bread, garners the fragrant leaves of oregano to strew in a Greek meat sauce, and picks the prolific mint to blanket a roasting leg of lamb.

But, more importantly, the cook who raises her own vegetables comes to appreciate the difference between vegetables fresh by minutes and fresh by days. These differences, sometimes subtle, must not be lost in the kitchen.

Ways of cooking

The ways to cook vegetables have changed as the "foreign" ways become our ways. These are the basics:

Boiling. This method is suitable for artichokes, asparagus, broccoli, cauliflower, corn, peas, and root vegetables such as potatoes, yams, carrots, beets, rutabagas, turnips, parsnips, winter squash, and onions.
Cook these vegetables in boiling salted water, covered, until tender. Drain and dress with butter or any one of your favorite seasonings.

Poaching is a variation of this method. An example is Vegetables a la Grecque (see page 88) where prepared vegetables are cooked in a large quantity of richly seasoned court bouillon. The liquid is then boiled down until reduced to a thick, flavorful sauce and spooned over the vegetables.

French steamer

Steaming. Appropriate vegetables for this cooking method include asparagus, broccoli, cauliflower, corn, spinach, Swiss chard, and peas. Place the vegetable in a French steamer (a container with perforations and flexible sides) or a colander and lower into a pan containing a small amount of boiling water. Cover and simmer, or let steam, until vegetables are tender. Cooking time is a few minutes longer than when the same vegetable is boiled. To serve, transfer vegetables from steamer or colander to serving dish and dress with butter or other seasonings.

Butter Steaming. This fast-cooking method lends itself to artichokes, asparagus, beets, broccoli, brussels sprouts, cabbage, carrots, cauliflower, celery, green beans, mushrooms, summer squash, peas, and turnips. Use a large frying pan. Place in it 2 tablespoons butter, 1/4 cup water, salt, and about 3 to 4 cups prepared vegetables, cut in small pieces or shredded, if appropriate for the vegetable. Cover and cook over fairly high heat until liquid is evaporated and vegetables are tender. (If necessary, add additional water to slow-cooking vegetables such as artichokes). Season with a desired herb, if you wish, and serve.

Braising. This is a combination method popular in the countries which border the Mediterranean. Suitable vegetables for it include green beans, brussels sprouts, cauliflower, mushrooms, peas, and zucchini. Parboil the selected vegetables in boiling salted water, then drain. Meanwhile, saute chopped onion and garlic in olive oil until soft. If desired, add chopped proscuitto, minced ham, or crumbled Italian sausage to the onion saute. Add the drained, parboiled vegetables and a few tablespoons water and heat until hot through, stirring.

Wok

Stir-Frying. The centuries old Chinese technique of cooking vegetables is still one of the best. It suits a wide range of vegetables, cut in small pieces or sliced on the diagonal. Use a wok or a large frying pan and place it over moderately high heat. Then add peanut oil or other desired oil. When the oil sizzles add salt and the prepared vegetable. Quickly stir-fry or toss using a wide spatula until the vegetable is coated with oil. Soft vegetables, such as spinach, cabbage, lettuce, watercress, tomatoes, and bean sprouts need no additional liquid and cook quickly in their own exuded juices. Mushrooms and zucchini may be covered for a minute or two and cooked without additional liquid until crisp-tender.

Additional liquid, such as stock or soy and water, must be added to semi-hard or hard vegetables. These include asparagus, broccoli, cauliflower, carrots, green beans, and celery. Cover pan and steam the vegetables until crisp-tender. Seasonings such as garlic and fresh ginger root may be added at the beginning of cooking.

Baking. Oven baking whole vegetables in their skins suits white potatoes, sweet potatoes, spaghetti squash, eggplant, and winter squash.

Deep-Fat Frying. Cooking sliced vegetables in hot oil is appropriate for white potatoes and sweet potatoes. Scandinavians drop parsley sprigs into hot oil and cook until crispy.

The Italians egg coat certain vegetables and deep fry for *frito misto.* The Japanese batter-dip vegetables for *tempura.* Suitable vegetables include green beans, eggplant, mushrooms, green peppers, cucumbers, zucchini, sweet potatoes, onions, asparagus, cabbage, cauliflower, broccoli, and artichoke hearts or stems. Be certain the vegetables are thoroughly dry before dipping into an egg or batter coating. Immerse the vegetables in hot oil, heated to 375°, and cook until the vegetables are golden.

French knife

Cutting vegetables

Another step in the preparation of vegetables that is important in both their cooking and their presentation is in the cutting.

Often the size of the cut determines the cooking time. In the stir-fry dishes of the Orient where flash cooking is a matter of minutes, the uniformity of size of each vegetable is most important.

Changes from the regular crosswise rounds or slices may change the taste in the mind of the beholder.

The diagonal cut brings a pleasing change to the presentation of hot buttered carrots, celery or cauliflower. Diagonal slicing works well with vegetables served on a relish tray with dips — such as celery, zucchini, carrots, asparagus and cucumbers.

Julienne match sticks are suitable for both carrots and potatoes. To do this, remove a thin strip off one side of the carrot or potatoes and lay the vegetable flat on the board. Then cut it into lengthwise slices about $1/8$ inch thick. Pile two or three slices on top of each other and cut the slices into strips about $1/8$ inch across, then cut into desired lengths.

A fan cut works well with zucchini. Using small to medium-sized squash, make lengthwise slices $1/4$ inch apart, cutting to within 1 inch of the end. After cooking in boiling salted water, the squash fan out slightly.

A Swedish way of slicing baking potatoes makes a handsome vegetable to ring a roast. Peel medium-sized potatoes and lay each one flat on a board. Slice down vertically making $1/8$ inch thick slices, cutting to within about $1/4$ inch of the bottom so each potato is whole. Brush with melted butter or oil and bake with a roast.

A French knife is an indispensable tool for chopping and slicing. Use the tip of the knife as a pivot, never lifting it from the cutting board. Relax your wrist and keep to a rhythm.

Let's glorify the fresh raw vegetable

What about a harvest garden party — and there should be many harvests.

Imagine a gathering in the garden when everyone picks, pulls, washes, slices and eats their way through the ripe harvest.

The day might be when there are peppers, tomatoes, celery, carrots and turnips for sure and celeriac, cardoon, Florence fennel and Jerusalem artichokes maybe. This happening should revolve around the hot pot of Bagna Cauda.

Sauces and serving ideas

BUTTER SAUCE, ITALIAN STYLE

The Italian Bagna Cauda, translated as "hot bath," is a robust garlic and anchovy butter sauce. It is served bubbling hot in a communal pot. Guests dip raw vegetables into it, just to coat them, not cook them. It makes a congenial appetizer for a party dinner, and one that is particularly effective served in the garden where there is lots of room for moving about and plunging vegetables into the tantalizing butter bath.

This is a dish that makes effective use of whatever the garden offers. You can include as few as two or three vegetables or as many as a dozen if the harvest is abundant. Feel free to increase the garlic if you are fond of it.

Bagna Cauda Sauce
$3/4$ cup butter
$1/4$ cup olive oil
2 to 3 cloves garlic, minced
8 anchovy fillets, finely chopped

Select a heat-proof container or sauce pot suitable for placing over an alcohol burner or candle warmer. Place in the pot the butter, oil, garlic, and anchovies and heat until bubbly. Wash vegetables and cut into bite-size pieces and arrange on a tray alongside. Include small bamboo skewers for skewering vegetables and dipping into the pot. Makes about 1 cup butter sauce.

Stir-fried shrimp and asparagus. *Wash 1 pound asparagus, break off tough ends, and cut in diagonal slices about $1/4$ inch thick. Cut 3 green onions in 1 inch lengths. Slice $1/4$ cup water chestnuts. Peel and devein 1 pound cooked shrimp. Mince 2 slices fresh ginger root, add to shrimp and toss.*
Heat 3 tablespoons peanut oil in a large frying pan or wok, add asparagus and 1 clove minced garlic and stir- *fry 2 minutes. Add onions, water chestnuts, and shrimp, and stir-fry 1 minute longer.*

Blend together 2 teaspoons cornstarch, 2 tablespoons water, 2 tablespoons sherry, and 1 tablespoon soy sauce, and pour into pan. Cook and stir until sauce boils and thickens. Turn out onto a serving dish and sprinkle with nuts. Makes 4 servings.

BASIL BLENDER SAUCE

The Italian *Pesto Sauce,* a puree of garden fresh basil, olive oil, garlic, and Parmesan cheese, is renowned as a sauce tossed with hot fresh egg noodles called *fettucine.* It is a savory encounter spooned over sliced tomatoes, hot corn-on-the-cob, and cooked zucchini or green beans, as well. Or dollop it on a steak, hamburgers, or minestrone, or mix it into a green salad, dressed with oil and vinegar. It freezes beautifully. A smart way to package it for freezing is to drop small mounds of pesto on foil placed on a baking sheet, then freeze. When solid, peel mounds from foil and package securely.

The authentic method calls for grinding the fresh leaves in a mortar with a pestle. A swifter contemporary version utilizes a blender instead.

Pesto

2¹/₂ cups fresh washed basil leaves
3 cloves garlic, peeled
3 tablespoons lightly toasted pine nuts
³/₄ cup olive oil
¹/₂ cup freshly shredded Parmesan cheese
Place in the blender container the basil, garlic, pine nuts, and oil. Blend until the leaves are pulverized. Add cheese and blend a few seconds longer. Use at once or package and freeze. Makes about 1³/₄ cups.

FRENCH PROVENCAL DIP

The Provencal garlic sauce, called Aioli, provides a robust dip for a supper platter filled with both raw and cooked vegetables and shellfish. An arrangement of the ingredients makes a stunning decoration on the table.

Basil

The sauce has gained great popularity in the south of France where it is a favorite dip for local and garden produce and the wealth of nearby seafood.

Purists would make the sauce in a mortar with pestle, but a blender simplifies the whole process.

Aioli Sauce

1 egg
3 tablespoons white wine vinegar
1 teaspoon each salt and Dijon-style mustard
4 large cloves garlic, peeled
1 cup peanut, safflower, or olive oil

Place in a blender container the egg, vinegar, salt, mustard, and garlic, and blend until smooth. With the motor running, gradually pour in the oil in a fine steady stream, blending to make a thick mayonnaise. Turn into a sauce bowl, cover and chill. Makes about 1¹/₄ cups.

Aioli sauce enhances a range of vegetables. Consider pairing it with hot or cold cooked artichokes and Italian green beans, hot cooked new potatoes, cooked carrots or asparagus, raw fennel, cherry tomatoes, red peppers, mushrooms, zucchini, and cauliflower. For shellfish, consider cold cooked shrimp, crab, or lobster, or such fish as cold poached halibut or turbot. Hard-cooked eggs are a fine addition, while salt cod is typically French.

To duplicate the supper platter, pictured, prepare the following ingredients:

Aioli Supper Platter

Trim 4 large artichokes and cook in a large amount of boiling salted water with 2 tablespoons lemon juice and 1 tablespoon oil for 40 to 45 minutes, or until tender, drain and serve hot, or chilled, if desired. Trim the ends from 1 bunch small carrots and peel. Cook in boiling salted water until tender, about 7 to 10 minutes; then drain. Snap the tough ends from ¹/₂ pound asparagus and cook in boiling salted water for 5 to 7 minutes, or until tender; drain. Cut 1 small red cabbage into wedges. Arrange the vegetables on a platter with 1 box cherry tomatoes, ¹/₂ pound mushrooms, and 1 bunch fennel. Add 1 pound cooked large shrimp. Serve with a sauce bowl of Aioli Sauce. Makes 4 servings.

Another time you might utilize the sauce on a more intimate scale at luncheon with shrimp, mushrooms, and cherry tomatoes. Or spoon it into a fish soup.

QUICK CLASSICS

Blender Hollandaise

Rinse out a blender container with hot water and drain. Place in it 3 egg yolks, 2 tablespoons lemon juice, and ¹/₄ teaspoon dry mustard. Blend until smooth. Heat ³/₄ cup butter until bubbly and slowly pour in a fine stream into the yolk mixture, blending constantly. Serve hot, at room temperature, or dollop chilled spoonfuls of sauce over hot asparagus spears. If desired, season with a dash of nutmeg or pinch of tarragon. Makes 1 cup.

Bearnaise Sauce

2 sprigs parsley
2 shallots finely chopped
¹/₄ cup tarragon vinegar
1 cup Hollandaise sauce
1 tablespoon fresh tarragon
¹/₈ teaspoon cayenne

Place parsley, shallots and vinegar in a saucepan and reduce to 1 tablespoon liquid. Remove from heat and allow to cool. Add reduced liquid to Hollandaise sauce and stir. Add tarragon and cayenne. Makes 1 cup.

i supper platter

Mornay Sauce

1 cup thick cream sauce
1 cup whipping cream
1 cup shredded Cheddar cheese
1/8 teaspoon cayenne
Salt and pepper

Place cream sauce and whipping cream in small saucepan. Mix well. Bring to gentle boil. Add cheese and cayenne. Allow to simmer until cheese is melted and sauce has smooth appearance. Salt and pepper to taste. Makes 1 pint.

GREEK CHEESE AND GREENS

The Greek country salad is another green salad that utilizes the pleasantly bitter greens such as chicory, escarole, and cress. The nippy bite of the greens are a perfect counterbalance to the creamy *feta* goat cheese and salty olives.

Greek Country Salad

1 head curly endive or 1 bunch cress
1 head Romaine or iceburg letttuce
1 cucumber, peeled and sliced
1 cup cherry tomatoes, halved
3 tablespoons capers
1 1/2 dozen Greek olives
6 tablespoons olive oil
2 tablespoons red wine vinegar
1 teaspoon fresh oregano or 1/4 teaspoon dried
1/2 teaspoon salt
3 to 4 ounces feta cheese

Tear greens into bite-size pieces and place in a large salad bowl. Add the cucumbers, cherry tomatoes, capers,

Escarole and hot sausage salad

and olives and mix lightly. Shake together the oil, vinegar, oregano, and salt and pour over. Mix well. Scatter over the crumbled cheese. Makes 6 to 8 servings.

HOT AND COLD SALAD

A fascinating Parisian salad is composed of chilled, slightly bitter greens tossed with hot smoky slices of sausage. It is a tantalizing combination and one that suggests unlimited variations. It works beautifully with fresh garden greens and locally available sausages.

Escarole and chicory (or curly endive) are choice greens to use. Appropriate sausages include Italian garlic, French blood sausage, Italian coteghino, Portuguese kielbasa, knackwurst, and strings of cocktail sausages.

Crisp garlic croutons, cherry tomatoes, and halved soft-cooked eggs are optional additions. Crispy nuggets of salt pork or bacon can be added at the last, lending a smoky overtone.

Escarole and Hot Sausage Salad

2 slices sour dough French bread
2 tablespoons butter
1 clove garlic, minced
1 bunch escarole or endive
2 kielbasa sausages or mild Italian garlic sausages
Boiling water
3 slices thick-sliced bacon, diced
1/4 cup olive oil
2 tablespoons white wine vinegar
1/2 teaspoon each salt and Dijon-style mustard

Cut French bread into small cubes and saute in butter with garlic until lightly toasted; set aside. Tear well-washed, crisped greens into bite-size pieces and pile into a salad bowl. Place kielbasa into hot water and heat just until hot through; drain. (Or place garlic sausage in simmering water and let simmer 20 minutes; drain.) Cook bacon until crisp, reserving the drippings. Meanwhile, shake together the oil, vinegar, salt, and mustard, and pour over the greens. Pour over 2 to 3 tablespoons of the reserved hot bacon drippings and mix well. Slice the sausage on the diagonal and arrange on top. Scatter over the croutons and bacon. Makes 6 servings.

FLAVORS BLEND IN BAKING

A beautiful baked vegetable melange from the South of France is Ratatouille. (The name is pronounced *rah-tah-too yeh*, in a rhythmical manner). Vibrant with eggplant, red and green peppers, tomatoes, and zucchini, the vegetables are bound together through gentle cooking in olive oil and garlic. In this recipe the vegetables are thoroughly cooked so the flavors meld.

This makes a marvelous side dish to accompany a dinner entree of roast leg of lamb. Or serve it cold as a luncheon salad with a paté, omelet, or quiche for a companion.

Ratatouille

About 6 tablespoons olive oil
2 large onions, thinly sliced
4 cloves garlic, minced
3 large zucchini, thinly sliced
1 red or green bell pepper, seeded and cut in pieces
1 large eggplant
3 medium-sized tomatoes
1 teaspoon salt
2 teaspoons fresh basil, chopped
1/4 cup minced parsley

In a large frying pan heat 3 tablespoons of the oil and saute onions until limp. Add garlic, zucchini, and pepper, and saute a few minutes longer. Cut eggplant lengthwise,

touille

then cut into 1½ to 2 inch pieces. Transfer sauteed vegetables and eggplant to a large casserole and drizzle over remaining oil. Peel tomatoes, dice, and mix in. Season with salt and basil. Cover and bake in a 350° oven for 1½ to 2 hours, or until vegetables are thoroughly cooked, basting the top once or twice with some of the pan juices. Sprinkle with chopped parsley. Makes about 8 servings.

MEXICAN MEDLEY

The Mexicans create a rival quick-cooking vegetable combination, this time emphasizing fresh corn kernels instead of eggplant. Named Colache, this brilliant medley again calls on such harvest-time vegetables as red and green peppers, zucchini, onions, and tomatoes plus ears of corn.

It makes a striking dish to accompany a Mexican dinner featuring chicken enchiladas or turkey mole. You might start with a guacamole salad and end with a flan.

Colache

1 medium-sized onion, finely chopped
1 each red and green bell pepper, seeded and diced
1/4 cup butter
2 zucchini, thinly sliced
2 yellow crookneck squash, thinly sliced
1/3 cup water
4 ears corn
1 large tomato, peeled and diced
Salt and pepper to taste

Using a large frying pan or Dutch oven, saute onion and peppers in butter until limp and glazed. Add zucchini, crookneck, and water. Cover and simmer 5 minutes.

Cut the corn kernels from the ears and add along with

When leeks go to seed

tomato. Cover and simmer 4 to 5 minutes longer, or until vegetables are tender. Season with salt and pepper to taste. Makes about 8 servings.

MEAL-IN-A-POT

Pot-au-feu, meaning "pot on the fire," is one of the earliest cooking methods. A selection of vegetables and some type of meat or poultry brew together in a slowly simmering flavorful broth. The result is an aromatic soup and a stunning meal on a platter to serve with sprightly condiments. It is a custom that is carried out in many countries.

The classic French dish is pictured. There are also the sauerkraut and beet root dishes of Russia, the corned beef and cabbage of New England, the *Puchero* of Spain, and the Italian *Bollito Misto,* redolent with spicy coteghino sausage.
For the peasant style French pot-au-feu, select a solid piece of meat such as a sirloin tip, boneless chuck or rump. For vegetables, choose from among carrots, onions, turnips, leeks, new potatoes, parsnips, and cabbage. Traditional condiments are freshly grated horseradish, Dijon-style mustard, coarse salt, and tiny gerkin pickles.

Pot-Au-Feu

1 pound cracked beef or veal shank bones
4 pound sirloin tip, rump, or boneless chuck roast
2 onions
4 cloves
1 bay leaf
1 clove garlic
6 whole peppercorns
2 teaspoons salt
½ teaspoon thyme
3 to 4 quarts water
1 bunch small carrots, trimmed and peeled
3 small turnips, peeled and halved
8 new potatoes
6 small leeks, washed, trimmed, and halved
Parsley for garnish
Condiments: freshly grated or bottled horseradish,
  Dijon-style mustard, coarse salt, small pickles

Using a large soup kettle (about 8 quart size), place the bones and meat in the bottom of the pan. Stud onions with cloves and put in the pan with bay leaf, garlic, peppercorns, salt, and thyme. Add water to almost cover the meat and heat to simmering. Remove scum and bring to a simmer again. Cover and simmer very slowly for 2 hours. Add carrots, turnips, and potatoes, and simmer 20 minutes longer. Add leeks and simmer 10 minutes longer, or until vegetables are tender.

To serve, lift out meat to a large platter and surround with vegetables; keep warm. Strain the cooking liquid and discard cooking seasonings; skim off fat. Pour broth into a tureen or individual soup bowls and serve as a first course.

Garnish the meat platter with parsley and slice meat. Accompany with condiments to pass at the table. Makes about 8 servings.

ONE ALONE OR MANY TOGETHER

Here vegetables cook in a richly flavored, aromatic court bouillon or broth. At the end of cooking, the broth is cooked down or reduced to create a sauce to spoon over the vegetables.

You may cook only one vegetable, such as mushrooms, carrots, leeks, or artichoke hearts, or you may prepare a succession of assorted vegetables, simmering each one

au-feu

separately, to serve on a buffet platter. The vegetables are good served hot, at room temperature, or chilled.

Vegetables Ala Grecque

3 cups water
1/3 cup each lemon juice and olive oil
1 teaspoon salt
1 shallot or green onion, minced
3 sprigs parsley
1 sprig fresh thyme and fennel or 1/8 teaspoon
  each dried thyme and fennel
6 whole peppercorns
Vegetables: 2 pounds button mushrooms or an assortment: artichoke hearts, crookneck squash, zucchini, leeks, eggplant, celery, endive, or red and green bell peppers
Watercress for garnish

Combine in a large saucepan or Dutch oven the water, lemon juice, oil, salt, and minced shallot. Place in a cheesecloth bag the parsley, thyme, fennel, and peppercorns and add. Cover and simmer for 10 minutes for seasonings to blend.

Add prepared vegetables, one at a time, as suggested below, and simmer as directed. Remove vegetables with a slotted spoon to a serving dish. Rapidly boil down juices until reduced to about 1/2 cup. Spoon over the vegetables. Serve hot, let cool to room temperature, or cover and chill. Garnish with watercress, if desired. Serves 8. **For mushrooms,** trim and wash. Add to broth, cover, and simmer 5 minutes. **For artichoke hearts,** use the diminutive artichokes, about 1 1/2 inches in diameter. Peel off outer leaves, halve, and scoop out choke. Add to broth, cover, simmer 25 to 30 minutes, or until tender. **For crookneck squash and zucchini,** trim ends and halve. Add to broth, cover, and simmer 8 to 10 minutes, or until

barely tender. **For leeks,** trim ends, cut lengthwise, and wash thoroughly. Add to broth and simmer 10 to 15 minutes, or until tender. **For eggplant,** cut in lengthwise wedges and leave peel on, if desired. Add to broth, cover, and simmer 8 to 10 minutes, or until tender. **For celery,** use celery hearts. Trim and halve or quarter bunches lengthwise. Wash thoroughly. Add to broth, cover, and simmer 20 to 25 minutes, or until tender. **For French endive,** quarter or halve the bunches. Add to broth, cover, and simmer 20 to 25 minutes, or until tender. **For red or green bell peppers,** quarter peppers lengthwise and remove seeds and ribs. Add to broth, cover, and simmer 10 minutes.

FLAVORED BUTTER

Herb and seed butters make fascinating spreads on a variety of breads. Try a garlic-parsley butter on a fine-grained egg bread or a robust shallot butter on a hearty rye or pumpernickel. A mixed fresh herb butter, composed of chopped chives, parsley, oregano, and marjoram is delightful on wholesome buttercrust or Dutch crunch bread. A quartet of seeds, each different in assertive qualities, dots this garlic butter, lending a snappy zest:

Seed Butter

1/2 cup butter
2 tablespoons finely chopped onion
2 cloves garlic, minced or mashed
2 teaspoons each poppy and sesame seeds
3/4 teaspoon each dill and caraway seeds

Beat butter until creamy and beat in onion, garlic, poppy, sesame, dill, and caraway seeds. Spread on slices of bread, place in a single layer in a baking pan, and heat in a 350° oven for about 8 minutes, or until hot through and butter melts.

Seeds lend sparkle to a variety of baked goods. Flavor your favorite pound cake, baked in a bundt pan, with sesame seeds and ground coriander, or caraway seeds and grated orange peel, or poppy seeds and lemon peel. Or scatter sesame or poppy seeds on yeast bread braids and rolls or sugar cookies.

PRESERVE THE SUMMER'S BOUNTY

There are almost as many kinds of pickles and recipes for pickling as there are good cooks in the world. This time we give you a simple way, using dill and garlic that grew nearby.

Dill Pickles

3/4 cup sugar
1/2 cup salt
1 quart vinegar
1 quart water
50 to 60 small cucumbers
Fresh dill
Garlic cloves

Combine the sugar, salt, vinegar, and water. Bring to a boil and let simmer 5 minutes. Pack cucumbers into hot, sterilized pint or quart canning jars, leaving 1/4-inch head space. Put a head (or flower) of dill and a garlic clove in each jar. Pour boiling brine over cucumbers, leaving 1/4-inch head space. Adjust caps.

Place each jar as it is filled on a rack in the canning kettle. Pour in hot water to cover jars 1 to 2 inches. Bring water to a boil. Reduce heat until a gentle boil and let boil for 15 minutes. Remove jars to a rack to cool. Makes about 3 to 4 quarts.

The indispensable herb

When it comes to growing herbs even the gardener with little experience shouldn't be intimidated by the word "herb." A herb is a plant from which you gather leaves, seeds, fruits, flowers, buds, bark or roots for seasonings, flavorings, scents, or enrichment of certain foods to make them more pleasing to the taste or smell. A "potherb" is a plant you cook in a pot. Growing herbs is in no way different from growing flowers or vegetables. The admonitions in the herb books about soil requirements read this way: This herb requires (or prefers) soil to be alkaline, dry, somewhat dry, moderately dry, fairly dry, light, moist, poor, rich, and fairly, moderately, somewhat of each. These are clues to the nature of the plant but obviously impossible to follow in a small herb garden.

In a mixed border, planted for color, you find plants of different soil "preferences" growing cheek to cheek. About the only allowance for wide differences is not to mix desert plants with tropicals.

If directions for growing herbs sound technical it's a good idea to forget to call them herbs and go about planting them as vegetables or flowers.
Of the many culinary herbs, annuals and perennials, these can be grown in exactly the same way as annual vegetables: anise, basil, chervil, corainder, dill, sweet fennel, false saffron, summer savory, sesame, parsley, chives, thyme, winter savory. Caraway is a biennial and is cultured so the seed crop can be harvested the second year.

Others are treated as perennials and are often grown with ornamentals: borage, marjoram, oregano, mints, sage, rosemary, tarragon.

One thing happens (or can happen) in a herb garden that is different from just growing a plant in the normal fashion. The herbs that are harvested by snipping leaves are *pruned* and made more compact—the same way boxwood is clipped into a hedge. This clipping or pruning made possible the fantastic knot gardens of the colonial days, sketched here.

The following good advice on harvesting, drying and winter care of herbs is quoted from a bulletin *Herbs for Culinary Purposes* by James A. Wott of Purdue University.

"Harvesting. Leaves of many herbs such as parsley and chives are harvested for fresh seasoning. Remove from the plant as soon as the plant has grown a good number of leaves.

"Herbs such as rosemary and thyme are harvested by clipping the tops at full bloom. Usually both leaves and flowers are harvested together.

"Basil, fennel, mint, sage, summer savory, sweet marjoram, tarragon, and winter savory are best harvested in the pre-bloom stage or near the time blooming starts.

"Chervil and parsley leaves can be cut and dried anytime.

"The seeds or fruits of anise, coriander, dill, and fennel are best harvested in the early stages of ripening before the seed heads shatter.

"Drying. Herbs may be dried by loosely tying in small bunches and hanging in a ventilated, dust-free room; by loosely spreading on a frame of hardware cloth, screening or cheese cloth; or by stripping off the leaves and spreading on flat trays. Dry in a cool room. Do not use artificial heat or allow exposure to sunlight both of which may impair quality.

"Dried leaf and flower material is commonly pulverized and placed in labeled jars to preserve aroma and flavors. If any moisture condenses in the jars, further drying is necessary. Foliage herbs include basil, sweet marjoram, sage, thyme, savory, tarragon, parsley, dill, fennel, mint, oregano, chervil and rosemary.

"Winter care. Some types of herbs may be potted in the fall and placed in the home for fresh winter use. Start with new plants such as cuttings or divisions. Reduce the amount of foliage according to the root loss suffered in the transplanting process. Place in a south window and care for them as regular houseplants. Some herbs respond better if they are left outdoors and subjected to freezing temperatures for 2 to 3 weeks before bringing indoors. Herbs may also be raised from seeds in window containers.

"The better potted herbs are basil, chives, mints, parsley, sweet marjoram, and rosemary."

If you wish to pursue the fascinating hobby of herb culture, consider joining one of the herb societies. For information write:

Mrs. R. H. Miller
Herb Society of America
300 Massachusetts Avenue
Boston, Ma. 02115

Dr. Elizabeth Moyer
National Herb Study Society
74 Trestle Glen Rd.
Oakland, Ca. 94610

If you have an urge to duplicate the old or create a new knot garden of herbs, it's a good idea to check the growing habits of the possible candidates to see how readily they can be shaped to a compact, definite form.

Sage, lemon thyme, spearmint, pep- *permint, santolina are often recommended. All will withstand clipping and grow more compactly when clipped. Mints spread wide unless roots are confined in pots or boxes.*

Parsley, basil, and chives are easy to handle in ribbon plantings.

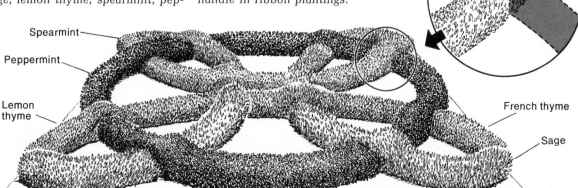

Spearmint — Peppermint — Lemon thyme — French thyme — Sage

ANISE

A native of Greece and Egypt and among the first European herbs planted in America. Famous for its distinct licorice-flavored leaves and seeds. Romans used seeds in cakes prepared for festive occasions. Also used in ancient times for its power to ward off the 'evil eye'.

Anise is a slow growing annual flowering 2½-3 months after planting. It grows to a height of 18-24 inches. Lower leaves are oval with serrated edges; upper leaves are longer and divided into 3 segments. Yellowish-white flowers are carried in tiny umbrella-like clusters.

How to grow. Does best if sown in place because of long tap root. Give it a warm sunny location. If planted in rows, thin plants 6-8 inches apart

Italians, the spirit of love . . . to Greeks, a symbol of hate and misfortune. The Romans who believed in communication with plants regarded basil as a stubborn, do-the-opposite character. Rather than sweet-talking when planting they cursed it, then prayed it wouldn't grow.

In gardens today basils are grown for their importance in hundreds of dishes and their beauty in flower borders and in containers.

Sweet Basil. An annual, 1-2 feet high, with leafy light-green foliage. Spikelets of tiny flowers white and often tinged with lavender. A spicy herb with a slight taste of pepper. 'Dark Opal' is a most attractive variety of sweet basil. It's an All-America Selection as an ornamental. Grows 12-18 inches high. Dark purple-bronze foliage, small lavender-pink flowers

Sauce, see page **82** for the recipe and its many uses.

BORAGE

A European and North African herb. Cited by the Roman naturalist Pliny for its ability to promote euphoria. He described it as the drug of Homer that "brought absolute forgetfulness."

An attractive annual 1-3 feet tall. Leaves are grey-green, star shaped flowers bright blue. Drooping flower clusters especially eye-appealing in flower borders and containers.

How to grow. Sow seeds in place. Difficult to transplant unless grown in pots. Takes sun or filtered shade. To stretch out the harvest, sow 3 times at 4-week intervals.

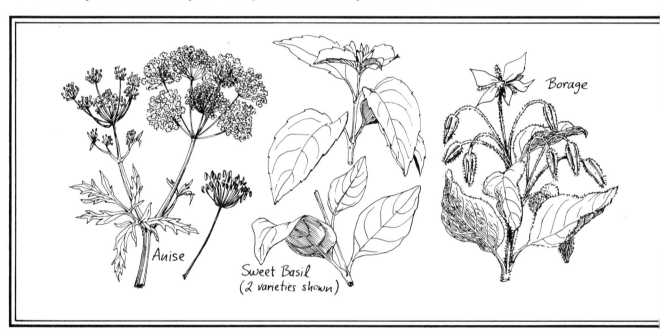

Anise

Sweet Basil
(2 varieties shown)

Borage

in rows 2 feet apart.

Harvest. Harvest seeds about one month after flowers bloom.

How To Use

This licorice-flavored seed is especially prized in breads and cookies. It goes into Scandinavian orange rye bread and Italian panettone, a sweet fruit-filled yeast bread. It flavors German Christmas cookies, such as *springerle* and *pfeffernuesse*. It lends zest to apple or pear pies and cooked carrots or beets.

BASIL

A native of India steeped in symbolism in ancient times. To Hindus, a protecting spirit of the family . . . to

in spikes. Much milder tasting than other sweet basils.

Bush Basil. A compact form of sweet basil 6-12 inches high. Milder in flavor. Tiny rounded leaves taper at the stems; flowers whitish in color.

How to grow. Easy to grow. Sow seeds in place after last frost or grow indoors and transplant. Give them sun. Pinch stem tips to promote bushier, more compact growth. Go easy with fertilizer; lush growth may reduce flavor.

Harvest. Gather leaves at pre-bloom or when blooming begins. May be preserved by freezing.

How to use

Beloved by the Italians, basil has gained fame in the Genovese *Pesto*

Harvest. Clip leaves before buds flower.

How To Use

The cucumber flavored leaf is pleasant minced in salads.

CARAWAY

Rich in history and folklore, ancient Arabs called the seeds "karawya." Thought to have originated in Asia Minor before spreading to other continents. Ancients believed caraway had the mysterious power to prevent theft of any object in which it was contained. Also used in love potions to keep lovers from becoming fickle.

Caraway is a biennial, the seeds are produced the second year. The first year it grows 8-15 inches high with bright green carrot-like leaves. It dies down in the winter and in the following spring. quickly grows to about 24 inches and shows off with clusters of greenish-white flowers. Seeds ripen about a month after flowering and the plant dies.

How to grow. The easiest way to get a seed crop is to sow seed in early fall. There is no need for a full season of growth for seed production the following summer. Give the plant room to grow. If planted in rows, thin plants 8-12 inches apart in rows 3 feet apart. Sow in place; long tapering roots are not suited to transplanting. In cold winter areas protect yearling roots with a mulch after the ground is frozen.

Harvest. Seeds ripen about a month

Assyrians and eaten either boiled or raw. Vinegar in which chervil seeds were soaked was believed to be a cure for hiccoughs.

An annual that lends beauty to flower borders or makes an attractive potted plant. Grows to height of 1-2 feet. Light green fern-like leaves resemble parsley, but milder in flavor with a slight taste of anise. Produces tiny white flowers in umbrella-like clusters.

How to grow. Sow in place or start seeds indoors in pots and then set out. Seedlings difficult to transplant. Prefers partial shade — such as from taller plants — and slightly moist soil. Easily grown indoors since direct sunlight isn't needed. Sow in early spring and thin plants 3-4 inches apart. For denser foliage, cut flower stems before bloom.

The best coriander came from Egypt, according to the Roman naturalist Pliny.

Fast growing annual that reaches height of about 1-2½ feet. Oval leaves on main stems have serrated edges. Leaves on side branches are feathery and more delicate. Parasol-shaped flower clusters are pinkish-white. Plant gives off odor some people find offensive.

How to grow. Easy to grow. Sow in place. Thin 7-10 inches apart. Takes sun or filtered shade.

Harvest. Harvest plants when 6 inches high. Or, pick leaves sparingly, beginning when plants are 4-6 inches tall. Gather seeds as they ripen in midsummer. Otherwise, weight of seeds will bend stems to the ground and fall off.

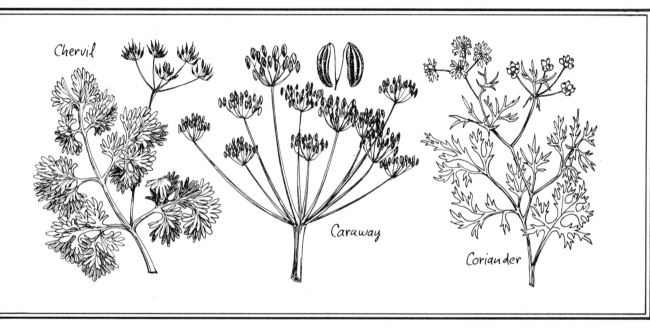

Chervil

Caraway

Coriander

after flowering to greyish-brown color.

How To Use

This sharply aromatic seed is popular in Middle European rye and pumpernickel breads, bread sticks and pound cakes. It goes into Hungarian goulash, borscht, pickled beets, and sauerkraut. It seasons coleslaw, pates, and cheese spreads, such as *liptauer*.

Sprightly raw apple slices are intriguing dipped into the seeds to coat lightly. It also refreshes meat stews and fish casseroles.

The oil, expressed from the seeds, flavors the liqueur kümmel.

CHERVIL

A native of Europe, Orient and north Asia. Grown in ancient times by the

Harvest. Pick leaves just before buds break. Green tender leaves may be cut and dried.

How To Use

This delicate, parsley-like herb is good in a variety of sauces: béarnaise, vinaigrette, remoulade, and sauce verte. Add it to a butter baste for broiled chicken or fish. Sprinkle it on pea and tomato dishes or cream soups. A pinch elevates scrambled eggs, omelets, and cheese souffles.

CORIANDER

Native to the Eastern Mediterranean. A biblical herb compared to manna, the food that mysteriously appeared to the children of Israel. Seeds have been discovered in Egyptian tombs.

How To Use

The fresh leaves of this herb are commonly known as cilantro or Chinese parsley. They are widely used fresh in Oriental, Indian, Caribbean, Portuguese, and Mexican dishes.

Cilantro is intregal to guacamole, Portuguese shellfish platters, Indian curries, Chinese soups and fish dishes, and the Oriental chicken entree that is baked in clay.

The dried herb, whole or ground is widely used in Scandinavian baking. It goes into Danish pastry, Swedish coffee cake, gingerbread, butter cookies, and rich egg custards. It also complements baked fish, meat balls, and roast pork or ham. It is essential to most curry powder and is used in Spanish dishes. Sausage manufacturers use it extensively.

DILL

Native to Southern Russia and the Mediterranean. Used as a drug in early times. Prescribed for variety of ailments ranging from insomnia to hiccoughs. Name thought to be derived from Norse word "dilla," meaning to lull. Probably refers to dill's supposedly soothing power.

Annual that grows to height of 2-4 feet. Lacy leaves light green in color. Tiny greenish-yellow flowers appear in parasol shaped clusters. Produces large quantities of seed.

How to grow. Sow in place in spring. Give it sun and well-drained soil. Stake tall growing plants.

Harvest. Pick leaves as soon as flowers begin to open. Gather seeds when useful in pickles, sauerkraut, and beet dishes.

FENNEL

There are two kinds of Fennel. One is generally grown as a herb for leaves and seed: Common Fennel or Sweet Fennel *(Foeniculum vulgare)*. The other is grown for its broad leaf stalks and bulbous base: Florence Fennel or Finocchio *(Foeniculum vulgare var. dulse.)* To confuse things a little, this Fennel is offered in some produce markets as 'Sweet Anise.'

The leaves and seeds of both have the same uses for seasoning. For the enlarged bulb and the heavy leaf stalks eaten raw, boiled, braised or used in salads, plant Finocchio. To get good sized stalks it is essential feathery leaves to 1½ inches long.

How to grow. Sow in place in full sun. Space rows 3 feet apart. Thin plants at 10-12-inch intervals. Stake when 18 inches tall to protect from wind.

Harvest. Pick stems just before flowers bloom; pick leaves when flowers start to bloom. Seeds turn brown when ripe and can be dried. Leaves may be preserved by freezing.

How To Use

The licorice-like seeds go into German and Scandinavian rye breads, cheese spreads, and vegetable dishes, such as beets, cabbage, and sauerkraut, and potatoes.

Drop a few seeds into vinegar or the court bouillon for fish or vegetables. Crush a few seeds for a Greek lentil soup or a spaghetti sauce.

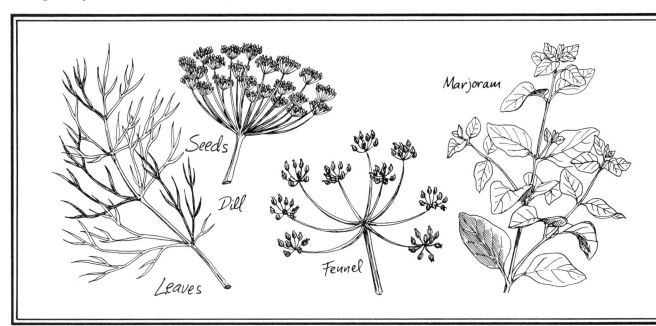

ripe—flat and brown in color.

How To Use

Dill is notable for both its seed and weed, the latter actually the leaf of the plant. The seed has a slightly bitter taste and fragrance, while the weed has a delicate bouquet.

Scandinavians in particular are fond of fresh dill weed. They use it freely nestled into Swedish *gravlax* (fresh salmon buried in sugar, salt, and dill), tossed into wilted cucumber salad, and sprinkled over new potatoes. It goes into tartar sauce or butter sauce for fish. It lends verve to broiled lamb chops and sweetbreads in cream. It is pleasant in pickled beets, potato salad, and tossed green salad.

The seeds have a place in cheese, yeast breads and rolls. They are also that it be treated as a cool weather crop. Sow seeds in summer for a fall crop. As plant develops pull soil up around base to blanch it. See page 78. You can give the Common Fennel the same treatment.

Common Fennel or Sweet Fennel.

The Common Fennel is rich in herb lore. Cultivated by Romans for its seed and tender stalks. Cited in ancient literature for its medicinal powers, including a cure for blindness and importance in reducing diets. In the Middle Ages, one of several herbs used to ward off evil spirits.

Tall growing perennial that lacks hardiness to survive cold winters. Most often grown as an annual. Reaches height of from 3-5 feet. Attractive in border areas with its bright-green hollow stems and flat clusters of golden flowers. Narrow,

MARJORAM

Thought to have originated in the Orient, though several species have been traced to Europe. Ancient history records a variety of medical uses. Prescribed in ancient Greece as a remedy for narcotic poisons, convulsions and dropsy. Marjoram found growing on a Greek grave meant the departed was enjoying happiness. Both the Greeks and Romans offered crowns of marjoram to young married couples.

Although there are several species of marjoram the most used and easiest to find is:

Sweet Marjoram. An attractive bushy plant in borders or container. Grows 1-2 feet high with small oval leaves — light green on top, gray-green underneath. Bears small knot-like clusters of white to pale lilac flowers.

How to grow. Although it's a perennial, treat as an annual in all but the warm weather areas.

Start seed indoors in late winter and set out after last frost.

Harvest. Leaves can be used anytime but for full flavor pick just before bloom.

How To Use

This sweet, spicy herb with a slight mint aftertaste is an asset to sauteed or stuffed mushrooms, butter-steamed zucchini, or fresh new peas. Add it to a red wine marinade for lamb shish kebab or a white wine marinade for broiled chicken. Sprinkle it into omelets and scrambled eggs, or spinach, clam, or onion

Orange Mint. Grows from 1 to 2 feet tall. Stems are reddish-green, leaves oval shaped with purplish edges. Lavender flowers appear in uppermost axils. Sometimes called bergamot mint, it has slight taste and smell of fresh oranges.

Peppermint. Grows to height of 3 feet with purple stems and green leaves tinged with purple. Tiny purplish flowers appear in thick terminal spikes 1-3 inches long. Oil is used in many products — chewing gum, confections, toilet water, soap, liqueur.

Golden Apple Mint. Grows to 2 feet tall with dark green leaves streaked with yellow. Flowers are pale purple in color. Aroma and flavor more delicate than spearmint.

and zucchini. Float a few sprigs in a citrus punch or steep some leaves in a tea-based punch.

Peppermint enhances mint sauce for lamb or veal, goes into iced tea, fruit salads, and mint ice.

OREGANO *(Origanum vulgare)*

A first cousin to sweet marjoram and fairly common to Asia, Europe and North Africa. Name derived from ancient Greek word thought to mean "delight of mountains." Likely refers to plants which often grew wild on hillsides.

Hardy perennial and good container plant. Often called wild marjoram. Forms leafy shrub-like plant from 2-2$\frac{1}{2}$ feet tall. Broad oval leaves have blunted tips. Pale pink flowers form in loose clusters or short spikes.

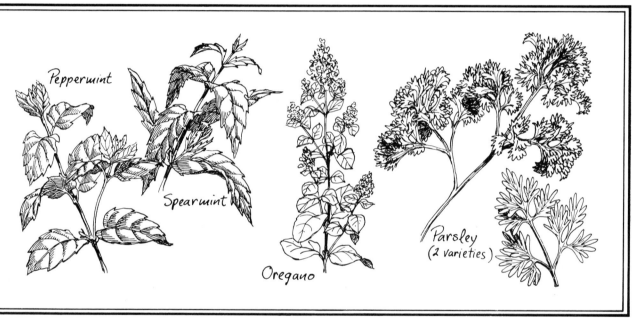

Peppermint

Spearmint

Oregano

Parsley (2 varieties)

soups. Rub it on pork or veal roasts before cooking.

MINT

Highly regarded by ancients and one of the more popular modern-day herbs. Pharisees used it to pay their taxes. Mints were used by Greeks as a smelling salt . . . a body perfume . . . and· to scent bath water. Also highly prized as a medicinal herb for curing a variety of ailments, including ulcers and skin diseases.

Aroma of mint comes from oils produced within the plant. The following—all hardy perennials—are among the more popular garden mints.

Spearmint. Grows to height of 1 to 2 feet. Has reddish stems and crinkly pointed leaves. Lavender flowers appear in 2-4-inch long spikes.

How to grow. Can start from seed, but division or cuttings are recommended. Will not grow "true" from seed. Often grown in containers in the soil because of spreading nature of root system. Takes sun or shade. Cut flowering stalks before they go to seed. Renew beds every 3-4 years.

Harvest. The more frequently the sprigs are cut the better the growth.

How to use

Spearmint is the most common garden mint. Sprigs of it make a pretty garnish on fresh fruit medleys, ices, melon, and lemon tarts. The Greeks crush a few leaves for their savory meatballs or a mixed vegetable stuffing for a whole eggplant or fish steaks. The crushed leaves add zest to coleslaw, potato dishes, carrots,

How to grow. Grow from seeds or divisions. Starts slowly, so starting seeds indoors helps assure good first-season growth. Give it full sun and well drained soil. Thin plants 10-12 inches apart. Cutting back flowers will stimulate growth of foliage. Replant when plants become woody in 3 to 4 years.

Harvest. Use fresh leaves as needed. Leaves may be preserved by drying.

How To Use

Sprinkle it over broiled lamb chops, roast leg of lamb, or steak along with a squeeze of lemon juice. Add it to spaghetti sauces and guacamole. It goes well on green beans or garbanzos. One expert says the best fried zucchini he ever ate had a liberal sprinkling of oregano on it.

PARSLEY

A native of Southern Europe and the Eastern Mediterranean. Ancient Greeks held it in high esteem. Crowns made of parsley were presented to winners at national games. Wreathes were worn at banquets to absorb fumes from wine and prevent intoxication.

Today most gardeners and cooks know the parsleys as attractive edgings for a flower border, a kitchen window plant and providers of garnishes and seasoning.

The seed catalogs offer 4 kinds:

'Moss Curled' or 'Triple Curled'. 70 days. Leaves are finely cut and deeply curled. Excellent for garnishing and culinary decoration. 'Deep Green' and 'Evergreen' varieties are similar to 'Moss Curled.'

in warm water for 24 hours before planting improves germination. Prefers partial shade. Thin 6-8 inches apart.

Harvest. Pick mature leaves from first-year plants. Harvest second-year plants before flowers bloom. Leaves can be dried and used as seasoning.

How To Use

The beautiful, vibrant green sprigs are most often used as a garnish. They have a real place in cooking as well.

Mince the herb and heat it with butter for a superb, simple dressing on asparagus, cardoons, artichokes, carrots, and new potatoes. Or spoon it over broiled or pan-fried fish. Or use as a baste for broiled shrimps or snails. Deep fry it in oil for a novel

Seedlings and young plants need frequent tip pinching to direct growth. Give it a dry sunny spot.

How to use

Rub rosemary into veal and lamb roasts or sprinkle it over chicken sautés. Tuck it in stuffings for fish or use small twigs as a baste for barbecued salmon. Greek cooks use it with abandon on barbecued chicken or lamb steaks or roast.

Sprigs of rosemary make a festive wreath surrounding a leg of lamb or roast chicken or turkey. Tuck zigzag cut lemon halves into the greenery.

SAFFRON (Crocus sativus)

A Mediterranean herb prized by ancients for its pleasing aroma and yel-

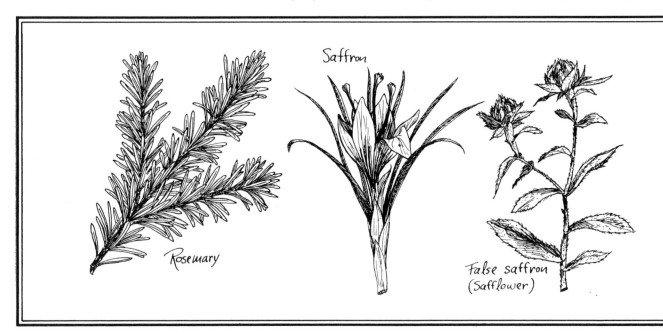

Rosemary

Saffron

False saffron (Safflower)

'Plain or Single'. 72 days. Bright green flat leaves are deeply cut but not curled. Standard variety for flavoring.

'Dark Green Italian'. 72 days. A flat leafed type. Heavy, glossy, medium dark green leaves of strong flavor. More attractive than 'Plain.'

'Hamburg' or 'Turnip Rooted'. 90 days. Forms a slender root 8-10 inches long resembling a slender parsnip. Used for flavoring soups and stews. Roots may be stored in sand for winter use.

How to grow. A biennial — producing foliage the first year, going to seed in the spring. Treat as an annual. A slow starter that may germinate poorly. (Transplants in pots available at garden stores.) Soaking seeds

garnish with meats.

Mince it and toss into an Italian salad or a cucumber and yogurt salad. Tuck some sprigs inside a chicken before roasting and scatter some minced parsley over a French-style beef stew.

Blend minced parsley and garlic with butter for a spread on sour dough or egg bread, then oven heat until hot through.

ROSEMARY

Rosemary is a hardy evergreen shrub in areas where winter temperatures stay above 5°. Normally grows to 4-6 feet with gray green foliage and pale blue flowers. Can be trained or clipped as a hedge. Dwarf forms grow to 2 feet, spread 3-4 feet. Useful groundcover where adapted.

low dye extracted from flower pistils. Shoes dyed saffron yellow were worn by Persian Kings. Also one of several ingredients used in ancient Egyptian perfume that was believed to be a cure for insomnia.

Two plants, a bulb and an annual are listed in seed catalogs as saffron.

True Saffron (Crocus sativus). Bulb. Lilac flowers appear September-November soon after planting. The saffron of commerce comes from the orange-red stigma. Plant bulbs in August about 6″ apart each way, and 4-6 inches deep.

False Saffron (Carthamus trinctorius). Annual. This is the oil-producing safflower. Resembles a thistle, 1½-2 feet tall. Orange-yellow flowers retain their color when dried and are used in dry arrangements. Flavor of the dried flowers from the flower head is very much like that of true saffron and is used in the same way. Plant seed after frost. Water regularly up to time flowers begin to form and then slack off.

How to use

This golden herb flavors and colors Spanish and Italian rice dishes. It tints Swedish-style holiday buns a pale gold and seasons bouillabaise and fish stews. It is popular in the Mediterranean and Latin American countries in sauces for fish, chicken, lamb, and pork.

GARDEN SAGE

A Mediterranean herb, the family name *Salvia* is from the Latin word meaning "to be saved." To ancients, a herb with wide-ranging medical

should be renewed every 3 to 4 years.

Harvest. Pick leaves before or at blooming. Cut back stems after blooming.

How To Use

This aromatic and slightly bitter herb is notable as a stuffing herb. Use it in stuffings for roast turkey, rabbit, chicken, pork chops, and baked fish. Rub it on pork, veal, or lamb before roasting. Use it in sausage patties or meat loaves. Knead it into herb bread and onion bread.

SAVORY

Native to the Mediterranean and Southern Europe, savory is perhaps one of the earliest cultivated herbs. Romans used it — along with other herbs — to flavor vinegar used in the

cuttings and divisions. Both plants like sunny locations, though summer savory likes drier soil. Thin summer savory every 8-12 inches; give winter savory more room — 12-15 inches from its nearest neighbor.

Harvest. Gather leaves from both plants from pre-bloom until blooming begins. When winter savory begins flowering, clip stems often to promote new growth.

How To Use

Savory goes well with all kinds of beans — in salads, soups, and vegetable dishes. Rub it over poultry before broiling and tuck it into poultry stuffings. It punctuates sweetbreads and kidney dishes. Strew it over baked or broiled fish and fish stuffings. A mild herb, it is particularly good in egg dishes and cheese souffle.

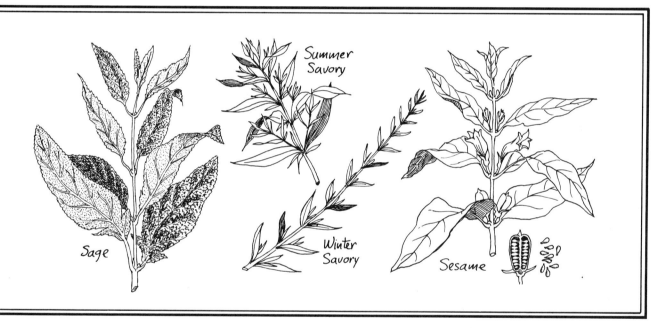

Sage   Summer Savory   Winter Savory   Sesame

uses — from mending broken bones to curing nervous disorders. The Chinese preferred it as a substitute for their own native grown tea.

A shrub-like perennial from 1 to 2 feet tall. Greyish-green oblong leaves heavily veined. Purple flowers appear in whorls on tall spikes. Varieties available having leaves marked with tints of yellow (Golden sage); reddish purple (Purple sage) and white and deep red (Tricolor sage). Makes a handsome low hedge around vegetable or herb gardens.

How to grow. Start from seed or cuttings. A slow starter, sow seeds indoors and transplant. Give full sun. Space plants 2 to 2½ feet apart. Plants eventually become woody and

same manner as we use mint sauces. Two species most often grown for food and seasoning are:

Summer Savory. An annual that grows to 18 inches high. Has erect, branching stems and gray-green leaves. Produces small pinkish-white flowers. Peppery-tasting leaves used in salads, soups and dressings.

Winter Savory. A shrub-like perennial about 15 inches high. Upper leaves are narrow, lower leaves rounder in appearance. White to lilac blossoms less than ¼ inch long. Weak stems tend to collapse, making plant suitable for edgings.

How to grow. Summer savory starts easily from seed and should be sown in place. Winter savory, a much slower beginner, often started from

SESAME

A herb native to Africa and Eastern Asia. East Indians called it "thunderbolt," alluding to its powers to open secret places. In classic times a herb of magic, associated with Hecate, queen of the witches. Sometimes called bene, from the Malay word meaning grain or seed. Today oil extracted commercially is used for salads and cooking, and seeds are widely used in confections, cakes and breads.

Annual. Grows to 3 feet with round glistening green stem and leaf stems, attractive green leaves and cream colored or pale orchid flowers from July to September. A decorative garden plant.

How to grow. Easy to grow. Sow seeds in place in sunny location. Thin seedlings 8-10 inches apart.

Harvest. Gather seeds when ripe — about a month after flowers bloom.

How to use

This nut-like seed is widely used in Oriental cookery in meat and vegetable stir-fries and crispy appetizers and cooky wafers.

Oven toasting enhances its nut-like flavor. Scatter seeds in a single layer in a shallow baking pan. Heat in a 300° oven for 10 to 15 minutes, or until lightly browned. Sprinkle toasted seeds over fresh fruit salads, creamy soups, broiled chicken, pan-fried fish, and vegetable dishes. Toss it into salad dressings for a tomato and avocado medley or a mixed vegetable salad.

Untoasted, add the seeds to cookies and pound cake before baking and sprinkle on breads and rolls.

with soil mulch. Small root pieces can be potted and set out the following spring. Make new plantings every 3-4 years.

Harvest. Leaves most flavorful when picked pre-bloom or just before blooming begins. Preserve by drying.

How To Use

Used with restraint, tarragon enhances all fish and shellfish dishes. It also enlivens poultry and veal. Add it to the marinades for barbecued fish and poultry. Blend it into butter for a dressing on asparagus and artichokes. It is integral to béarnaise sauce and green goddess salad dressing. Roll it up in an omelet or sprinkle it on a crab or tomato cocktail. Steep it in vinegar for a tantalizing, aromatic flavor. A pinch goes well in chicken or crab soups and fish chowders.

cover with dark green ¼-inch leaves with a caraway scent and clusters of rose-pink flowers. Seed is difficult to germinate; propagate by division or cutting. Plant in full sun. Trim to control growth.

Common Thyme. A perennial also called garden thyme. A shrub-like plant from 8-12 inches high. Has slender, woody branches and tiny gray-green leaves less than ¼ inch long. Lilac or purplish flowers grow on stem ends in loose spikes. Though there are several species of thyme, the garden form is recognized as the most flavorful.

Lemon Thyme. Perennial. Also grown for leaves. Good ground cover. Golden-green leaves have a lemon scent. Pinkish flowers bloom in July. Grow same as garden thyme.

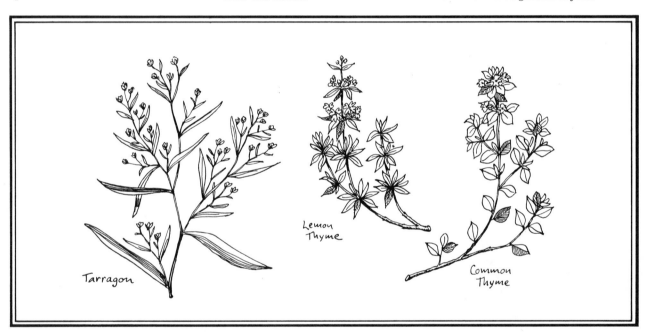

Tarragon — Lemon Thyme — Common Thyme

TARRAGON

A Southern European native, its roots were once used as a cure for toothaches. Cited in 17th century literature as being "friendly" to the head, heart and liver. According to legend, tarragon could be grown from roots of radishes or sea onions laced with flax seeds.

Tarragon holds its own in the flower border and is most attractive in pots. Grows to height of 2 feet. Fine, dark-green leaves have pointed tips. Extremely small whitish-green flowers are tightly clustered.

How to grow. Perennial, grown from cuttings or divisions. Rarely sets fertile seed. Takes partial shade. Protect roots in cold climates by covering

COMMON THYME

Native to the Mediterranean. Steeped in symbolism in ancient times it signified courage, elegance and energy. Prized for its medicinal powers, it was believed to be a cure for toothaches, snakebites, skin diseases, nervous disorders and many other ailments. Used in broths and sauces by the English in the 17th century. In North American gardens by 1721.

Of the many thymes, in bush form and ground cover, three add flavor to the kitchen.

Caraway Thyme. Perennial. Leaves are used fresh or dried. A ground

How to grow. Germination is inconsistent. May be sown indoors, or start from cuttings. Likes dry soil and lots of sun. Thin plants 8-12 inches apart. Keeping plants well clipped prevents them from becoming woody. Renew every 3-4 years.

Harvest. Clip tops of plants when in full bloom.

How To Use

The strong, warm clove-like flavor of thyme goes well in gumbos, bouillabaise, and clam chowder. It is in tune with onions, carrots, and beets. It uplifts stuffings for turkey or duck and sauces and butters to go with fish. It flavors slow-cooking beef dishes and court bouillon for vegetables.

Borage

Basil

Fennel

Variegated creeping thyme and rue

Good ideas from good gardeners

RAISED BEDS FOR SPECIALTIES

From a gardener with all the space he wants to use:

I can't say enough for raised beds, and we will more than double the number we now use. They give me the ability to plant small quantities of certain vegetables without lousing up the garden rows. Specialities such as garlic (so little is needed) do well. We grow our shallots there, too, although we are about to double our planting and move them out into a full-size garden row. Raised beds are perfect for spring onions because you want only a few feet at a time. We have 2 of our beds reserved for herbs, one for perennials and the other for annuals.

GOPHER PROTECTION

Two families of gophers practically

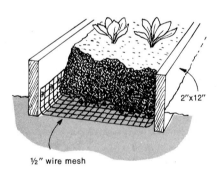

½" wire mesh

ruined our garden last year. This year we have gopher-proofed one section by building a 12-inch deep raised bed and lining the bottom of the bed with ½-inch mesh wire.

GROWING PLANTS TO SET OUT

I use an old styrofoam box—the kind you buy to keep things cool. Punch holes in the bottom for drainage. Fill it half full with a mixture of 1 part soil, 1 part peat moss and 1 part sand. Mix thoroughly. Place it on the south side of the house. Cover with clear sheet of plastic. Remove cover on warm days.

COFFEE CANS

I am sure you have many ideas already. Hotkaps I am not crazy about as they can blow away if not carefully anchored and they sometimes get the plant too hot. We have had good luck with respect to late light frosts with 2-pound coffee cans, both tops and bottoms removed.

We put them over our tomatoes, eggplants and peppers and leave them for a couple of weeks. Occasionally the tips of the leaves get burnt by the hot metal on contact but the damage is not permanent. We also use on cabbage plants, not against frost but as protection against bugs. The advantage of the open-ended

can is that you don't have to lift every morning and replace each night. Of course it's not protection against a heavy frost but one would not normally be putting out tender plants that early.

BIRD PROTECTION

I made a cover of aluminum fly screen. Built portable frames 14 inches wide and 7 inches high and 9 feet long for my peas and beans and smaller ones 7 inches wide for carrots, beets and lettuce. I store them in the winter and bring them out for the first seed sowing. They're very simple.

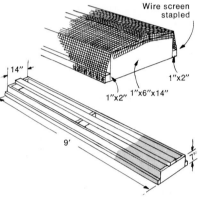

Length should be 1/2, 1/3 or 1/4 the length of a full row. Just staple the wire to frame. A heavy stapling gun is ideal and very fast. The 7-inch height is adequate. After plants are 6 inches tall, birds don't do much damage. The first year we used 1-inch mesh chicken wire. It didn't stop the mice. Small birds squeezed through and couldn't get out again. No trouble after covering with the aluminum fly screen.

Black plastic stops weeds, acts as a mulch and slows evaporation. It increases yields of many warm weather crops, especially melons.

"Soaker" hose is very effective for watering young plants (Cos lettuce here). It's portable and provides slow irrigation in long rows.

Coffee can waterer with holes punched in sides. No need to trench, no erosion, less weeds. Drains slowly, confines water to roots.

PLASTIC NETTING

For the first time, plastic bird netting was used to protect newly planted corn, peas and beans; nuisance birds such as brown thrashers we completely foiled, and replanting was not needed for the first time in many years.

CONE PROTECTION

Cone

I have manufactured by own "hot caps" by forming a cone out of plastic hardware cloth and a long pointed stick attached. It gives protection from frost and wind without danger of the heat build-up typical of hot caps. Furthermore I can make the size fit the plant.

"WHAT VARIETY IS THAT?"

We try out new varieties in a rather cautious fashion. The trial plantings are small in comparison to the ones we have had success with. To make sure that we have the name of the variety at harvest time we keep a record on a garden map or on stakes.

Seed packets on stakes quickly fade out in rain or sprinkling or are lost. We've tried several methods from writing on stakes with a waterproof marker, to protecting seed packet. You can put seed packet or written label between sheets of plastic (art

supply stores carry plastic sheets suitable for this purpose.) Or use mat-surface scotch-type tape to cover package. Or use lacquer in a spray can. Fasten to stake with double-sided tape or white glue.

WOOD LABELS

What works best for me are wooden marking stakes from the nursery. I mark them with an ordinary indelible pencil. They stay put in the ground better than plastic strips and the writing doesn't smear. Over the winter I leave them face-up in the garden or other sunny spot—sun and moisture bleach the indelible ink out of them by spring.

DON'T WORRY ABOUT CLODS

Some gardeners work too hard in spading and raking soil for a seed bed. I don't cheat on the depth of spading but a few clods and small rocks don't bother me. When preparing seed bed for rows $2^1/_2$ to 3 feet apart I don't worry about clods between the rows.

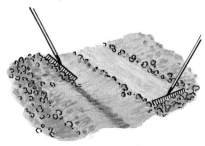

A clod-free strip can be quickly developed in very rough soil by hoeing up a ridge 4-6 inches high, then raking it down, pulling the clods off

in the process. The row can be left slightly mounded if excess water is apt to be a problem.

HANDY PANELS

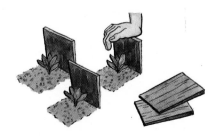

I hate to see transplants of anything wilt even temporarily. So when transplanting the thinnings from lettuce, beets and the like, I give them part shade for a few days. With small plants I stick a shingle at an angle to stop the hot sun. The best protection is with latticed panels. I make them 2 feet wide and 3 feet long.

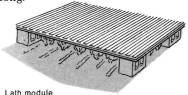
Lath module

NIGHTTIME WARMTH

We built a plastic A-frame (see p. 6) and found a way to keep it warm on cold nights. We put large plastic bleach bottles full of water inside the A-frame. The sun warms the water during the day. At night it slowly gives off heat and keeps the A-frame several degrees warmer than the outside air.

This photo and next show unusual circular garden planting, good for rough areas which otherwise might need terracing. Watering is done

from the center with "bubblers" or raised spray-type sprinkler. Cuttings are put in center for composting.

Gallon-size plastic jugs with bottoms cut out are useful as mini-greenhouses and insect protectors for tender young plants.

ICE CREAM SCOOP

For setting out transplants of lettuce, tomatoes, cabbage and the like, I prefer the ice cream scoop over the trowel. I can get the same depth in each planting hole fast and easy.

(Setting out lettuce in peat pots. Holes every 6-10 inches.)

WATERING MANY CONTAINERS AT ONCE

In hot, windy weather my son and I spent almost an hour watering our 24-plant container garden. The plants were in a light soil mix and we watered slowly. We tried putting a couple of inches of sand on top of the planter mix so we could water a little faster without floating the mix away. It helped, but our best idea was the use of a length of galvanized eave trough (roof gutter) capped at both ends.

We laid it across the rims of a dozen containers in a row and used a roofing nail to punch a hole in the bottom of the trough for each container. Now we flood the trough and it irrigates many pots at once. We also fertilize with liquid fertilizer this way. If we move a container out of the row, we plug up the unused wa-

ter hole with liquid solder from a tube. When not in use, the trough can be stored.

LITTLE RED WAGON

The little red wagon is a very practical gardening aid. In addition to simple transport from garage to garden and back again of small tools, fertilizers, containers and such we use it in early spring for indoor-outdoor movements of plants in pots in the transplant stage. We give them sunlight during the day and move them in the garage at night for frost protection.

INDOOR LETTUCE

From an apartment dweller: I found that 'Ruby' leaf lettuce makes a beautiful house plant. I plant it in an 8-inch centerpiece bowl, keep it near a window well-watered and fertilized, harvest a salad about once every three weeks all winter.

TOMATOES AND LATE FROST

We extend our tomato season by as much as three weeks by laying a wide strip of black plastic over each row at night. This year we will do the same with peppers and eggplants.

Having frosts September 20-30 we lose a lot of fruit unless we protect it this way.

MORE TOMATO TRAINING

We solved the problem of keeping tomatoes off the ground without staking and very little tying and pruning. I built 2 frames to place over 12 plants, set 26 inches apart in a 27-foot row. They're rugged and have lasted 8 years. Here's a sketch of how they are made:

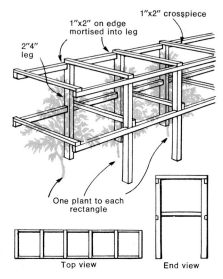

ROTATION

Recommended by everyone, like motherhood, but more difficult to achieve, for the amateur. I have shown you my system of dividing garden into quarters and planting all that was in quarter #1 this year in quarter #2 next year, etc. The ace-

One way to keep a melon from getting sunburned. A simply constructed "A" frame, pictured, can be moved from place to place.

Here a wooden frame covered with chicken wire over lettuce, carrots, chard, peppers. It's used for staking and protection from birds.

The start of a barrel of Chinese pod peas. In 2 or 3 months the plants will have grown up the strings to top point on stake.

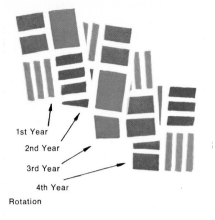

1st Year
2nd Year
3rd Year
4th Year
Rotation

tate overlay I use with my garden layout is not so much for record keeping as it is for planning. I find it invaluable.

HIP-POCKET TOOLS

For gardening in boxes and pots the ordinary tools I could buy were too big and clumsy. I carry a 2-inch putty knife and a pair of scissors and that's all. I can harvest beet greens, prune tomato plants, thin carrots, lettuce by snipping rather than pulling. The putty knife is a spade, cultivator and hoe all rolled into one. It's perfect for blocking out transplants in a flat.

COSTS MORE—WORTH MORE

The best investment I have made in gardening equipment is the professional heavy duty wheelbarrow. Its beautifully balanced and easy on the back. Moving dirt, compost, sand,

peat moss — all bulky stuff — is no strain. And to the kids it's Puffer Bill's train and the magic garden ride.

NO DIRT, NO WORMS

I have found a way to bring smiles to the gal in the kitchen. The vegetables I bring in are really clean. After kitchen inspection there's no dirt or worms in the sink.

I use a large pail of water and a wire basket using either or both to suit the vegetable. Spray from the hose

will take care of most of the dirt from root vegetables in the wire basket. Some may need a wash in the pail. A couple of shakes and whirls in the wire basket gets rid of excess water.

CLOTHESPINS

Spring-clip clothespins are useful when handling seed packets in the garden. Clip them on partly used packets — fold the top back — so the rest of the seeds won't spill out.

PARCEL POST STORAGE

We mounted the large parcel post size mailbox on a 5-foot high post alongside the main path in the garden. It gives us handy storage for insecticides, gadgets, twine, small tools, markers etc. It's weatherproof and high enough to keep things out of reach of small children. This year we trained a cucumber to climb up the post.

OLD RULE

A seed company told us: When seeds fail to germinate, some gardeners are sure that the fault must be in the seed. Actually it's almost impossible to buy seed that will not germinate. It is not uncommon to see 90% or more of the seeds produce excellent plants. Gardeners do, and should, sow more seeds than are usually needed for the final stand. This excess is good insurance against less than perfect soil conditions, and other hazards. The old rule for sowing corn, beans and peas still has some validity: "One for the blackbird, one for the crow, one for the cutworm and one to grow."

A strawberry container offers another kind of harvest when planted with Japanese cucumber, herbs and pink banana squash.

A half cylinder of 6" mesh wire is placed in container for use in staking 'Patio Pik' cucumber.

Bushel basket is ideal for "Potpourri Salad" basket. This one planted with radish, red lettuce, endive and parsley.

When the whole family gardens

We visited many gardens where children were involved in one way or another in vegetable growing, or more precisely, where they were invited to join in the fun when the parent or parents gardened.

We also learned a lot about children and gardening from our panel of gardeners. Each family had its own idea about the place of children in the garden. Some parents with an absorbing active interest in gardening excluded the children without realizing they were doing so.

Other parents, with a shallow interest in the garden but with generous praise for anyone who could grow anything, often found themselves watching a very busy and determined pint-sized gardener—the official gardener of the family.

"Historical and cultural aspects of vegetables and their by-products can easily be illustrated. Gourds are not only decorative, but were used as ladles and bowls. Corn leaves soaked in water can easily be woven into ropes or baskets like those used by native American Indians. Or they can be made into corn husk dolls like those pioneer mothers made for their daughters.

"Exacting educational or productive goals should not take precedence over the *process* of learning. Children learn in infinite ways, and often self-corrective methods are the most stimulating. Allow some plants, for example, to go to seed or grow less palatable sizes. A zucchini that's as big as your arm is a delight to behold, however tough to eat. Scarlet runner beans quickly get a foot long, and in our experience, this meant (to the novice gardener) the bigger the better. But soon the same child would begin to set his own standards of quality."

In the following pages we have taken bits and pieces of the projects of many families and sorted them out into four groups, and created a family to represent each group.

The "No-Nonsense family". They like to look at the vegetable garden as a source of food. Food with the good

Our experience with the Children's Adventure Garden gave us some understanding of how a talented teacher can stimulate the child's interest in gardening.

In the booklet *A Child's Garden, A guide For Parents and Teachers**, Carol Malcom who worked with the children the first year, makes these observations:

"Encourage a child to grow crops which he himself may not prefer to eat. Often these (like summer squash) become very appealing when the size and abundance of yield are the product of his own hand. Also, crops can be traded, or community baskets for sharing and trading can be encouraged. Often children will avidly grow crops which grandmother will appreciate, or Mom really likes.

"Parents should be encouraged to let the child follow his vegetables into the kitchen, and let him cook them when possible. Some of our kids cooked a vegetable stew of their combined harvest of beans, peas, corn, and radishes —and claimed it was delicious.

fresh taste, food to freeze or store, food to can, preserve, pickle. We found these families on a suburban lot, a "place in the country", anywhere there was room to return to the land.

The "Seed family". They discovered seeds—seeds to play with, seeds to eat, seeds to sow.

The "Mixed-up family". They are convinced that vegetables and flowers and herbs and bulbs can be mixed. And the mixture will furnish beauty to the eye and good taste to the table.

The "Teachers family". Parents of Tom (7), Dick (5), Debbie ($3^1/_2$) have read that "a child does half his learning before he is four years old, another 30% before he is eight, and only 20% during the remaining years of elementary and secondary education."

*For a free sample copy of *A Child's Garden, A Guide For Parents And Teachers*, write Public Relations – ORTHO, 200 Bush Street, San Francisco, California 94120.

They return in the cool of the evening with their loot from the pumpkin patch—the giant sized 'Big Max' and half-dozen 'Jack-o-lanterns.'
Below: The root view box shows underground action of green onions. For more about the box see page 110.

When the camera tries to explain the earthy pleasures of family gardening there is always one "pride-of-harvest" snapshot, and one showing baby helping daddy (who never yells "don't"), and one of a vegetable freak. Missing in all are the many hours of just growing up, by the vegetables and the kids.

About the "No-nonsense Family"

We caught a family in the moving-to-the-country stage and joined them in developing their first vegetable garden. It would be one of our major test gardens. In it we could not only try out varieties we had only read about but we could watch a family without any experience in growing vegetables go about growing them on a grand scale.

In the photographs on the preceding two pages you meet the Jack Chandler family in the raised-bed portion of their garden, in a show-off harvest in the wheelbarrow and on their way from the melon patch on a pre-Halloween evening. The garden has been a success in crop production and family involvement. The childen accepted the garden as part of the business of living in the country and took on responsibilities in planting, weeding, watering and even selling the excess. But as you can see, the line between work and play in a garden is not always sharp.

Two vegetables in the test garden that made the greatest hit with the children were the egg-sized eggplant and

lecting through the young daughter's fascination with bean seeds — her jewels. They found themselves buying packets of bean seeds by seed color from descriptions in the catalogs. They favored such varieties as 'Horticultural' — like a wren's egg; 'Christmas Lima' — striped with carmine; 'Dixie Butterpea' — red speckled with dark carmine; 'Tendergreen' — purple, mottled tan.

Seeds of the multicolored 'Rainbow' or 'Indian' corn were strung as necklaces. (Dampen kernels until soft, thread with needle, dry rapidly to harden and prevent rot.)

One of the seed favorites was the marigold. The seed has the look of an Indian's bark canoe. Seeds sown when the weather warms deliver color that associates well with peppers and eggplants.

Seed catalogs became gift catalogs as far as this young lady was concerned.

Seeds the *Yearbook of Agriculture* 1961 became a favored reference book. And they learned to agree with the author of these lines in the introduction:

"The details of the surface relief of many seeds are even

Edible seed collection (untreated seeds);
(Left, top to bottom) 1 Indian Corn (pink) 2. Indian Corn (tiny brown) 3. Mexican Pumpkin 4. Squash 5. Flax 6. Dill 7. Mustard 8. Sesame 9. Fennel 10. Caraway 11. Lentils 12. Garbanzos 13. Fava

(Right, top to bottom) 1. Pencil Pod Black Wax 2. King of the Garden Lima 3. New Kidney Stringless Wax 4. Romano 5. Bush Kentucky Wonder 6. Soybeans 7. Mung Beans 8. Black Beans 9. Missouri Wonders 10. Azuki Beans

an egg-sized cantaloupe. Seed of the cantaloupe came from the Nichols Nursery and was described in their catalog this way: "cantaloupe, producing fruit that only weigh 10 ounces each. Egg-shaped fruits with smooth, shiny golden-yellow skin. White crisp flesh that is sweet and very aromatic."

We cut the little melons length-wise in quarters and ate the rind and flesh together. Great fun for the children and everyone.

The eggplant that produced fruit that any hen would envy was the showpiece of the garden. The plant, shapely and well-branched, displayed 30 little eggs, too beautiful to eat.

About the "seed family"

The "Seed Family" stumbled into the hobby of seed col-

more beautiful in design and precision than the mass of the seed as a whole. Often you can find minute surface characters of surprising kinds. Surfaces that appear plain and smooth to the unaided eye may be revealed under a good hand lens to have beautiful textures.

"Surfaces may be grained or pebbled. They may have ridges like those of Doric columns. They may bear geometric patterns in tiny relief, forming hexagons, as in a comb of honey, or minute dimples may cover the surface. Some irregular surface patterns of surprising beauty sometimes appear under the lens. Surface may be a dull matte, or highly glossy, or anywhere in between.

"Last but not least in the beauty of seeds are their surface colors. They may be snow white or jet black. The color may be a single solid one, or two or more may be scattered about at random. Colors may form definite patterns that are distinctive and characteristic of the species and variety. The colors may be almost any hue of the rainbow — reds, pinks, yellows, greens, purples — and shades of ivory, tan, brown, steely blue, and purplish black."

From beans the collection spread to all types of seed. A page from the collection is photographed at left. It brings together many of the seeds we eat, as is, or cooked, roasted, sprouted or parched.

Naturally, the collecting led to experimenting. Seeds, unlike shells or rocks, are alive. As you see them they are resting — dormant. All they need is moisture, air and warmth to break into active growth. In experimenting with seed germination the "Seed Family" learned that moisture without air is fatal. To germinate seed for observation of the miracle of growth they used the seed-doll method described below.

Most seeds will germinate in the dark and can be planted 1/2 to 2 inches deep depending on kind of soil and temperature. However some of the very small seeds require light, or are benefitted by light for germination. 'Curly Cress' or Pepper Grass is a good example.

Try this experiment with Cress:

Sow seeds on the surface of moist soil in three flower pots. Quickly cover the seed in 2 of the pots with 1/4 inch of moist soil. Do not cover the seeds in the other pot. To prevent soil from drying out, cover all 3 pots with a plastic film. In a few days seedling will appear in the pot with the uncovered seeds. No seedling will appear in the

other pots. However if you draw a stick through the soil covering the seeds, seedlings will appear in a few days where you have scratched the soil.

Soaking seeds. By experimenting the family learned that soaking seed of most varieties not only did not hasten germination but was a dangerous procedure.

Rice and other water plants will germinate under water with a very low supply of oxygen. But seeds of most vegetables need both air (oxygen) and moisture to germinate.

An overnight soak of bean seeds in warm conditions can completely ruin them. Long soaking without air ferments and kills the seed.

Cabbage seeds will not germinate if even a film of water surrounds the seeds.

If the spongy covering of spinach seeds is filled with water for any length of time, seeds will not germinate.

Seed scatterers. Our seed family developed a habit of scattering seed without fuss or fear. Any piece of open ground became fair game. They sowed the seeds like they were sowing lawn seed, raked them in and sprinkled them in the same way as they would start a lawn. Some patches were used to supply young plants for greens. A square foot or two of beets, for example, were harvested when the beet tops were 3 or 4 inches high to supply a meal of greens and baby beets.

Mystery planters. Collections of old seed packets and spilled seeds were mixed together and planted in "mystery" planter boxes. The result: first the radishes, and then a jumble of beets, chard, beans, and carrots. A harvest of the early ones at a very young stage made room for a good pulling of beets and carrots. Three bean plants were given a pole to climb on.

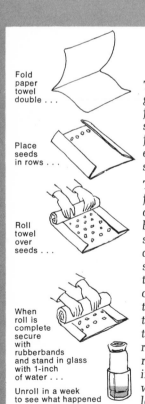

Fold paper towel double . . .

Place seeds in rows . . .

Roll towel over seeds . . .

When roll is complete secure with rubberbands and stand in glass with 1-inch of water . . .

Unroll in a week to see what happened

HOW TO MAKE A SEED DOLL

The seed-doll method of germinating seeds is useful where quantities of seedlings are required for examination by several youngsters, as in a schoolroom.

Take a paper towel folded double. In a row, one inch from the doubled edge, place the seeds, 1/2 inch or more apart. When the row is set, roll the towel over the seeds. Place the second row of seeds and roll to cover. Continue until the roll is complete. Hold the roll together with a rubber band. Place the roll in a glass with an inch of water. Add water when needed. Take a look in a week and see what has happened.

Cress seeds sprout where soil is scratched

PLANT YOUR INITIALS

The cress experiment outlined above, suggests the possibility of sowing cress in pots or wider containers such as flats, and "writing" on the soil surface. Seeds will sprout wherever the pencil exposes them to light.

SEED VIEW JAR

Use pint jar and a 4 by 8 inch blotter. Fill jar with water to saturate blotter. It will stick to glass. Pour out all but 1 inch of water. Place seeds between blotter and jar. Add water when it goes below 1-inch level.

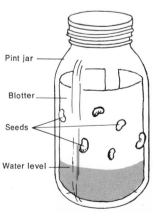

Pint jar

Blotter

Seeds

Water level

Midget varieties. Many of the midget varieties found their way into the garden. The dwarf short vines of 'Patio-Pik' cucumbers were grown in hanging baskets. The 'Little Leaguer' variety of cabbage with round, softball sized heads were tucked into the flower border.

About the "Mixed Up Family"

In the language of gardening, the word "ornamental" is used to distinguish plants used for beauty in the landscape from plants used for food and fiber. But many plants serve a dual purpose. And so you have edible ornamentals and ornamental edibles.

We can recall several garden scenes in which the family ignored the distinction between vegetables and ornamentals.

Spearmint in a pot sunk to the rim in a spot right under the garden faucet.

In a damp shady spot: Parsley, chives and mint. Grow the mint in a sunken pot to keep roots in bounds.

Corn in a large patio planter looking as tropical as ginger lilies.

A bed of curly kale rivaling the beauty of a bed of ferns.

A groundcover of parsley with daffodils dancing above.

Rhubarb chard combined with white Sweet William.

A border of beets and carrots along a walk. Harvest young beets for greens. Tops of the variety 'Ruby Queen' are short, dark green turning to red. 'Burpee White' produces large, shiny medium green leaves. Leaves of 'Burpee Golden' carry a slight orange tint.

The ferny foliage of asparagus in the back of the flower border or planted to show its delicate tracery against a house wall.

Cabbage becomes beautiful in the flower border. Especially interesting are the crinkled Savoy types and the red cabbages.

Okra shows its hibiscus relationship in leaf and flower in the flower border.

No-nonsense vegetable gardeners are not blind to the beauty of vegetables in the landscape. One such gardener wrote us: "Our garden is largely utilitarian and we concentrate our aesthetics on two 8x8 raised beds where there are all kinds of possibilities. Beyond that we do a long row of sunflower along our north fence (of the garden); easy and very striking. Also, borage is great — out of the way against a fence or wall as it is so prolific. Attracts bees like mad, which we need here. Finally, scarlet runner bean over a trellis.

"Squash, pumpkins and melons are groundcovers on a grand scale.

"I think eggplant and peppers are two of the most elegant plants in our garden."

Sunflower, Gourds and Scarlet Runner Beans

The plantings in the family gardens followed no pattern. But all of the time-honored plantings that children enjoy were repeated more than once.

The giant sunflower was used in many ways. In one large garden they were planted to form a 2-row windbreak. In a small garden they substituted for bean poles. Sunflower seeds were planted 2 weeks before the pole beans.

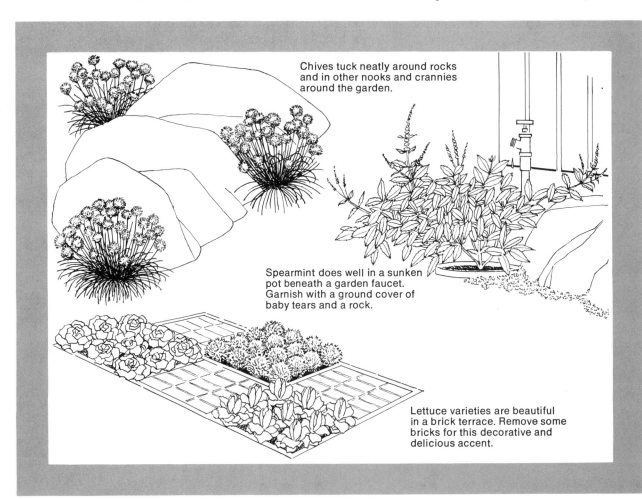

Chives tuck neatly around rocks and in other nooks and crannies around the garden.

Spearmint does well in a sunken pot beneath a garden faucet. Garnish with a ground cover of baby tears and a rock.

Lettuce varieties are beautiful in a brick terrace. Remove some bricks for this decorative and delicious accent.

(With this advantage they will stay ahead of the beans and support them as they climb.)

We picked up the following recipe for roasting sunflower seeds from a county agent in Washington state: Hang the sunflower heads in a dry location with good air circulation. Tie a cloth bag around each head to catch any seeds which might drop during drying. When seeds are dry, mix thoroughly 2 cups of unwashed seeds, 1/2 teaspoonful Worcestershire sauce, 1 1/2 tablespoons melted butter, and 1 teaspoon salt. Place in a shallow baking pan and roast for one hour at 250°. To insure even browning, shake the pan several times during the process. Place seeds in a plastic bag and store in the refrigerator. Squash and pumpkin seeds can be roasted the same way.

Gourds, squash, cucumbers, pole beans, anything that would grow rapidly to create a hide-out or camouflage a fort was welcomed by the 5-7-year old play set. The same concrete reinforcing wire as used with tomatoes (see page 62) makes good "walls" to support the vines. Bean and gourd tunnels, teepees and "houses" were found here and there. See page 68 about gourds.

Drying Ornamental Gourds. To make sure that gourds will keep their natural beauty, do this: Pick when fully ripe. Take care not to bruise the gourd. Wash in a strong disinfectant. Spread the gourds on a raised screen in a cool dry place. Make sure there's air space between gourds. To speed up drying of the inside, punch a hole with an ice pick in the end of the gourd. Turn the gourds every few days through the drying period. Two weeks should do it.

Scarlet Runner. This bean occurs wild at altitudes of about 6,000 feet in Guatemala where perennial forms have been domesticated and are still cultivated for green and dry beans. It forms fleshy tubers which are boiled and eaten.

Although a plant of the humid uplands in the tropics it is less sensitive to cool summers than the common bean. It is grown successfully in Britain and throughout the United States.

In seed catalogs it is listed more frequently as a flowering vine than as a vegetable.

It is worth a place in the landscape with or without beans. Yet the beans are more than acceptable as string beans when young and as green shelled. Scarlet Runner will grow rapidly to 10 to 20 feet to form a dense yet delicate-appearing vine. Its bright scarlet, sweet pea-shaped flowers, appearing all summer long, are borne in long sprays of 10 to 20 or more.

Pods grow 6 to 12 inches long. Seeds are large, up to an inch, dark purple with red marking.

It climbs by twining stems and can be trained on poles, wire mesh or strings, to cover arches, fences, arbors, trellises.

Indoors, the growing of vines from sweet potatoes and avocados brought home from the market can continue the gardening experience. To grow a sweet potato in water in a glass jar, stick 3 tooth picks into the potato at equal distances around it. These will hold the potato half in and half out of the jar. Fill the jar with water until it is above the end of the potato. Sprouts will grow from the portion above the jar in about 2 weeks (unless the sweet potato has been given the no-sprout treatment) and you have a lush vine in 6 weeks.

Parsley, chives, and mint in a sunken flue tile. Let the tile show a little to enrich this miniature garden and to confine the roots.

Brighten your spring with daffodils dancing flamboyantly above a ground cover of parsley.

Oh what a measuring stick am I!

Our "Teachers Family" knows that learning-time and play-time are one and the same. So if any part of gardening could be turned into a game, a lot of learning fun might be had by all. The vegetable gardener is asked to be a measurer in almost every garden operation — "Add 3 pounds of fertilizer per 100 square feet," "sprinkle 2 pounds of fertilizer per 100 feet or row," "plant 3 inches apart in rows 18-24 inches apart," "spread 2 or 3-inch-thick mulch over 100 square feet." Certainly in these directions there must be all the elements needed for many games of "How much?," "How wide?," "How long?."

The trouble is that many teacher-parents don't want to think in the simple terms of measurement. They will tell you, "All directions are too complicated," "I'm no good with fractions."

Let's take some of the measurement problems from simple to complex and solve them as we go.

Let's take a young guy of 5 or 6 and play a few games. First let's give him a measuring stick he can be proud of — a lance to kill a dragon — when he's not measuring the distance between rows of spinach.

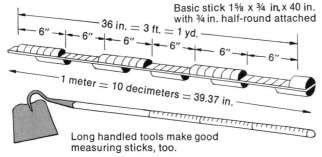

Basic stick 1⅝ x ¾ in. x 40 in. with ¾ in. half-round attached

36 in. = 3 ft. = 1 yd.

6"   6"   6"   6"   6"   6"

1 meter = 10 decimeters = 39.37 in.

Long handled tools make good measuring sticks, too.

You might as well put the centimeter-meter scale on the side opposite the inch-foot-and-yard. In not too many years he will be using the Metric System.

With this measuring stick he transforms himself into a live measuring machine.

How long is my finger? . . . to the first joint? . . . 2nd joint . . . whole thing? How deep do you want the pea seeds?

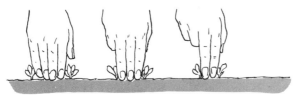

How wide are my fingers? All four? . . . three? . . . two? How far apart shall I plant the bean seeds?

How far can my fingers space? Thumb to index finger? . . . thumb to little finger? What's the distance between rows of radishes?

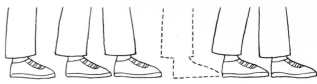

How long are my shoes? . . . two shoes, heel to toe? How far apart do you want the rows of beans?

← ? →   ← 10 ft. →   ← 15 ft. →

How long is my pace? How many paces to go 10 feet? 15 feet? How long shall we make this row?

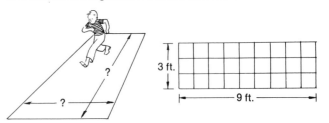

3 ft.   9 ft.

How big is my garden? 3 at one end, 9 feet at one side. Will someone please multiply? So it's 27 square feet.

What's a square foot?

← 1 ft. →   1 ft.

Now the counters in the game are wooden squares or 12" x 12" floor tile or any other material that can be handled.

And then we lay out 9 of the squares.

And we have a square yard.

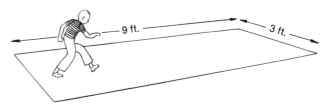

9 ft.   3 ft.

And just for fun we check the width and the length by pacing it off.

So we look at our 27 square foot garden. Then read the label on the fertilizer bag. "Apply 3-4 pounds per 100 square feet." What part of 100 is 27? Well, ¼ of 100 is 25 square feet, and that's close enough to 27 to cheat a little and take ¼ of 4 pounds and spread 1 pound. But we have no scale!

If we did have a scale, we would find that one pint of

any of the dry-mixed fertilizers weighs just short of a pound. And one pint of water weighs a pound. So, with a pint of either water or dry fertilizer we can set up our "table of equivalents" in liquid measurements and forget the scale.

Now if you have cooked, put up fruit or measured liquor into a glass you close your eyes and see an ounce, cup, pint and quart jar.

But our young man hasn't handled things called pints or quarts or jiggers. A pint isn't a pint in our game until he has poured 2 cups of water into a pint jar.

So we gather together and place before him pint and quart jars, coffee cans, two sizes of milk cartons, a measuring cup, tablespoon and a half-gallon watering can.

The young fellow we worked with was a veteran role player. You might meet him as Superman in the morning and G.I. Joe at noon. He had no trouble being *Mister Pint*. And it seemed obvious to him that his young sister was a cup, his mother a quart. So, you see, it takes 2 sisters to make *Mister Pint*. (You take it from there.)

Of course if the table of equivalents as visualized here is easy to handle, the role playing may have a short life.

So we read the label on our bag of fertilizer. It says "Prior to planting apply 4 lbs. of fertilizer to 100 sq. ft., or 2 lbs. to 50 feet of row."

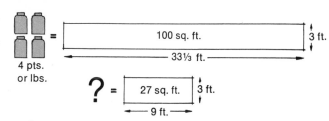

Right here we decide not to quibble about a foot or two. If it takes 4 pounds to cover 100 sq. ft., one pound will cover $1/4$ of it or 25 sq. ft. And for the vegetables in the 27 sq. ft. that's close enough. So you pour one pint into the coffee can. Sprinkle it evenly over the 27 square feet. Water it in, and you have followed directions.

How about directions for 2 lbs. for 50 feet of row when you have 18 ft. of row?

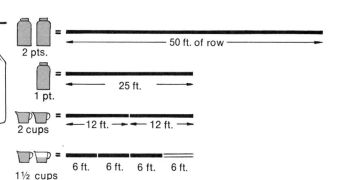

And how about the cubic foot game? Take the problems of "covering the soil with a 2-inch thick layer of peat moss or sawdust, or ground bark." How much will I need? How many 1 cubic foot bags?

Have you looked at a cubic foot lately? One way to see a cubic foot is to find a 1" x 12" board 1" thick and 12' long and cut it into 12 pieces.

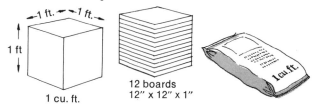

Stack them up, stand back and take a look. There is one cubic foot. It looks a little different than the 1 cubic foot bag. But they are equal.

And then we look at the 3' x 9' garden, with its 27 square feet.

How much will your stack of 12 cover?
Answer: 12 square feet 1" thick.

And how much 2" thick? Answer: 6 sq. feet.

So how many bags do we buy?
Answer: 5 bags will cover 30 sq. ft. So we will buy five, that's close enough.

Root View Box

With a box designed to bring the below-ground action of plants into view, the plant world takes on a new dimension.

According to teachers using the box, the vegetable world comes alive in the eyes of the children. Roots and tops are seen as one. Roots develop rapidly. There's a day-to-day change to sustain interest.

To get full exposure of root growth, the window or viewing side of the box must be slanted enough to force the roots to grow against the window.

Manufactured root view boxes are now available — complete with built-in automatic watering and soil mix.

One way to make the box is diagrammed below. The dimensions are not critical. The box can be any length. We like to use a 2-foot long box. It's easy to move around but long enough to show off a dozen root vegetables. With two boxes you can compare growth in different soils or with different rates or methods of fertilizing.

To make sure of success, use one of the scientifically blended "soil" mixes: Jiffy-Mix, Peat-Lite, Redi-Earth, U.C. Mix, Super Soil, Pro-Mix. Thoroughly dampen the mix before filling the box. Fill to near the top and water thoroughly to settle the soil. Sow seeds 1/4 inch from the glass or plastic. Cover the box with a plastic film to slow evaporation. Moisten top of soil when it becomes dry.

The window should be covered with a wood panel or a dark cloth drape except at viewing times, since roots of many plants tend to grow away from the light source. Boxes can be used to show many features:

How roots develop in an ideal soil.
How roots develop in a problem soil.
How water moves through various soil types.
How plants respond to fertilizers.

With two or more boxes you can set up a number of soil tests. For example, compare plant growth of lettuce in the synthetic soil with growth in your garden soil or with your garden soil mixed with compost or other organic matter.

Or test one method of fertilizing against another. For example, try fertilizing with a liquid fertilizer at the rate and frequency called for on the label in one box and in the other apply at 1/2 the amount called for but twice as often.

Observation of the root growth of tomato transplants will tell you a lot about planting tomatoes. Plant one as you would any other vegetable and in the same box plant another deep in the soil. Watch to see if roots form all along the buried stem as well as spreading out from the root ball.

Experiments in rooting cuttings will open young eyes to another miracle. A piece of geranium or coleus "mother" plant, stuck into the planter mix will form roots and produce a duplicate of its mother. In growing cuttings, cover the box with polyethelene film to prevent the cuttings from drying out.

If the boxes must remain indoors at all times include chives, cress, leaf lettuce, endive and parsley in your planting. All of the root crops — carrots, beets, turnips — will need sunlight or an indoor grow-light.

After the box has been in use for a month, some light fertilization will be necessary. Use a liquid fertilizer at the rate called for on the label.

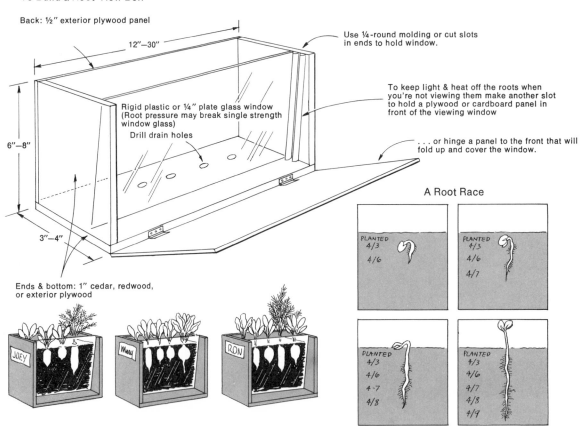

To Build a Root-View Box

Back: 1/2" exterior plywood panel

12"—30"

Use 1/4-round molding or cut slots in ends to hold window.

To keep light & heat off the roots when you're not viewing them make another slot to hold a plywood or cardboard panel in front of the viewing window

Rigid plastic or 1/4" plate glass window (Root pressure may break single strength window glass)

Drill drain holes

. . . or hinge a panel to the front that will fold up and cover the window.

6"—8"

3"—4"

Ends & bottom: 1" cedar, redwood, or exterior plywood

A Root Race

PLANTED 4/3 4/6

PLANTED 4/3 4/6 4/7

PLANTED 4/3 4/6 4-7 4/8

PLANTED 4/3 4/6 4/7 4/8 4/9

Good reading

There is a surprising amount of free and almost free vegetable-gardening information.

Information at the local level is available from the office of the County Agricultural Agent. See phone book for listings of county departments—check "Agriculture."

GOVERNMENT PUBLICATIONS

Write Superintendent of Documents, Government Printing Office, Washington, D. C. 20250 for:

List of Available Publications of the U.S.D.A., Bulletin No. 11, 45¢.

Minigardens for Vegetables, H & G Bulletin No. 163, 15¢.

Indoor Gardens with Controlled Lighting, H & G Bulletin 187, 15¢.

Write Publications Division, Office of Information, U.S. Department of Agriculture, Washington, D.C. 20250 for: *Suburban and Farm Vegetable Gardens*. Bulletin G 9. Free.

Good handbook. *The Home Vegetable Garden.* No. 69. Brooklyn Botanic Garden, 1000 Wash. Ave., Brooklyn, NY 11225. $1.50.

What's edible? Paperback reprint of the classic *Sturdevant's Edible Plants of the World.* Dover Publications Inc., 180 Varick St., N.Y., N.Y., 10014. $5.00.

ABOUT SEED CATALOGS

We take advantage of the seed companies and send away for more catalogs than we really need. They renew our hopes for a better garden and for a world where everything is superlative.

Many of the catalogs are valuable garden books with cultural directions and good ideas tucked in with every vegetable listed.

In talking with our fellow gardeners we found more than a few who used catalogs to track down varieties recommended by their State Experiment Stations.

Some gardeners look to the garden stores and seed racks for 90 percent of their supplies and look to the catalogs for items of special interest.

Some curious minded gardeners search the catalogs for the new and unusual in the belief that the search for new kinds of vegetables should never stop.

And there is the growing number of gardeners looking for vegetables to fit into their adventures in international cookery.

The following list of companies are offering a 1974 catalog. The seed business is not static. There may be a change or two in the 1975 list.

(2) Breck's of Boston, BB5 Breck Bldg. Boston, MA 12210. 128 pages, 5½ x 9½. Accent on seeds and accessories. Established 1818.

(3) F. W. Bolgiano & Co. Inc. 411 New York Ave., N.E. Washington, D.C. 20002. Vegetables 18 pages. Features All America Selections. How and When to plant information.

(4) Burgess Seed & Plant Co. Box 2000, Galesburg, MI 49053. 68 pages. 8½ x 11. Vegetables 26 pages. Varieties especially selected for home gardeners. Many unusual items.

(5) W. Atlee Burpee Co. (Free from your nearest Burpee branch): Philadelphia, PA 19132. Clinton, IA 52732, Riverside, CA 92502. 166 pages, 6 x 9. When seed catalogs are mentioned most people think "Burpee."

(6) D. V. Burrell Seed Growers Co. Box 150, Rocky Ford, CO 81067. 96 pages, 8½ x 4¼. Seed growers. Special emphasis on Melons, Peppers, Tomatoes and varieties for California and the Southwest.

(7) Comstock, Ferre & Co. Wethersfield, CT 06109. 12 pages, 8½ x 11. Vegetables, 11 pages. An informative guide to variety selection. 40 varieties of herbs. Founded 1820.

(9) Farmer Seed & Nursery Co. Faribault, MN 55021. 84 pages, 8 x 10. Complete. Special attention to midget vegetables and early maturing varieties for Northern tier of states. Established 1888.

(10) Henry Field Seed And Nursery Co. 407 Sycamore St., Shenandoah IA 51601. 128 pages, 8½ x 11. A complete catalog. Wide variety selection. Many hard to find items, good tips for vegetable gardeners.

(12) Gurney Seed & Nursery Co. 1448 Page St., Yankton, SD 57078. 64 pages, 15 x 20. Emphasis on short-season North country varieties. Accent on the unusual items.

(13) Joseph Harris Co. Moreton Farm, Rochester, NY 14624. Box 432, Gresham, OR 97030. 84 pages, 8½ x 11. Vegetables, 39 pages. The look of authority, and so considered.

(14) The Chas. C. Hart Seed Co. Main and Hart Streets, Wethersfield, CT 06109. 24 pages, 7 x 10. Vegetables, 16 pages orderly arranged. 20 herbs. Established 1892.

(16) J. W. Jung Seed Co. Station 8, Randolph, WI 53956. 70 pages, 9 x 12. Everything for the garden. Vegetables, 18 pages. Attention to Experiment Station introductions.

(17) D. Landreth Seed Co. 2700 Wilmarco Ave., Baltimore, MD 21223. 56 pages, 7 x 10. Vegetables, 32 pages. Washington and Jefferson were customers of this seed house. "America's oldest." Established 1784.

(18) Earl May Seed & Nursery Co. 6032 Elm St., Shenandoah, IA 51601. 88 pages, 9½ x 12½. Wide choice of varieties. Features All-American Selections.

(19) Nichols Garden Nursery, 1190 No. Pacific Highway, Albany, OR 97321. 88 pages, 8½ x 11. Written by an enthusiastic gardener and cook who has searched the world for the unusual and rare in vegetables and herbs.

(20) L. L. Olds Seed Co. 2901 Packers Ave. Box 1069, Madison, WI 53701. 80 pages, 8 x 10. Vegetables, 30 pages, carefully written guide to varieties. All America Selections.

(21) Geo. W. Park Seed Co., Inc. Greenwood, SC 29646. 116 pages, 8¼ x 11¼. A guide to quality and variety in flowers and vegetables. Includes indoor gardening. The most frequently "borrowed" seed catalog.

(23) Seedway (formerly Robson Quality Seeds), Hall, NY 14463. 35 pages, 8½ x 11. Vegetables, 19 pages. Informative, straightforward presentation.

(25) Harry E. Saier, Dimondale, MI 48821. 32 pages, 5½ x 9. Vegetables, 19 pages. General catalog 75¢. Ask for Vegetable catalog—it's free. Accent on the unusual. Wide selection of herbs.

(26) R. H. Shumway Seedsman, 628 Cedar St., Rockford, IL 61101. 92 pages 10 x 13. Complete. Founded 1870. Catalog has maintained some of the "good farming" 1870 look.

(27) Stokes Seeds, Box 548 Main Post Office, Buffalo, NY 14240. 150 pages, 500 different vegetable and 800 different flower varieties. Emphasis on short season strains. Canadian & European introductions.

(28) Otis S. Twilley Seed Co. Salisbury, MD 21801. 64 pages, 8½ x 11. Clear, helpful presentation with special attention to Experiment Station releases, and disease resistant varieties, for varying climatic conditions.

(31) Glecklers Seedmen, Metamora, Ohio 43540. 2 pages. 8½ x 14. Listings, brief descriptions of unusual, strange vegetables. Yearly supplements.

NOTE

Looking for a scarce or hard-to-find vegetable variety? Check the "parent" vegetable. There you will find many unusual types mentioned, with catalog numbers following them in parenthesis. These are the same as the numbers in parenthesis above — showing you which seed companies to write to for the catalogs you want.

Index